AN INTERPERSONAL PERSPECTIVE ON CLASSROOM MANAGEMENT

Effective classroom management is an essential skill for teachers and student teachers alike. Packed full of practical examples and evidence-informed guidance, this book offers a comprehensive approach to classroom management that emphasises the importance of building positive teacher-student relationships and fostering a supportive classroom climate that promotes student well-being, engagement, and learning.

Drawing from interpersonal theory, 40 years of research in the field, and the authors' own experiences as teachers and teacher educators, this book offers a deeper understanding of classroom dynamics and provides strategies for navigating various classroom situations. Insightful real-life examples and hands-on practical strategies are provided throughout, as well as tools, individual and team assignments, and best practice for addressing teacher-student interactions and relationships. Its contents will help both novice and experienced teachers manage classrooms for the benefit of student development. It effectively guides readers around teacher relationships and styles, interactions during a variety of classroom situations, responding to challenging student behaviours, and creating a psychologically safe classroom.

This book is an essential read for teachers, student teachers, and teacher educators across all education grade levels and subject areas who are seeking to enhance their classroom management knowledge, skills and courses. The book caters to educators at different stages of their careers, from novice teachers aiming to establish a solid foundation to experienced educators interested in refining their interpersonal approaches to classroom management.

Theo Wubbels is emeritus professor of educational sciences at the Faculty of Social and Behavioural Sciences of Utrecht University in the Netherlands. He has been involved for over 40 years in teaching and research on teacher-student relationships, learning environments, and staff development in primary, secondary, and higher education.

Perry den Brok is professor of education and learning sciences at the Department of Social Sciences of Wageningen University and Research in the Netherlands. He is also teacher educator, supervises several PhD students, and head of the group on education and learning.

Luce Claessens is an associate professor at the Department of Education at Utrecht University in The Netherlands and director of the teacher education programme for primary education. She teaches on interactions in class and research in schools.

Tim Mainhard is professor of educational sciences and head of the primary teacher education programmes at Leiden University. He teaches classroom management and research methods.

Jan van Tartwijk is professor of education and vice-dean for graduate education at the Faculty of Social and Behavioural Sciences at Utrecht University in the Netherlands. He teaches in the university's graduate school for teacher education and is involved in research projects on teacher-student communication, teacher expertise, and curriculum and assessment.

AN INTERPERSONAL PERSPECTIVE ON CLASSROOM MANAGEMENT

Building Teacher Relational Capacity

Theo Wubbels, Perry den Brok, Luce Claessens, Tim Mainhard, and Jan van Tartwijk

LONDON AND NEW YORK

Designed cover image: Image credit: © Sarah Hoyle

First published 2026
by Routledge
4 Park Square, Milton Park, Abingdon, Oxon OX14 4RN

and by Routledge
605 Third Avenue, New York, NY 10158

Routledge is an imprint of the Taylor & Francis Group, an informa business

© 2026 Theo Wubbels, Perry den Brok, Luce Claessens, Tim Mainhard, and Jan van Tartwijk

The right of Theo Wubbels, Perry den Brok, Luce Claessens, Tim Mainhard, and Jan van Tartwijk to be identified as authors of this work has been asserted in accordance with sections 77 and 78 of the Copyright, Designs and Patents Act 1988.

All rights reserved. No part of this book may be reprinted or reproduced or utilised in any form or by any electronic, mechanical, or other means, now known or hereafter invented, including photocopying and recording, or in any information storage or retrieval system, without permission in writing from the publishers.

Trademark notice: Product or corporate names may be trademarks or registered trademarks, and are used only for identification and explanation without intent to infringe.

ISBN: 978-1-032-91465-7 (hbk)
ISBN: 978-1-032-91467-1 (pbk)
ISBN: 978-1-003-56346-4 (ebk)

DOI: 10.4324/9781003563464

Access the Support Materials: www.routledge.com/9781032914671

Typeset in Interstate
by SPi Technologies Private Limited, India (STRAIVE)

CONTENTS

About the Authors   vii
Acknowledgements   viii

1 Introduction   1
Teacher August   1
Teacher Tonia   2
Teacher Dion   2
Teacher Renz   3
Topic of This Book   4
A Journey from Discipline Problems to Student Development   5
Organisation of This book   6
Sources   7

2 Teaching and Classroom Management   9
Looking at Teaching   9
Classroom Management   12
The Importance of Positive Relationships Between Teacher and Students   15

3 The Interpersonal Conceptual Framework   19
Teacher and Students Influence Each Other   19
Content and Relationship   25
Agency and Communion   26
You Are Always Communicating Agency and Communion   28
The Interpersonal Circle for the Teacher   29
The Interpersonal Circle Student   34

4 Gaining Insight into Behaviour, Interactions, and Relationships   37
Observing Behaviour with the Interpersonal Circle   37
The Questionnaire on Teacher Interaction (QTI)   40

5 Teacher Interpersonal Relationships and Styles   48
Changes Over Time   48
The Relationship Colours the Meaning of Behaviour   49
One-on-One Relationships with Students   53
Types of Teacher-Class Relationships   56
Development of Relationships   64
Teacher's Interpersonal Style   67

6 Complementarity in Interactions — 73
- Two Complementarity Patterns — 73
- Complementarity in Communion — 74
- Complementarity in Agency — 76
- Complementarity in the Combination of Agency and Communion — 77
- Professional Teacher Behaviour and Complementarity — 83

7 Non-verbal Communication in Interactions — 88
- Communicating Communion Through Non-verbal Cues — 88
- Communicating Agency with Non-verbal Cues — 92
- Combination of Non-verbal Behaviours — 95
- Non-verbal Cues in Multicultural Classrooms — 96
- Aligning Verbal and Non-verbal Messages — 96

8 Maintaining, Directing, and Redirecting Student Behaviour — 99
- Maintaining Desired Student Behaviour — 100
- Directing Student Behaviour — 108
- Redirecting Undesirable Student Behaviour — 113

9 Responding to Challenging Student Behaviours — 122
- Reappraising Negative Emotions — 122
- Student Disruptive Behaviour — 124
- Student Remarks — 131
- Disappointing Student Performance — 133
- Student Emotional Expressions — 134
- Students with Special Needs — 136

10 Dealing with Situations That Are Important for the Classroom Atmosphere — 141
- Teaching Moments That Are Important for the Classroom Atmosphere — 141
- Managing Whole-Class Teaching Moments — 142
- Starting the Lesson: Setting the Tone for Success — 145
- Whole-Class Instruction — 148
- Managing Individual or Group Work — 149
- Whole-Class Instructional Conversation — 151
- Transitions Between Lesson Parts — 153
- Ending of the Lesson — 154

11 Answers to Frequently Asked Questions about Teacher-Student Interactions and Relationships — 157
- Results in Earlier Chapters — 157
- Overview of the Current Chapter — 158
- What is in the Teacher-Student Relationship for Students and Teachers? — 158
- Do Behaviours and Relationships Differ Between Countries and Cultures? — 161
- Are Teacher-Student Relationships Associated with Class, Teacher, or Student Characteristics? — 166
- Can Good Interpersonal Behaviour Be Learned? — 167

Appendix 4.1 — 172
Appendix 4.2 — 175
References — 178
Index — 183

ABOUT THE AUTHORS

Theo Wubbels is emeritus professor of educational sciences at the Faculty of Social and Behavioural Sciences of Utrecht University in the Netherlands. He has been involved for over 40 years in teaching and research on teacher-student relationships, learning environments, and staff development in primary, secondary, and higher education. He is fellow of the American Educational Research Association.

Perry den Brok is professor of education and learning sciences at the Department of Social Sciences of Wageningen University and Research in the Netherlands. He is also teacher educator, supervises several PhD students, and head of the group on education and learning. His research interests are teaching and teacher education, innovation in higher education, learning environments, and the professional development of teachers in secondary and higher education.

Luce Claessens is an associate professor at the Department of Education at Utrecht University in the Netherlands and director of the teacher education programme for primary education. She teaches on interactions in class and research in schools. Her research interests are relations and interactions in class, teaching and teacher education, and professional development of teachers.

Tim Mainhard is professor of educational sciences and head of the primary teacher education programmes at Leiden University. He teaches classroom management and research methods. His research focuses on social dynamics in classrooms and the role of teacher-student relations in students' and teachers' well-being and motivation.

Jan van Tartwijk is professor of education and vice-dean for graduate education at the Faculty of Social and Behavioural Sciences at Utrecht University in the Netherlands. He teaches in the university's graduate school for teacher education and is involved in research projects on teacher-student communication, teacher expertise, and curriculum and assessment.

ACKNOWLEDGEMENTS

Many people have played important roles in designing and completing this book.

Numerous teachers and their students from various countries have inspired us, collaborated with us in our research, and helped us understand how results of our studies can be applied in the classroom.

More than 20 PhD students were involved in the research underlying this book, and their work has been invaluable to its content. Their names are listed in Chapter 1 (see p. 7).

Our colleagues Hans Créton, Herman Hooymayers, Mieke Brekelmans, and Jack Levy have been deeply involved with us in writing, thinking, and discussing interpersonal relationships in education for many years. They were integral members of the group that developed the ideas presented in this book.

We are deeply grateful for the invaluable feedback we received on earlier versions of Chapters 6, 7, 8, 9, and 10 from Ridwan Maulana, Mei Liu, Rekha Koul, and Xiaojing Sun. Their insights have greatly enriched the book, ensuring its relevance across diverse educational contexts worldwide.

For the activities on the website accompanying this book, we acknowledge Thom Somers for his work in the teacher education programmes at Utrecht University and the HAN University of Applied Sciences. He developed much of the educational material that inspired us, some of which has been used and adapted for inclusion on the website. Additionally, Adrienne Westermann and Els Laroes created activities at Utrecht University's teacher education programme, which have also been incorporated into the website in modified form.

It is about a year ago that we published a book in Dutch on classroom management with Telos Publishing. We are grateful to René Kneiber and Hilly Drok for their support in publishing that book and allowing us to adapt it into the current book.

At Routledge, we owe thanks to Anna Clarkson who paved the way for us to reach out to our helpful editor Bruce Roberts and the editorial assistants Maddie Gray and Lauren Redhead.

1 Introduction

Spend a day observing a secondary school class, and you will quickly notice how the atmosphere shifts dramatically depending on the teacher leading the lesson. The same group of students can experience entirely different dynamics—from focused and lively to chaotic or tense—depending on the approach and interaction style of the teacher.

To illustrate these contrasts, we present four examples of such classroom dynamics. While these examples are based on real observations, we've slightly exaggerated the situations to emphasise the differences. This approach helps highlight how varying interpersonal styles can influence the energy, relationships, and overall environment in the classroom.

Teacher August

August is the kind of teacher students look forward to learning from. His lessons are well-structured yet relaxed, striking a perfect balance between clarity and comfort. Students always know what's expected of them—both in behaviour and effort, whether in class or at home. August manages his classroom with confidence and genuine care, taking the time to understand his students' perspectives and what matters to them.

He focuses on students' strengths, emphasising their successes over their mistakes, and celebrates their achievements with positive reinforcement. His enthusiasm is contagious, not just for the subject he teaches but also for the students themselves. This passion creates an environment where students enjoy tackling their tasks and find joy in learning.

To his students, August isn't just a "nice teacher"; he's one they truly respect. They feel supported, motivated, and challenged in his classroom, and many credit him as one of the best teachers they've ever had. An authoritative figure with a warm approach, August has mastered the art of teaching with both heart and skill.

DOI: 10.4324/9781003563464-1

2 An Interpersonal Perspective on Classroom Management

Teacher Tonia

Tonia, like August, genuinely cares about her students, showing interest not only in their schoolwork but also in their lives outside the classroom. She makes an effort to connect with what matters to them and considers their preferences and interests. However, Tonia's classroom authority differs significantly from August's approach.

For Tonia's students, the boundaries of what's acceptable in class often feel unclear. Rules seem fuzzy, and as a result, students frequently drift away from the lesson's focus. They chat quietly among themselves, play games, or work on assignments for other classes, with little intervention from Tonia. Instead of addressing the distractions, she often raises her voice to be heard over the background noise but rarely enforces structure.

When students do ask for help, Tonia is patient to a fault—explaining concepts repeatedly, even for those who weren't paying attention earlier. This cycle reinforces a dynamic where both Tonia and her students mostly keep to their own paths, neither deeply engaging nor fully committing to the classroom experience.

Students appreciate Tonia for her kindness and the considerable freedom she gives them. However, they also feel she struggles to maintain control, describing her as a teacher who is perhaps too nice and unable to assert authority effectively.

Teacher Dion

Dion's approach stands in stark contrast to August's authority and Tonia's friendliness. Unlike either of them, Dion exhibits much less interest in his students—both in their academic work and in what matters to them personally. His interactions are often marked by disapproval, not just of the students' behaviour but, at times, of the students themselves.

Dion frequently expresses frustration with his class, criticising both their actions and their performance. He calls for order regularly, but his attempts often fail to elicit cooperation. Instead of settling down, students sometimes argue back, escalating the tension and disorder in the room. When pushed, Dion's reactions can become harsh, with angry outbursts, threats of punishment, or the frequent use of disciplinary actions—sometimes unfairly directed at students who weren't at fault.

The result is a chaotic and uncomfortable classroom environment, where conflicts between Dion and his students are common. Students frequently ignore the rules, engage in disruptive behaviour like taking items from each other or wandering around, and show little focus on the lesson material. This ongoing power struggle creates an almost hostile atmosphere, with both teacher and students occasionally acting in ways that verge on aggression.

For the students, Dion comes across as distant and unapproachable. Many describe him as unpleasant and ineffective at maintaining order. As a result, most view him as one of their least favourite teachers.

Teacher Renz

Renz, like our first teacher August, keeps tight control over his classroom, ensuring students understand exactly how they're expected to behave. However, while August inspires respect and engagement, Renz is perceived as strict rather than a true leader. Students in his class wouldn't dream of speaking out of turn or skipping homework–any misstep is met with a sharp reprimand.

The classroom atmosphere under Renz is far from warm. It's focused heavily on performance and competition, leaving students perpetually on edge. Mistakes or underperformance rarely go unnoticed, as Renz is quick to point out when students fail to meet his high standards–which, in his eyes, is often. Unlike August or Tonia, Renz shows little interest in his students' lives or personal experiences, creating a disconnect that further fuels the tension.

In Renz's classroom, students work hard, but not out of a love for learning or the material. Their diligence stems from fear rather than motivation, and they know there's no room for creativity or initiative.

His rigid expectations and lack of warmth make Renz a divisive figure among students. Some see him as their least favourite teacher, describing his approach as cold and intimidating. Yet, for high-performing students who thrive on structure and clarity, Renz's methods can be reassuring. They appreciate knowing exactly where they stand and what's expected of them. For these students, Renz's demeanour is less of a burden and more of a challenge they're willing to meet.

The atmosphere in the classrooms of these four teachers varies dramatically, each offering unique dynamics that shape the learning environment. This book is designed to improve (student) teachers' understanding of the intricacies of classroom atmosphere, relationships, and interactions. By gaining this insight, teachers can strive to cultivate an environment as effective and engaging as August's.

Among the four, August's classroom stands out as having the most positive atmosphere. Research consistently shows that classrooms with the kind of teacher-student relationship exemplified by August foster the highest levels of student motivation and learning. His balance of authority, warmth, and engagement creates an environment where students feel supported and inspired to achieve their best.

The research backing these findings is outlined in the last section of Chapter 2 and explored in greater detail in Chapter 11.

Topic of This Book

This book invites you to explore the dynamics of classroom atmospheres in primary and secondary schools, focusing on the teacher's role in fostering a productive and positive environment. Adopting *an interpersonal perspective*, it examines how interactions and relationships between teachers and students shape lessons and classroom management.

> **To Keep in Mind**
>
> Under the *interpersonal perspective* on teaching, we understand a way of viewing the lesson and the behaviour of the teacher and students that focuses on interactions (chains of successive behaviours) and relationships between the teacher and students. We also refer to this as *looking through the interpersonal lens*.

This book is for anyone eager to strengthen their interactions with students, enhance teacher-student relationships, and create a thriving, positive classroom atmosphere. It is tailored for both prospective teachers, their educators, and mentors in teacher training programmes and schools, as well as experienced teachers who will also find its themes practical, relevant, and thought-provoking. Combining actionable strategies with in-depth insights, this book equips educators with the tools they need to succeed.

Although the book originates from research and practices in the Netherlands and other Western countries such as the UK, USA, and Australia, its scope goes beyond a purely Western perspective. Our aim is not to promote Western ideologies but to share evidence-based ideas informed also by diverse, multicultural classrooms and global experiences. Contributions from other contexts, including Brunei, Singapore, Turkey, and China, have enriched the approach and examples included.

That said, the core theories and strategies are rooted in Western practices and examples, more specifically, often come from North-Western European contexts, reflecting their origins while remaining adaptable for classrooms worldwide. This acknowledgement invites readers to interpret and apply the insights in ways that resonate with their unique cultural and educational contexts. After all, interpersonal theory has a universal significance. Its principles apply in different cultural settings, offering valuable guidance for educators worldwide.

A Journey from Discipline Problems to Student Development

The research underlying this book was started in 1979, sparked by the challenges novice teachers face with classroom discipline—issues that remain particularly acute in secondary education. These difficulties often lead new teachers to leave the profession prematurely.

Initially, our focus was on helping novice teachers navigate these discipline challenges, with the primary aim of retaining them in the profession. At the time, there was less emphasis on the well-being and development of students. However, as our understanding evolved, we began to explore how classroom management and interpersonal dynamics contribute to both teacher effectiveness and student growth.

This dual focus shapes the text of this book. On one hand, we aim to equip novice teachers with practical strategies for classroom survival. On the other, we provide tools to help both new and seasoned teachers create a positive and nurturing environment that fosters student development. This blend of practical guidance and research-backed insights offers a comprehensive approach to mastering classroom interactions.

> ### Background Information
>
> #### *The Development of Teachers in the Early Stages of Their Careers*[1]
>
> There are various descriptions of the evolution of the thoughts and concerns of teachers during their professional careers. Concerning the early stages of the career, all of these descriptions refer back to the seminal work of Frances Fuller. In her publications from the 1960s and 1970s on the development of novice teachers, she defined four stages in the concerns of teachers.
>
> During teacher training, aspiring teachers are primarily concerned about their *own development* as students until they actually start teaching. They think like students and not yet from the perspective of a teacher. This may lead them to be highly critical of the teachers they observe.
>
> After commencing actual teaching, for example during internships, they enter the second phase. Their concerns shift to *survival*, focusing on mastering the subject matter, controlling the class, and earning the students' appreciation. Questions they ask themselves include, "Can I create an orderly atmosphere in the class?," and "Will the students listen to me; will they like me?"
>
> Once they demonstrate the ability to create a positive class atmosphere, they enter the third phase, *mastery*. Concerns shift to performing well as a teacher, focusing on effectiveness. Concerns in this stage are less emotionally charged than in the survival phase, allowing space for contemplating the best pedagogic approach: "How can I ensure that the students learn as effectively as possible?"
>
> In the final stage of Fuller's model, teachers *establish stable routines*. They become more concerned with pedagogy: "What is my impact on the students' development?" For the first time, they make conscious considerations about the best ways to stimulate students' learning and development.
>
> In this phase, concerns about the effectiveness of *school policies* come to the forefront. Teachers question how well their school is organised and in what ways the school can best contribute to the development of the students.

Organisation of This Book

Contents

- Chapter 2 discusses the theoretical background of our distinct approach to teaching and classroom management emphasising the critical role of *strong teacher-student relationships*. It sets our approach apart from others.
- Chapter 3 lays the foundation of our approach by introducing the *principles of interpersonal theory*, including a key insight: You are always communicating when you are with someone else, even in silence. The chapter also explains the *Interpersonal Circle*, a framework for analysing behaviour, interactions, and relationships.
- In Chapter 4, we explore tools *to map behaviour and interactions* based on the Interpersonal Circle like the *Questionnaire on Teacher Interaction (QTI)*, which assesses how students and teachers perceive their relationships.
- Chapter 5 focuses on the characteristics of *positive and less desirable relationships*, also exploring how interactions, relationships, and teacher styles *evolve over time*.
- Chapter 6 delves into *complementarity*, a concept that highlights how teachers and students influence each other, often unconsciously.
- Chapter 7 discusses the role of *non-verbal behaviour* in shaping perceptions of behaviour, a theme revisited in later chapters.
- Chapters 8, 9, and 10 offer practical guidance for teachers to *maintain*, *direct*, and *redirect* student behaviours in various classroom situations.
- Chapter 11 presents research findings on interpersonal theory in education.

Although there is a certain order and structure to the chapters, they can be read independently. However, we recommend reading Chapters 2 and 3 first, as they cover the foundational concepts we use.

Since the book primarily reflects classroom dynamics in Western contexts with an emphasis on North-Western Europe, we have taken care to include discussions on cultural differences in behaviour, interactions, and relationships. These insights are woven into several chapters to provide a broader perspective. For instance, Chapter 7 touches on the varying interpersonal meanings of non-verbal behaviours across cultures, while Chapter 11 examines research findings from diverse countries. This inclusion enriches the book with examples and insights that extend beyond Western frameworks.

Practical Features

Every chapter includes classroom examples—mostly general, applicable across primary and secondary education. Key points are emphasised in **To Keep in Mind** boxes, while **Background Information** boxes provide extra context. Each chapter concludes with an **In Sum** box.

Most chapters include references to activities allowing you to engage in self-directed practice. These activities and two appendices can be found in the support material accompanying this book: www.routledge.com/9781032914671. These exercises help you to analyse and improve your interpersonal behaviour with students. Improving interpersonal skills takes practice—a lot of it. It should follow a structured approach, for example:

- Analyse your current teaching practices.
- Identify areas for growth.
- Set specific behavioural goals.
- Practice these goals in teaching.
- Seek feedback from peers to refine your approach.

Recording yourself during lessons and reviewing the footage can be a very effective way to reflect on your teaching style and classroom interactions. Sharing these recordings with a trusted colleague for feedback takes it a step further. Their external perspective can often reveal nuances that are hard to notice when you are immersed in the moment.

Feedback from colleagues is very valuable—they can offer insights into how your approach resonates with students and point out areas for improvement that might otherwise go unnoticed. Since you are actively engaged in teaching, maintaining a clear view of your behaviour can be challenging. A colleague's observations provide that much-needed distance, offering a fresh lens to help you grow and refine your skills.

With every activity, icons indicate the character of the activity, as in Figure 1.1.

Sources

This book draws heavily on over four decades of our own research, conducted in collaboration with a wide range of colleagues. The findings are documented in numerous doctoral dissertations, including those by: Tom Adams (2023); Wilfried Admiraal (1994); Mieke Brekelmans (1989); Hans Créton and Theo Wubbels (1984); Romi de Jong (2013); Perry den Brok (2001); Luce Claessens (2016); Monika Donker (2020); Marloes Hendrickx (2017); Tim Mainhard (2009); Heleen Pennings (2017); Jan van Tartwijk (1993); Hanneke Theelen (2021); Xiaojing Sun (2019); Ietje Veldman (2017); and Anna van der Want (2015). Our work is also documented in a range of reviews in handbook chapters (e.g., Wubbels, Brekelmans, den Brok, & van Tartwijk, 2006; Wubbels, Brekelmans, den Brok, Wijsman, Mainhard, & van Tartwijk, 2014, Wubbels, Mainhard, den Brok, Claessens, & van Tartwijk, 2023).

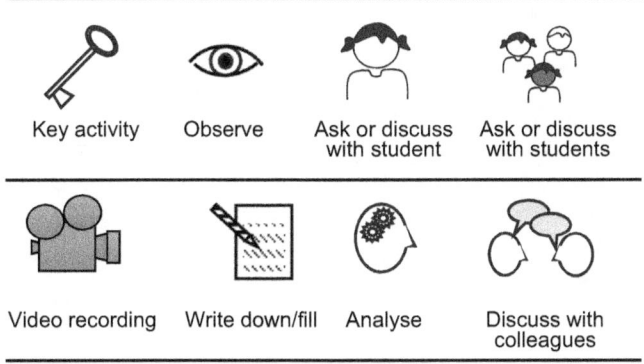

Figure 1.1 Icons indicating the character of the activity

In addition to our own contributions, this book incorporates findings from international research, and we provide detailed references throughout. Practical experience gained from mentoring both novice and experienced teachers, as well as students in teacher education programmes, has also deeply informed our work.

In Sum

This book:

- Offers an interpersonal approach to teaching and classroom management.
- Assists (student) teachers in gaining a deeper understanding of the atmosphere, relationships, and interactions in the classroom.
- Offers practical guidelines based on interpersonal theory to teach as effectively as possible as demonstrated by the authoritative teacher.
- Originated from teacher educators' practical experiences and an extensive body of research on teacher-student relationships.

Note

1 Van Tartwijk et al. (2017).

2 Teaching and Classroom Management

The interpersonal perspective offers a unique lens for understanding teaching, setting it apart from other approaches like the pedagogical or curriculum-focused perspectives. It offers specific strategies for classroom management different from for example behavioural and ecological approaches. In this chapter, we explore what distinguishes the interpersonal perspective from other perspectives and why it matters. We then delve into the profound impact of positive teacher-student relationships—like the one August demonstrated in Chapter 1—on the well-being and growth of both students and teachers. These relationships are not just a "nice to have"; they are at the heart of a thriving classroom.

Looking at Teaching

> Mrs. Phelix begins her lesson on electricity with an engaging hands-on activity: Students are tasked with building simple circuits using batteries and light bulbs. As the circuits come to life, she poses thought-provoking questions to tap into their existing knowledge and encourage curiosity. Yet, the classroom energy doesn't flow quite as smoothly. While some students eagerly participate, others lose focus, fail to listen to their peers or the teacher, and even offer off-topic responses.

In moments like this, the classroom becomes a dynamic environment where many interactions unfold simultaneously. Questions are asked, explanations are given, students collaborate (or do not), and the teacher adjusts her responses to student behaviour. Each action triggers a chain reaction—students observe and react, shaping the collective rhythm of the lesson.

Different Perspectives

When analysing such a lesson, there are many ways to focus your attention and form an opinion about what worked well and what could be improved. For example, you might zoom in on the lesson structure and the quality of the instructional discussion. Did Mrs. Phelix start with a strong opening question? Did she overestimate her students' prior knowledge? Were her responses to their answers constructive? Did she ask the right follow-up questions to deepen the discussion? Observing with these types of questions means taking a *pedagogical perspective*.

DOI: 10.4324/9781003563464-2

Alternatively, you might examine the content itself. Was the material appropriately challenging? Did the lesson align with the curriculum and its goals, and with the sequence in the textbook? This approach involves looking at the situation through a *curriculum lens*.

Another way to look at the lesson is by focusing on how Mrs. Phelix interacted with her students. Did she appear confident or uncertain? Did she control the flow of the class tightly, or did she allow students to take the lead? Was her demeanour friendly and engaging, or more formal and distant? What was the overall classroom atmosphere like? In this case, you are taking an *interpersonal perspective*, which is central in this book.

In truth, teaching can be viewed from many angles—e.g., student motivation, self-regulation, or group dynamics. Each perspective is like a unique pair of glasses that filters what you notice in the lesson. For instance, if you put on the curriculum lens, you might focus on the sequence of topics and overlook subtle classroom dynamics, such as a student whispering a snide remark to a peer. Just like adjusting to a new pair of glasses, it takes practice to observe effectively through these different perspectives.

Background Information

The Nature of the Classroom Environment[1]

In the 1980s, Walter Doyle identified six key factors that highlight the complex and dynamic nature of classrooms. These factors capture the situational characteristics of classrooms that both teachers and students navigate daily.

Multidimensionality

Classrooms are bustling with a variety of tasks, events, and participants. Students come from diverse cultural and social backgrounds, with varying preferences, abilities, and goals. Teachers must simultaneously address these differences while managing the classroom as a whole.

Simultaneity

Events in the classroom often happen at the same time. For example, while a teacher is presenting a topic, a student may whisper to a peer, requiring the teacher to multi-task—monitoring student behaviour and comprehension while continuing the lesson.

Immediacy

Classroom events move at a rapid pace, often requiring teachers to respond instantly. There is little time to pause and reflect on decisions, making quick thinking and adaptability essential skills.

Unpredictability

No two days in the classroom are the same. The way activities unfold varies with each class, lesson, or moment, sometimes influenced by factors that are difficult to predict or explain.

> **Public Nature of Teaching**
>
> Teaching is a highly visible role. Students observe and react to everything a teacher does, even actions that may not be directly intended for them. This dynamic creates a unique level of accountability for teachers.
>
> **Shared History**
>
> Over time, teachers and students develop a shared history of interactions and events. These past experiences shape classroom routines, habits, and norms, influencing future interactions and expectations.
>
> Together, these factors illustrate the complexity of the classroom environment. They highlight why teaching demands not only energy but also significant cognitive effort. Teachers must constantly balance immediate demands with long-term goals, navigating the multidimensional, simultaneous, and unpredictable nature of their work—all while maintaining a positive and productive atmosphere for learning.

Examining Teaching from the Interpersonal Perspective

When examining teaching from the interpersonal perspective, five key elements come into focus: Behaviour, interactions, teacher-student relationships, teacher-class relationships and classroom atmosphere, and the teacher's interpersonal style. Underneath, we will delve into each of these elements and what they entail.

- *Behaviour*: Behaviour refers to the specific actions a person takes at a particular moment. These can include non-verbal behaviours such as gestures, raising a hand, smiling, or making eye contact, as well as verbal expressions. For instance, a teacher nodding in agreement or offering a verbal cue like "good point" are examples of behaviours that play a role in shaping the classroom dynamic. Behaviours convey interpersonal messages. In this example, the teacher's nod conveys an interpersonal message of appreciation of the student.
- *Interactions*: Interactions are sequences of actions and reactions between the teacher and a student—or between the teacher and the entire class in which interpersonal messages are exchanged. Consider this example: A student shouts a comment across the room, the teacher raises an eyebrow and looks at the student, and the student quietly returns to their work. Interactions can be brief, as in this scenario, or extended, covering the course of an entire lesson. Interactions are not limited to one-on-one exchanges. Students often observe how the teacher interacts with others and adjust their own behaviour based on these observations. For example, a teacher's response to a single student's disruptive behaviour may influence the collective atmosphere of the class.
- *Teacher-student relationships*: The teacher-student relationship refers to the overall dynamics and perceptions that develop between the teacher and an individual student. The nature of the relationship is associated with the answer to questions like, "Does the teacher consistently show kindness and respect toward this student?" "Does the student view the teacher as supportive or approachable?"

It is important to distinguish between the general relationship and momentary behaviours. For example, asking, "Is the teacher being friendly to this student right now?" pertains to behaviour or interaction, whereas asking, "Does the teacher maintain a positive relationship with this student?" addresses the broader relationship.

Teacher-class relationships and classroom atmosphere: When you consider all the individual relationships a teacher has with their students, they collectively contribute to the teacher-class relationship. This relationship shapes the overall atmosphere in the classroom. A teacher might have a specific sense of the class as a whole—whether the group feels harmonious, motivated, or challenging. This perception reflects the teacher's connection with the collective class. Additionally, the classroom atmosphere is influenced by the dynamics among students themselves, as peer relationships and interactions can amplify or detract from the environment created by the teacher.

The teacher's interpersonal style: Every teacher brings a unique interpersonal style to their classrooms—a general, consistent way of interacting across lessons and student groups. Some teachers are naturally more controlling or structured, while others adopt a relaxed and flexible approach. Some teachers maintain a consistently warm and approachable demeanour, while others may adopt a more formal tone. This interpersonal style becomes a defining characteristic of teachers' presence and can significantly influence how students perceive and respond to them in different settings.

> **To Keep in Mind**
>
> *Behaviour* is what someone does at a particular moment.
> *Interactions* are sequences of teacher and student behaviours: Actions and reactions.
> *Relaltionships with students and class* involve the general way in which a teacher and student or class interact with each other and how they perceive each other.
> *Interpersonal Style* is how a teacher generally comes across to students in various classes.

Classroom Management

The title of this book, *An Interpersonal Perspective on Classroom Management: Building Teacher Relational Capacity*, highlights our focus on the interpersonal behaviours and strategies of teachers that influence classroom management, either directly or indirectly.

In defining classroom management, we draw upon the comprehensive framework provided by Carolyn Evertson and Carol Weinstein in their influential *Handbook of Classroom Management* (2006).[2] They define classroom management as encompassing everything teachers do to establish an environment that fosters both the intellectual growth and socio-emotional development of students. This perspective includes not only teachers' actions but also their thoughts and beliefs about teaching and learning.

Many approaches to classroom management focus heavily on responding to disruptions or addressing problematic student behaviour. While managing misbehaviour is undeniably important, this narrow view overlooks other critical aspects of classroom management. Our interpersonal approach adopts a more comprehensive perspective. It not only addresses how teachers can effectively respond to challenges but also emphasises proactive strategies for building strong teacher-student relationships, cultivating a positive classroom atmosphere, and encouraging cooperative and respectful student interactions.

By broadening the scope, we aim to equip teachers with tools to support both the academic and emotional well-being of their students, ensuring a harmonious and engaging classroom environment. This expanded view challenges the notion of classroom management as mere discipline and reframes it as a dynamic, relational process that lies at the heart of effective teaching.

Books on classroom management often draw from a broad range of theories or practical strategies. For instance, Tom Bennett's *Running the Room*[3] combines ideas from behaviourism, group formation theories, behavioural economics, and attribution theory. Our approach, however, takes a more focused path: We primarily explore classroom management through the lens of *interpersonal theory*.

By consistently applying this perspective, we aim to deepen your understanding of the interactions between teachers and students, and how teachers can actively shape those relationships through their behaviour. This focus allows us to illuminate aspects of classroom management that may not be as thoroughly explored in other resources.

While our book does share advice you may find elsewhere, framing it within the interpersonal framework clarifies *why* and *how* certain strategies influence the classroom environment and may help to solve classroom issues. With this deeper understanding, you can more easily remember and apply the advice in real-life situations. Interpersonal theory connects seemingly simple strategies, like using rewards or managing disruptions, to the larger goal of fostering a positive classroom atmosphere. As the saying goes, "Nothing is as practical as a good theory."[4]

Our concentrated focus on interpersonal dynamics means other valuable perspectives—such as those related to motivation or curriculum design—are only briefly touched upon. Classroom management is a multifaceted domain, and several other approaches to fostering a productive learning atmosphere in classrooms and schools are recapitulated in the background information that follows. While our primary lens is interpersonal, we will occasionally touch upon these alternative frameworks to provide a more well-rounded view.

Background Information

Four Other Approaches to Creating a Positive Classroom Environment[5]

Creating a positive classroom environment involves multiple strategies, each offering unique insights and methods. The following are four approaches to classroom management additional to the interpersonal one, which often intersect and complement one another.

External Behaviour Control[6]

The oldest approach to classroom management has its roots in behaviourism, with B. F. Skinner considered its founder. At the core of this behavioural approach to classroom management is the *external regulation of student behaviour by the teacher*. Disruptions to order are perceived in this approach as problematic student behaviour that needs to be suppressed or transformed into more desirable behaviour. This is primarily achieved through the prevention of undesirable behaviour, and teaching and rewarding desired behaviour. Other important strategies in this approach are ignoring undesirable behaviour and withdrawing privileges in response to such behaviour. One of the most well-known applications in this line is the popular Positive Behaviour Support (PBS).[7] The most controversial aspect, also within PBS, is the use of punishment for undesirable behaviour, as it can have negative consequences and may not teach alternative behaviour. Especially in special education and in cases of severe behavioural problems, the behavioural approach remains meaningful, often based on a thorough, systematic analysis of the antecedents of problematic behaviour.

Internal Behaviour Control[8]

In contrast to external control, this approach centres on fostering *students' internal regulation* of their own behaviour. It encourages students to develop self-motivation and socio-emotional skills to navigate classroom dynamics independently. This approach to classroom management aims to support students with behavioural issues in regulating their own behaviour. The goal is for students to become motivated to engage in socially and appropriate behaviour and to develop the necessary skills to do this. This implies that they need to internalise the societal norms and values for appropriate conduct. This is achieved, for example, by training students in socio-emotional skills, including understanding their own behaviour and its consequences for others, taking responsibility, providing care for others, and being able to set boundaries and stand up for themselves in a socially acceptable way. In addition to promoting individual socio-emotional development, the focus is on creating a caring classroom community that addresses the needs and desires of each student, and where everyone is a valued part of that community. In such an environment where every student is appreciated, they can feel secure and develop control over their behaviour.

Favourable Ecology[9]

The ecological approach focuses less on individual behaviour and more on *optimising classroom processes, organisation*, and *the physical environment*. The key question is how the many processes occurring in a lesson can be optimised and streamlined to create a pleasant and effective working atmosphere. This approach primarily emphasises preventing distraction and problematic behaviour rather than dealing with it. There is considerable attention in this approach to moments in lessons when issues in the (work) atmosphere may arise, such as at the beginning of the lesson or during transitions between different lesson components, as well as in establishing and enforcing rules and carrying out procedures. The arrangement of the classroom (placement of chairs and cabinets, walkways, pictures on the wall, etc.) is also important in this regard: Does everyone know what needs to happen, and are the materials easily accessible without causing distractions? According to this approach, effective classroom managers have eyes in the back of their heads and consistently convey to students that they are aware of what is happening in the class.

Motivating Curriculum[10]

The curricular approach to classroom management emphasises the role of *engaging and meaningful lessons* in preventing undesirable behaviours. It assumes that when students are actively involved in learning, disruptions decrease naturally. The fundamental assumption is that when students are engaged in tasks that align with their needs and preferences, they are less likely to exhibit problematic behaviour or disrupt the order in the classroom. Through a well-thought-out pedagogical approach, efforts are made to render learning enjoyable and meaningful for the students.

While each of these approaches offers distinct strategies, they are not mutually exclusive. Effective classroom management often draws from multiple perspectives, combining elements of behavioural reinforcement, self-regulation, ecological awareness, curricular engagement, and interpersonal perspectives to create a holistic and adaptive learning environment.

The Importance of Positive Relationships Between Teacher and Students

Humans are social beings. Positive relationships with others are crucial for everyone. When people feel they belong to a group and have positive, friendly interactions with others in that group, they feel better, are happier, more motivated, and healthier. This holds true for everyone in various environments: At home, in a club, and at work. Strong positive relationships at school are essential for both students and teachers. For students, it has positive effects on their motivation and learning processes; for teachers, positive relations are related to well-being and reduce the chances of burnout. To teach effectively, it is crucial to comprehend and navigate interpersonal dynamics.

Background Information

Basic Human Needs[11]

According to Deci and Ryan's Self-Determination Theory (SDT) humans have three basic psychological needs: *Relatedness, competence*, and *autonomy*. These needs influence motivation and engagement. The following is an overview of these needs and how they relate to classroom environments for both students and teachers.

The *need for relatedness* refers to the human desire to belong, form connections, and experience familiarity with others. Students are more motivated when they feel a sense of relatedness with their teacher and peers. This book emphasises relatedness and provides numerous strategies to help teachers strengthen connections with students.

The *need for competence* reflects the desire to feel capable, efficacious, and experience progress. Students are intrinsically motivated when they believe their efforts

> lead to meaningful success. To foster competence in the classroom, you should provide challenging yet achievable tasks. Students should encounter tasks that push them to grow while remaining attainable with effort. Recognising and celebrating small successes, especially in the early stages of teacher-student communication, helps building relationships with a class. You can use faultless learning strategies for students with limited success experiences. Assign guided tasks that guarantee success to help rebuild their confidence and belief in their abilities. The sense of competence is critical to establishing trust and motivation, particularly for students who may doubt their capabilities.
>
> The *need for autonomy* represents the human drive to act independently, make choices, and feel in control of one's own actions. Autonomy fosters motivation when individuals feel their actions are self-directed. To promote autonomy in the classroom, good strategies are allowing students to complete tasks in their own way, encouraging creative problem-solving and initiative. You can provide open-ended clues or prompts rather than prescribing rigid instructions and encourage self-expression by letting students voice opinions and ideas. Also, being overly strict, revealing answers prematurely, or micromanaging students' actions are counterproductive for promoting autonomy. Autonomy requires careful balancing: Teachers need to guide students without undermining their ability to explore and make decisions independently.

Chapter 11 in this book will provide a more detailed exploration of scientific findings on teacher-student relationships. For now, the following overview highlights how crucial it is for teachers to focus on building and maintaining positive relationships—not only for the benefit of their students but also for their own professional satisfaction and well-being.

The Importance of Positive Relationship with Teachers for Students[12]

A positive teacher-students relationship is associated with better student motivation and academic performance. Students engage more, perform better on tests, and have more positive emotions. This applies to all types of students, ages, and educational formats and levels. Research indicates that a good relationship with teachers is particularly crucial for students facing challenges either inside or outside of school. Furthermore, the way a teacher interacts with a student during class influences the student's social standing within the group. As students receive more negative comments during class and are corrected more frequently by the teacher, the likelihood of them having poor relationships with classmates increases. Teacher-student relationships thus have multifaceted effects.

A positive relationship includes not solely being friendly and kind; clear expectations, clear guidance and rules that are consistently enforced constitute the second pillar of positive teacher-student relationships. Predictable and clear interactions with students bring calm to the classroom, help maintain focus, and encourage motivation to engage in tasks. When everything is permitted, students may find it challenging to stay on task and experience autonomy. Many students disengage under such circumstances. The ideal teacher, according to students and teachers themselves, has a significant impact on the classroom dynamics, in a friendly way (as illustrated by teacher August in Chapter 1). In this book, we pay considerable attention to achieving a good combination of guidance and friendliness in teaching. In the interpersonal perspective, we refer to these two aspects as teachers' Agency and Communion (as will be introduced in Chapter 3).

The Importance of Positive Relationships with Students for Teachers[13]

On the one hand, *interactions and relationships with students* are a reason why many teachers enter the field of education. On the other hand, teachers can also face difficulties with interactions in the classroom and experience negative relationships with students. If you have to correct students and find it challenging to be friendly in class, the likelihood of dissatisfaction with your lessons *and* your work increases. Teachers who can take charge in the classroom and easily maintain a friendly rapport with their students tend to be more satisfied with their lessons and find more joy in their work.

> **To Keep in Mind**
>
> For the motivation and academic performance of students, as well as the satisfaction of teachers with their work, it is essential that students perceive the teacher as *taking charge and friendly*.

How you perceive your own lessons is linked to the expectations placed upon you—especially the expectations you set for yourself. If you feel you are not friendly enough or not providing enough guidance, teaching can be challenging. It is exhausting to act kindly when you do not genuinely feel it or when you are actually upset. Dealing with this is referred to as emotional labour. The more emotional labour you must perform, the less enjoyable your work becomes, and the more challenging it is to be in front of the class. Therefore, it is also crucial for teachers themselves to have a positive atmosphere in the classroom.

> **In Sum**
>
> The interpersonal perspective offers a relational perspective on teaching and classroom dynamics, characterised in terms of the interactions and relationships between teachers and students.
>
> The interpersonal perspective stands apart from other perspectives on teaching (e.g., pedagogical or curricular) and other approaches to classroom management (e.g., external and internal control).
>
> Teachers' interactions and relationships with students are important for the motivation and academic performance of students, as well as the satisfaction of teachers with their work.
>
> It is key that students perceive their teacher as friendly and authoritative.

Notes

1 Doyle (1986).
2 Evertson and Weinstein (2006).
3 Bennett (2020).
4 Lewin (1952).
5 Wubbels (2011).
6 E.g., Landrum and Kauffmann (2006).
7 Crone et al. (2015).
8 E.g., Elias and Schwab (2006).
9 E.g., Doyle (2006).
10 E.g., Hickey and Schafer (2006).
11 Ryan and Deci (2000).
12 Wubbels et al. (2014 and 2023).
13 Spilt et al. (2011).

3 The Interpersonal Conceptual Framework

When exploring interactions and relationships in the classroom, having a shared vocabulary is essential for meaningful discussions with colleagues or others. Clear and precise terms not only enhance understanding but also ensure that your ideas are conveyed effectively. This chapter introduces key concepts for analysing relationships and interactions in the classroom, using *interpersonal theory*[1] as a framework. Developed from the 1950s onward by pioneers such as Harry Stack Sullivan and Timothy Leary, this theory provides valuable insights into human connections. Timothy Leary's work,[2] in particular, laid the groundwork for the research programme behind the *Interpersonal Circle for Teachers* that we will explore here.

We begin this chapter by examining classroom dynamics through the lens of interpersonal theory, focusing on how teachers' and students' behaviours influence one another throughout a lesson. Next, we delve into the flow of *interactions–chains of successive behaviours–* and consider how perceptions shape responses. It is important to recognise that even when observing the same behaviour, teachers and students may interpret it differently. These perceptions, not the behaviour itself, drive reactions within interactions. Importantly, teachers *can only alter interactions by adjusting their own behaviour*.

We then unpack fundamental principles of communication. For instance, *you cannot not communicate* when in the presence of others, and *every message carries both* a content and a relationship aspect. This relationship aspect can be understood using two key dimensions: *Agency* and *Communion*. Finally, we bring these concepts together by introducing the *Interpersonal Circle*, a framework that illustrates how Agency and Communion intersect to shape relationships in the classroom. This circle serves as a powerful tool for understanding and improving teacher-student interactions.

Teacher and Students Influence Each Other

Chains in Interactions

> I was already feeling a bit tense and nervous as I entered the classroom, slightly late, and the class was already seated. The students immediately asked a few questions, and I wasn't sure if I should address them individually right away or discuss things later with the entire class. I answered a few questions but postponed others, which seemed to

DOI: 10.4324/9781003563464-3

make the students even noisier and more restless. This made me feel even more nervous, and it seemed like the students became even more excitable because of this.

(Cheryl, student teacher)

In this example, Cheryl reflects on a classroom moment, describing how the behaviours of her students and herself formed a sequence of mutual influence. Her unease amplified the students' restlessness, which in turn intensified her nervousness. This dynamic highlights a core principle of the interpersonal framework: *Classroom interactions are a continuous stream of mutually influencing behaviours*. Understanding this chain of interactions is key to deciphering how both positive and challenging classroom atmospheres develop.

Who Is to Blame?

Teachers and students, however, do not always think about lessons in terms of these interaction chains. More commonly, they frame undesirable situations in terms of *blame*:

- A teacher might sigh, "Today, the class was impossible to manage; they were so noisy."
- Meanwhile, students might complain, "The teacher seemed angry today, or uninterested. She didn't even answer our questions."

This tendency to search for blame can lead to a vicious cycle of mutual frustration, further deteriorating the classroom atmosphere.

Focus on the Teacher's Behaviour

Searching for the one to blame is a futile path for improving the situation and often worsens it. A more constructive approach is the one Cheryl demonstrates in her reflection. By recognising how her own actions contributed to the situation, she takes the first step toward improvement. Within the interpersonal framework, *resolving classroom challenges begins by focusing on the teacher's behaviour*—not because the teacher is "at fault" but because it is the aspect of the interaction that they can most directly and effectively control. The teacher's own behaviour is their most powerful tool (and, probably, the only tool) for shaping the classroom atmosphere. By adjusting their actions, teachers can break negative cycles and foster a more positive and productive environment.

Background Information

Vicious Circles in Interactions in System's Theory

We borrow the emphasis on sequences of behaviours of teacher and students from the systems theory on communication that was developed by the Palo Alto group.[3] They have previously described vicious circles in problematic family situations and between couples. For example:

- "You never really tell me what's on your mind!"

- "Well, you never listen to me, when I do say something, you immediately go on the defensive and claim that what I'm saying isn't true."
- "Yeah, but that's because you don't show what's really bothering you."
- "..."

In educational situations, it could look something like this:

- "You don't do your homework."
- "You don't clearly assign it either."
- "That's because you all are so busy. You don't listen carefully."
- "That's because you can't maintain order."
- "Yes, but you all come into the classroom acting crazy."
- "..."

How You Come Across Shapes the Chain of Interactions

In the classroom, the impact of a teacher's actions is not determined by the behaviour itself but by how it is perceived by the students. Their *responses are shaped by their interpretation of the teacher's actions* rather than the teacher's intentions, emotions, or thoughts. The same principle applies to teachers: They react based on their perception of student behaviour, which may not align with the students' actual intentions or emotions. These mismatched perceptions can easily lead to misunderstandings.

Jere slouches in his chair, yawning, disengaged, and unresponsive during the lesson. The teacher repeatedly tells him to sit up straight, which prompts Jere to sigh audibly and adjust his position slightly without fully changing his posture. The teacher interprets this as Jere being disrespectful and intentionally ignoring him, growing increasingly irritated. However, Jere is simply exhausted and frustrated with other students.

A French teacher enjoys using light sarcasm to maintain a playful atmosphere, teasing students with comments like, "Is that chewing gum in your mouth, or just your braces?" While the teacher sees this as friendly banter, many students find her humour intimidating and fail to perceive it as intended.

In Joan's 5th-grade class, students are noisily working on independent math tasks. After asking for silence several times, Joan grows frustrated and announces, "I'm really disappointed that you're not doing your best today." While some students quiet down, others continue talking, perhaps unaware of Joan's irritation.

In each of the scenarios, the chain of interactions is influenced by perception rather than intention. Students respond based on how they interpret the teacher's behaviour, which in turn shapes the teacher's reaction.

Teacher and student interactions form a continuous chain of behaviours, perceptions, and responses. The teacher's behaviour is perceived by students in a particular way. Their perception shapes their behaviour (and their mood), which is then interpreted by the teacher, influencing how the teacher feels and reacts, and so on. This cycle unfolds moment to moment, creating a dynamic interplay of actions and reactions.

22 An Interpersonal Perspective on Classroom Management

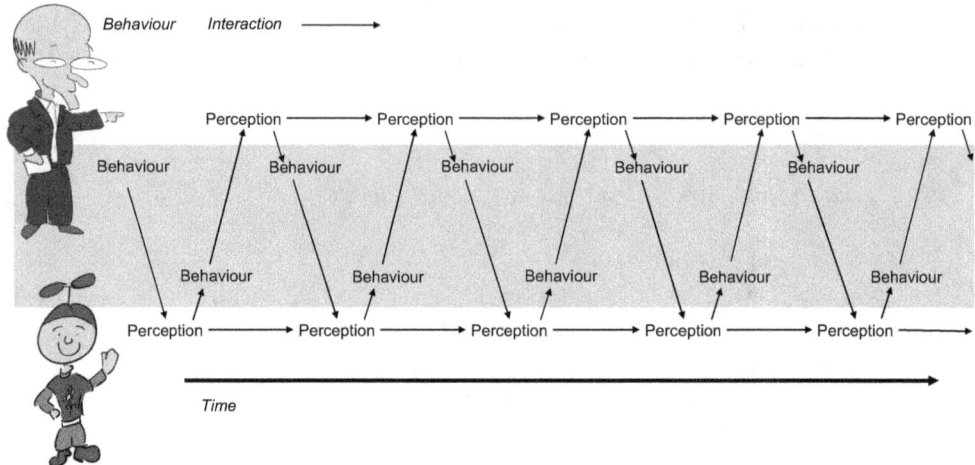

Figure 3.1 Sequence of teacher's and students' behaviours and perceptions from moment to moment

Figure 3.1 illustrates this process, showing how the teacher's behaviour affects the students, how their perceptions influence their responses, and how these responses, in turn, impact the teacher's subsequent actions. These mutual influences, represented by arrows in the figure, highlight the complex, ongoing nature of classroom interactions.

Understanding this chain of interactions is essential for navigating classroom dynamics effectively. By reflecting on how their behaviour is perceived, teachers can take steps to break negative cycles and create a more harmonious and productive classroom environment.

Thoughts, Emotions, and Intentions

In a classroom, emotions, intentions, and thoughts are invisible to others. These are components of internal processes—mental, emotional, and physiological—that shape how individuals interpret and respond to the world around them.

Thoughts represent a cognitive interpretation of external events. For example, a student might think, "The teacher wants us to be quiet." *Emotions* involve an emotional valuation of events ("It's annoying that we have to be quiet—we were just working well in our group") and may also manifest physiologically, such as through a quickened heart rate or tension. These thoughts and emotions influence behaviour. For instance, if a student perceives that the teacher wants silence, they are likely to stop talking. However, if they believe the teacher does not mind them chatting, they are far more likely to continue. In this context, *how* something is communicated becomes just as important as *what* is being said.

> Sheila wants to ask a question, but the teacher doesn't notice her. Sheila might feel consciously ignored, even though the teacher is simply focused on addressing another student. Despite the teacher's intention to be helpful, their unintentional behaviour creates the impression of neglect, which could lead to frustration or misunderstanding.

Intentions are even more difficult to infer than emotions. As in Sheila's case, no matter how good someone's intentions might be, they are irrelevant if the perceived behaviour does not align with those intentions. Behaviour always takes precedence in shaping another person's response. If this mismatch persists, misunderstandings are almost inevitable.

Students and teachers continuously respond not to each other's thoughts, emotions or intentions but to their perceptions of outward behaviour. This underscores the importance of awareness in communication. By considering how their actions might be interpreted, teachers can minimise misunderstandings, fostering clearer and more positive interactions.

Perceptions of Behaviour Differ

Research highlights an interesting phenomenon: Students in the same classroom may perceive their teacher's behaviour differently.[4] For instance, when a teacher says, "It really needs to be quiet now," one student might interpret this as the teacher being angry or displeased, while another might think, "She's about to start the lesson." These varying perceptions arise from several factors.

- *Teacher stereotypes*: Students tend to hold generalised beliefs about teachers, often shaped by past experiences or cultural norms. These stereotypes might include assumptions such as, "Teachers always want to be nice and to maintain control," or "Teachers love hearing themselves talk." Such preconceptions influence how students interpret a teacher's actions.
- *The teacher-student relationship*: The quality of the relationship between the teacher and each student plays a significant role in shaping perceptions. As we will explore in more depth in Chapter 5, a friendly teacher-student relationship increases the likelihood

that a teacher's actions are interpreted positively. For instance, a gentle reprimand from a trusted teacher might feel more like constructive guidance, while the same reprimand from a less-trusted teacher might feel harsh or unfair.

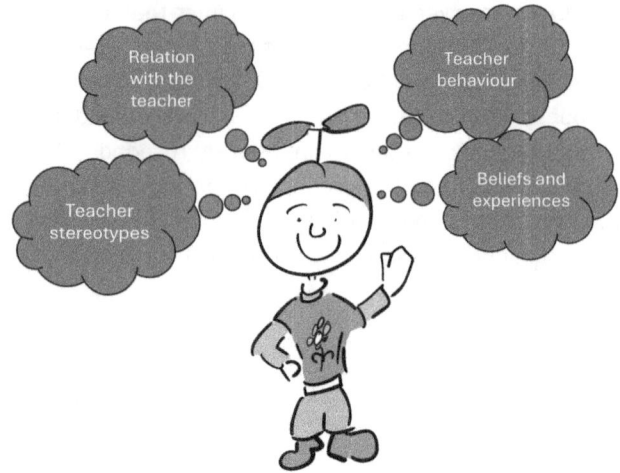

Meaning assigned to behaviour: Students naturally assign meaning to their teacher's actions. If a teacher does not respond to a student's raised hand, one student might assume the teacher is distracted, while another might think the teacher is uninterested or dismissive.

Individual beliefs and experiences: Personal factors like a student's background, emotions, and stress levels also colour their perceptions. For example, a student dealing with significant stress at home may be more sensitive to tone and more easily irritated by a teacher's behaviour, even if it is intended neutrally or positively.

> **To Keep in Mind**
> – Lessons are not isolated events but sequences of teacher and student behaviours that influence one another.
> – Students and teachers continuously respond to their perceptions of behaviour, not to each other's emotions or intentions. Students may interpret your actions differently than you intend.
> – Different students may perceive behaviour differently, based on their experiences.
> – Your behaviour is the most effective starting point for improving interactions.

In **Activity 3.1**, you can practice analysing interactions in your own lessons.

Content and Relationship

Two Aspects of Communication

In examining classroom interaction, it is key to consider the *content* and *relationship* aspects of behaviour.[5] Understanding these two elements is vital for interpreting and delivering effective interpersonal messages.

The *content aspect* of communication refers to the explicit, substantive message being communicated. This could involve instructional material or direct statements such as, "Grab your book." This usually verbally expressed element represents the *what* of the message. Non-verbal behaviour can be used also for content communication, such as a thumbs-up gesture as a response after correctly solving a mathematics problem.

The *relationship aspect* conveys the nature of the interpersonal connection, the *how* of the message. It reflects how the speaker feels about the other person and the relational dynamics, such as dominance, friendliness, or dissatisfaction. For example, a teacher's tone, body language, and facial expressions may reveal whether they are supportive, frustrated, or indifferent—often unintentionally. Just as teachers convey relationship messages to students, students reciprocate through their behaviour. A student may communicate respect and cooperation, or alternatively, frustration and defiance.

Communicating Relationship Messages

While content is primarily communicated through language, verbally, relationship messages are mostly deduced from non-verbal behaviour. This includes body posture, facial expressions, gestures, whether or not eye contact is made, physical proximity to others, how someone utilises the available space in the presence of others, and the non-linguistic aspects of speech such as volume, intonation, pauses, and pitch. Take the phrase "Grab your book" as an example. When said with a cheerful tone and a smile, it communicates friendliness and encouragement. However, the same words yelled with a stern expression convey anger and irritation.

> **To Keep in Mind**
>
> Non-verbal behaviour encompasses various elements, such as smiling, moving your arms, leaning towards a student, fidgeting with your hands, and so on. To bring order to this multitude of elements, we distinguish seven channels of non-verbal behaviour:
>
> – Body posture.
> – Facial expressions.
> – Gestures.
> – Eye contact.
> – Physical proximity to others.
> – Utilisation of available space when others are present.
> – Non-linguistic aspects of speech, such as volume, intonation, pauses, and pitch.

The fact that the relationship aspect is primarily communicated non-verbally does not mean that this aspect cannot also be conveyed through language. This is clear when you consider sentences like "I appreciate that," or "I'm in charge here." Communication of interpersonal messages through language is often rather explicit. Then it is generally clear what you mean for example, when you say: "I'm in charge here." However, when this is said with a nervous smile, then another message might be conveyed.

The most straightforward relationship messages are those where verbal and non-verbal messages are aligned. Saying "I'm in charge here" while standing upright, and speaking with a clear, confident tone reinforces the message. "I like what you're doing" to a student who just picked up something another student dropped, is most convincing when you say this with a smile on your face and enthusiastic body language. Conversely, delivering the same message without eye contact or with a muted tone significantly weakens its impact.

Non-verbal communication for conveying relationship messages often has the advantage of being more subtle and unobtrusive than verbal communication, supporting the flow of the lesson. For instance, a quick smile directed at a student who answers correctly can encourage engagement without interrupting the lesson. You easily can do this frequently while you continue the instruction, and you thus at the same time support a positive classroom atmosphere. Such non-verbal signals also give you flexibility when you want to correct a student in class. A subtle glance or raised eyebrow at an off-task student can redirect behaviour without drawing attention to the disruption or embarrassing the student. This is much less empathic than telling the student to stop and get back to work right away. Another example is when a teacher wants students to speak up, it can be effective for the teacher to take a seat, signalling an invitation for the students to take the floor.

While non-verbal communication has its benefits, it also comes with challenges. Students may not always notice or interpret non-verbal cues as intended. In cases where non-verbal cues are missed or ignored, reinforcing the message through additional non-verbal actions (e.g., standing closer) or explicit verbal communication (e.g., directly addressing the student) may be necessary. We will discuss this further in Chapter 8.

Activity 3.2 lets you observe the effectiveness of the non-verbal behaviour of experienced teachers.

Agency and Communion

According to interpersonal theory, the relationship aspect—that is, the interpersonal message—of an individual in interaction with another can be described universally[6] using two dimensions. In the classroom, we refer to these as *Agency* and *Communion*. These dimensions are both necessary and sufficient to characterise interpersonal dynamics.[7]

The Interpersonal Conceptual Framework   27

Agency describes the degree of influence and control communicated in an interaction. It aligns with concepts like assertive (versus passive) and is closely tied to *authority*, *status*, and *power*. In the classroom, Agency manifests as the teacher's actions to guide behaviour, establish expectations, and maintain a structured environment. For instance, teachers display high Agency when they audibly raise their voices and stand tall with arms spread to command attention at the beginning of a lesson. It is important to distinguish Agency *in relationships* (e.g., the teacher's inherent authority or status) from Agency *in behaviour* (e.g., actively structuring student activities). A teacher might choose not to exercise their authority in certain moments, yet their status remains clear to students. For example, students may enter the classroom quietly because they respect the teacher's authority, even if the teacher does not visibly enforce control at that moment.[8]

It is key to make a clear distinction between guidance in the interpersonal climate and in the learning process. These two forms of guidance can overlap but serve different purposes. Misunderstandings can arise when they are conflated. For example, a teacher can assign an open-ended task with minimal instructions (low guidance in the learning process) but deliver these instructions firmly, with a serious facial expression (high interpersonal Agency).

Communion refers to the level of emotional closeness, friendliness, or warmth expressed in interactions. It ranges from connection and care to hostility and distance. Numerous different concepts refer to forms or aspects of Communion, such as *care*, *affection*, *fondness*, *sympathy*, and *support*. For example, smiling and expressing genuine interest in a student's question shows high Communion. An irritated or dismissive response, even if unintended, demonstrates low Communion. Also, for Communion, teachers with a good classroom atmosphere and a positive relationship with the students do not always demonstrate Communion in every action.

Students are particularly sensitive to interactions with low Communion. For example, an unfriendly joke or a frustrated response to a question can outweigh several positive interactions. When low Communion moments occur, it is important to restore the relationship promptly to maintain trust and a supportive atmosphere (see the second section of Chapter 9).

In the relationship between teachers and their students, both high Agency and high Communion are important for the learning and well-being of students, as demonstrated in Chapter 2. High Agency establishes authority, ensuring order and focus. High Communion fosters trust, connection, and emotional safety. Teachers may not always demonstrate both dimensions equally in every interaction. However, building and maintaining a positive classroom climate depends on managing this combination well over time.

In **Activity 3.3**, you can practice estimating the level of Agency and Communion from a teacher's non-verbal expression.

You Are Always Communicating Agency and Communion

According to interpersonal theory, *you cannot not communicate*. Whether intentional or not, all behaviours exhibited in the presence of others convey an interpersonal message, reflecting both Agency and Communion. This includes both verbal and non-verbal communication, and even in moments of perceived neutrality or silence, an interpersonal message—an indication of what the relationship looks like—is always present.

Even routine actions like explaining a topic or organising a classroom activity carry interpersonal meaning: A teacher can explicitly express such a message, for example, by saying to a student, "I am glad you're here" (high Agency and Communion). However, non-verbal cues such as facial expressions, posture, tone of voice, and proximity often carry even more weight than spoken words. A smile during instruction might convey kindness or approachability, but depending on the context, it could also be interpreted as uncertainty. Frowning when students have not completed their homework could communicate disappointment or even frustration.

Non-verbal Behaviour

You can avoid conveying content by not saying anything, but it is important to remember that non-verbal behaviour is constantly present and unavoidable. Even when you believe you are entirely focused on delivering content, you are also sending interpersonal messages—whether positive, neutral, or unintended. For instance, if you explain something in great detail, students might perceive this as supportive and concern for them, but it can also be seen as low trust in their understanding. When a teacher remains seated at their desk and avoids looking at students as they enter the classroom, they might unintentionally communicate stress, disinterest, or a lack of warmth. Conversely, standing up to greet students with a smile signals friendliness (Communion), setting a positive tone for the lesson.

The fact that you, as a teacher, are always communicating non-verbally and that students derive interpersonal messages from it, can pose challenges, such as when you unintentionally reveal something non-verbally that you would rather not like to communicate. For example, if a teacher unconsciously holds low expectations for a student, this can be conveyed through subtle non-verbal cues like limited eye contact, a flat tone of voice, or reduced enthusiasm[9]. Students may interpret this as a lack of confidence in their abilities, which can damage their self-esteem and negatively impact their performance.

Awareness and Adjustments

Being constantly "on display" as a teacher means that every behaviour matters. To optimise your interpersonal messages, you need to cultivate awareness of how your actions might be interpreted. For instance, if you notice yourself unconsciously communicating low expectations for a student, consider reevaluating your assumptions. Adjusting your mindset can help you project more supportive and empowering interpersonal messages.

To Keep in Mind

- Every behaviour has both a content and a relationship aspect—the interpersonal message.
- When the content and relationship aspects do not align, the relational aspect takes precedence.
- The interpersonal message can always be described with precisely two dimensions: Agency and Communion.
- All behaviours exhibited when others are present convey an interpersonal message; you cannot not communicate.
- Awareness and intentionality in both verbal and non-verbal behaviour are critical to communicating interpersonal messages.

The Interpersonal Circle for the Teacher

The last concept of the interpersonal theory to be discussed is the *Interpersonal Circle*, a framework for organising interpersonal descriptors of behaviours along the two dimensions Agency and Communion. This circle visually represents how behaviours can be categorised and interpreted based on their interpersonal meaning.

Organising Interpersonal Descriptors

Interpersonal descriptors, such as "kind," "strict," or "accommodating," can be arranged based on their similarities. When words that are similar (e.g., "friendly" and "helping") are positioned close together, while opposing descriptors (e.g., "friendly" and "hostile") are placed far from each other, a circular structure emerges (see the left in Figure 3.2).

To simplify the structure, the circle is divided into eight sectors, based on the intersecting dimensions of Agency (vertical axis) and Communion (horizontal axis). On the right side of Figure 3.2, you can see the eight prototypical words we selected for the *Interpersonal Circle for the Teacher*: Directing, Helping, Understanding, Compliant, Uncertain, Dissatisfied, Confrontational, and Imposing.

Each sector represents a unique combination of the two dimensions. For instance, imposing behaviour consists of relatively low Communion and a significant amount of Agency. Understanding behaviour is relatively high in Communion and exhibits limited Agency.

Horizontally opposite sectors refer to behaviours that exhibit the same degree of Agency but differ in Communion. For example, Imposing and Directing, both reflect high Agency, but Imposing has moderately low Communion while Directing has moderately high Communion. Understanding and Dissatisfied both show moderately low Agency, but Understanding has high Communion, while Dissatisfied has low Communion. Sectors vertically opposite each other have a similar

30 An Interpersonal Perspective on Classroom Management

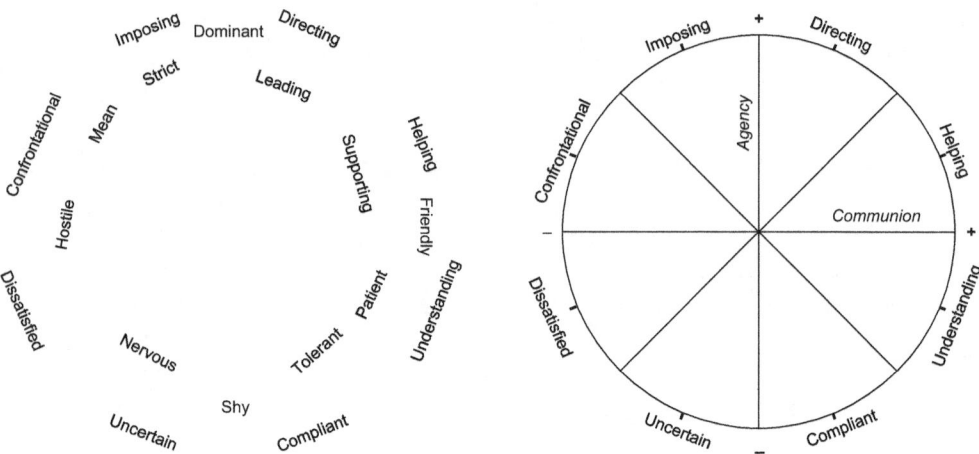

Figure 3.2 Arranging interpersonal messages in a circle (left) and the Interpersonal Circle teacher (right)

degree of Communion while these differ in Agency. For example, Imposing and Uncertain are moderately low on Communion, but Imposing is high and Uncertain low on Agency.

Agency and Communion are also referred to by their extremes: *Assertive* and *Passive* for Agency, and *Cooperative* and *Oppositional* for Communion. Therefore, Agency allows you to determine whether the teacher's behaviour is Assertive, as in Directing, or Passive, as in Uncertain or Compliant behaviour. With Communion, you indicate whether you are aiming to cooperate with the students or whether you position yourself opposite to them.

Behaviour Within the Circle

Teacher (and student) behaviour is not only categorised by its combination of Agency and Communion in the Interpersonal Circle, but also by its intensity. The intensity of behaviour is visualised in the circle by the distance from the centre. The further a behaviour is positioned from the centre of the circle, the greater its intensity.

For example, consider helping behaviour in Figure 3.3, positions 1, 2, 3, and 4. Position 1 (low intensity) involves a teacher providing minimal assistance, such as a quick non-verbal check-in (e.g., a nod or smile to indicate encouragement). This reflects a subtle, light-touch approach to support. Position 4 (high intensity) depicts the teacher providing extensive, overt help, such as speaking to the student in a very friendly and supportive manner, deeply engaging to understand and solve the student's problem. This may involve significant effort, possibly even taking over tasks from the student to ensure a resolution. Position 2 and 3 are in between these two extreme intensities.

The centre of the Interpersonal Circle represents neutral or minimal behaviour, and the outer edges reflect maximum. Behaviours closer to the centre are subtle and less forceful, often involving non-verbal communication. Behaviours near the outer edge of the circle are overt and may require greater effort or emotional investment. Quite often, these might be not appropriate.

The Interpersonal Conceptual Framework 31

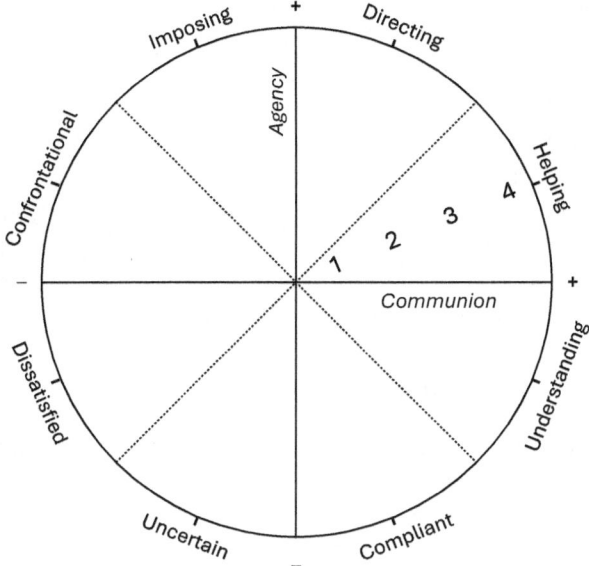

Figure 3.3 Behaviour in the Interpersonal Circle teacher with four different intensities and the same ratio of agency and communion

Background Information

Intensity in Leary's Framework

Within Timothy Leary's work, the position of behaviour within the circle can indicate both the intensity and the frequency of the exhibited behaviour. In Figure 3.3, position 4 can signify either someone providing very strong assistance or someone offering help very frequently. Similarly, position 1 can represent either light assistance or infrequently providing help. Leary refers to behaviour close to the origin as adaptive behaviour, while behaviour at the periphery of the circle is considered pathological behaviour. In terms of frequency, someone who constantly helps others is considered to exhibit pathological mothering behaviour.

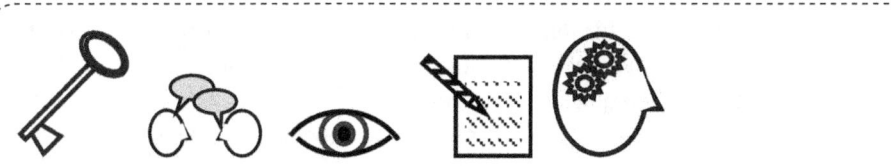

In **Activity 3.4**, you can practice placing teacher behaviours in the Interpersonal Circle.

Relationship Between Agency and Communion

The dimensions of Agency and Communion are independent of each other. This means that a teacher's level of Agency does not necessarily dictate their level of Communion, and vice versa. You can exert influence in a friendly manner (as seen in Helping behaviour) but also in an unfriendly manner (as exhibited by Confrontational behaviour). Similarly, you can be close to students with high Agency (Directive behaviour) or with low Agency (Compliant behaviour).

While Agency and Communion are independent, according to interpersonal theory, certain combinations of these dimensions are more compatible than others, particularly at extreme intensities. For instance, extremely friendly behaviour (such as overly helping or understanding behaviour) may not coexist well with exceedingly high Agency, while extremely assertive behaviour tends to be lower on Communion than the most extreme Communion.

The tendency of certain combinations of Agency and Communion being more likely than others explains why the Interpersonal Circle is a circular, rather than a square, framework.

Functional and Dysfunctional Behaviour

From research, we know that a relationship with students characterised by high degrees of Agency and Communion, in the upper-right corner of the circle as with the teacher August in Chapter 1, is important for a positive classroom climate as well as the well-being and learning of the students (see Chapter 11). While behaviours with high levels of Agency and Communion (in the upper-right corner of the Interpersonal Circle) are generally conducive to a positive classroom climate and student learning, behaviours from other sectors of the circle can also be *functional* if applied appropriately.

Functional behaviour refers to actions that align with engaging students in the learning process and creating a positive classroom environment. Behaviours on the right side of the circle, such as helping, understanding, and adapting, are usually seen as positive and self-evidently functional. These behaviours clearly promote cooperation and emotional closeness, contributing to students' well-being and engagement.

For behaviours on the opposite, left side of the circle, functionality may be less obvious, but strict or corrective actions can also be functional when applied thoughtfully and with low intensity. Its functionality depends on the situation and the intensity of the behaviour. For instance, during chaotic moments, imposing behaviour may help establish order, but if used frequently or in intense ways, it may come at the expense of students' intrinsic motivation. Even confrontational or corrective behaviour with low intensity to redirect disruptive students can be necessary and appropriate. High-intensity corrective actions like shouting or humiliating a student are dysfunctional and do not belong in the classroom, as they damage the teacher-student relationship and the classroom climate.

It is crucial to consider that behaviours with low Communion (e.g., corrections or confrontations) can quickly harm relationships with students—a good rapport with the class takes time to build but can deteriorate quickly. When you have displayed such oppositional behaviour, restoring the relationship is crucial: For example, by explaining your behaviour to the class, for instance, if you were feeling tired or momentarily confused.

Effectively employing teacher behaviours on the left side of the circle demands a high level of professionalism. For example, you must be able to accurately assess how your behaviour comes across and what its impact on students is. Some teachers confuse confrontational behaviour (with rather low Communion) with imposing behaviour where Agency is the most prominent. They think to act strictly, but their students perceive them as confrontational and hostile. In Chapter 6 (pp. 81-82), we will elaborate on the importance of this distinction.

Your *behavioural repertoire* is the foundation for flexible responses to students in many different situations. A professional teacher possesses a broad repertoire of behaviours across the circle, enabling them to switch flexibly between behaviours across the circle as the situation demands.

In practice, teachers naturally have stronger repertoires in certain sectors of the circle. For example, a teacher comfortable with high Agency may easily direct students but struggle with understanding behaviours. Recommendations for behaviour should consider these individual differences to avoid backfiring. For example, suggesting someone to be *a bit stricter* might work well for one person with a strong repertoire in the upper left corner of the circle but backfire for another who faces difficulties in displaying high Agency.

In sum, functional teacher behaviour is not limited to one part of the Interpersonal Circle; it depends on context, intensity, and the teacher's ability to adapt what behaviour is functional. While high Agency and Communion are generally ideal, behaviours from other sectors of the circle can also be effective when applied judiciously and often with low intensity.

Further exploration of functional and dysfunctional behaviours in specific situations will be provided in Chapters 8, 9, and 10.

You can reflect on the value of behaviours in different parts of the Interpersonal Circle in **Activity 3.5**.

The Interpersonal Circle and Teaching Methods

The Teacher Interpersonal Circle provides insight into the interpersonal dynamics of classroom interactions, but it is not intended to serve as a *pedagogical framework*. Teaching methods and interpersonal behaviours are independent concepts. For example, all possible teaching methods can be executed in a friendly or unfriendly manner. Also, a teaching method does not directly dictate the degree of Agency and Communion in the relationship. For example, in project-based learning, you can provide clear explanations about the purpose or be strict about usage of mobile phones for searching the internet or, alternatively, offer no structure at all. Additionally, the utilisation of specific teaching methods (such as working in open learning spaces) does not inherently imply that the teacher will have little or no Agency.

To Keep in Mind

The Interpersonal Circle:

- Categorises interpersonal behaviour along two dimensions: Agency and Communion.
- Maps relational guidance.
- Is not a pedagogical framework.

Interpersonal Time Scales and Components

The components in the interpersonal analysis of teaching—behaviour toward a student and toward a class, interactions between teacher and students, relationships with a student and with a class, and the teacher's interpersonal style—develop at different time scales, as we introduced in Chapter 2. The Interpersonal Circle Teacher can be applied to all these components and thus on distinct time scales. You can use it to describe:

Behaviour (moment-to-moment actions): What someone is doing at a particular moment, for example, a teacher showing dissatisfaction (low Communion). Or a student asking a question (high Agency).

Interactions (chains of actions and responses): Teacher behaviour elicits students' responses, forming brief interpersonal exchanges. For example, the teacher directs a student (high Agency), and the student complies (low Agency). Or vice versa: The teacher showing dissatisfaction with a student's behaviour in response to incomplete homework.

Relationships: The relationship between a teacher and a student reflects patterns of interaction over time. For example, a teacher's consistent use of behaviours high in Agency and Communion (upper-right corner of the circle) may establish a supportive, authoritative relationship with a student.

Interpersonal Style: A teacher's interpersonal style reflects their typical way of relating to students across different classes. For example, a teacher who consistently builds relationships during their career emphasising high Agency and Communion.

It is important to make clear distinctions between these components.

Momentary behaviour vs. established relationships: The character of the relationship differs from momentary behaviour. For example, a teacher with a positive relationship (upper-right section of the circle) might temporarily display dissatisfaction (left side of the circle) due to a specific incident. Conversely, repeated displays of high Communion behaviour can help restore a relationship characterised by low Communion.

Individual students vs. the class as a whole: Teachers can interact differently with individual students and the class as a whole. For example, a teacher may praise the entire class for completing homework (right side of the circle), while expressing dissatisfaction with specific students who did not complete their assignments (left side of the circle). Likewise, teachers have a *relationship* with an individual student and the class as a whole.

The Interpersonal Circle Student

Similar to the Interpersonal Circle Teacher, the Interpersonal Circle Student is based on the dimensions of Agency and Communion. It provides a framework to describe and categorise student behaviours in the classroom using these two axes (see Figure 3.4). Based on interviews with teachers and students, the eight prototypical terms on the circle are now chosen to describe *student behaviour* characteristic for the eight sectors of the circle. For instance, behaviour with high Agency and moderate Communion is labelled as Proactive, and when high Agency coincides with moderate oppositional behaviour, we refer to that as Competitive in relation to the teacher.

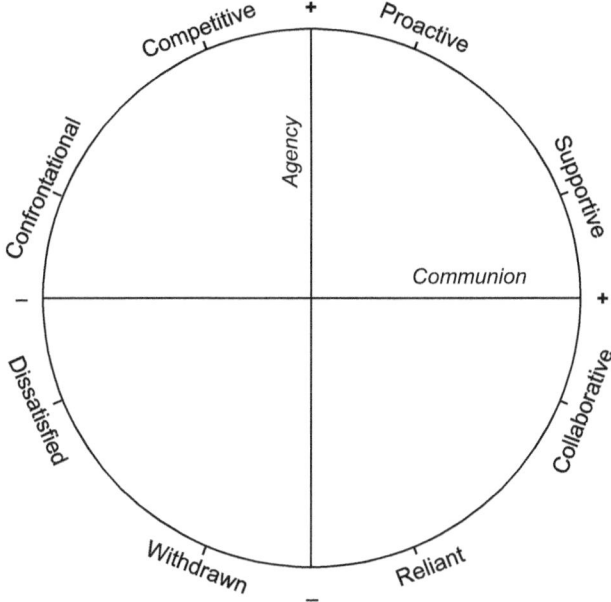

Figure 3.4 The Interpersonal Circle student

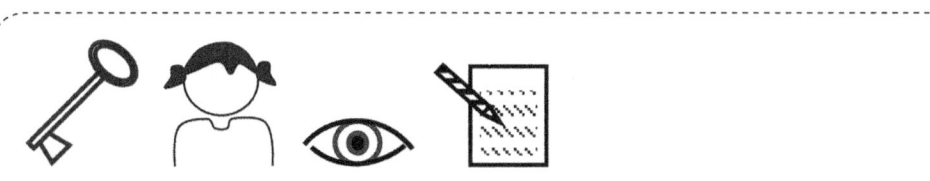

In **Activity 3.6**, you position student behaviours in the Interpersonal Circle.

In sum

Teachers and students:

- Influence each other during the lesson in chains of successive behaviours called interactions.
- May have different perceptions of each other's behaviours.
- Respond based on these perceptions, not the actual behaviour.

Teachers' behaviours:

- Are their only means to change interactions.
- Always convey content and relationship messages.
- Can be described using two dimensions: Agency and Communion.

The Interpersonal Circles Teacher and Student are models on which all teacher and student behaviours, interactions and, relationships can be plotted along the dimensions Agency and Communion.

Notes

1 Horowitz and Strack (2010).
2 Sullivan (2013), Leary (1957).
3 Watzlawick et al. (1967).
4 Den Brok (2001), Levy et al. (1993, 2003).
5 Watzlawick et al. (1967).
6 Blatt and Luyten (2010).
7 Leary (1957), Lonner (1980).
8 Burgoon et al. (2022).
9 Timmermans et al. (2018).

4 Gaining Insight into Behaviour, Interactions, and Relationships

Reactions to behaviour are based on perceptions of behaviour. After all, only behaviour is visible to the person with whom you communicate. You may have *intended* to communicate something quite differently from how it is *perceived*. For teachers, it is crucial to carefully assess whether what they intended to convey in the classroom (for example, it should be safe for students to ask questions) is actually perceived by students in that way (for example, if I ask a question, I might be laughed at).

In this chapter, we discuss how you can investigate the interpersonal meaning and significance of your behaviour, interactions, and relationships in the classroom. You can gain insight into these aspects in various ways. First, you could think about it (referred to as *reflection*, providing the *teacher's perception* of their own behaviour). Also, you could ask students what they think about certain behaviour or their relationship with you as a teacher (the *student's perception* of the teacher's behaviour). Finally, instead of using students' perceptions or opinions, you might ask someone else to *observe* in your classroom.

Activity 4.1 will help you gain insight into how students perceive your behaviour.

Observing Behaviour with the Interpersonal Circle

In Chapter 3, we discussed that you are *always communicating*. At any given moment, both teacher behaviour and student behaviour can be located on the dimensions of Agency and Communion within the Interpersonal Circle. The position on the Agency dimension depends on the answer to the question, *Who determines what happens in the classroom at a given moment?* Is it the teacher or the students who determine(s) or are both trying to take charge of the situation? You can use a five-point scale to score both for the degree of Agency:

DOI: 10.4324/9781003563464-4

38 An Interpersonal Perspective on Classroom Management

The teacher has no control at all over what happens in the classroom **Low Agency**				The teacher has complete control over what happens in the classroom **High Agency**
1	2	3	4	5
The students have no control at all over what happens in the classroom **Low Agency**				The students have complete control over what happens in the classroom **High Agency**
1	2	3	4	5

For the Communion dimension, the key question is *how friendly are teacher and student(s) towards one another?* Key words are friendliness or unfriendliness, rejecting versus approving and connecting, or, in other words, Oppositional or Cooperative:

The teacher acts unfriendly and expresses rejection of the students **Low Communion**				The teacher acts friendly and connects with the students **High Communion**
1	2	3	4	5
The students express rejection towards (the behaviour of) the teacher **Low Communion**				The students express approval of (the behaviour of) the teacher **High Communion**
1	2	3	4	5

To Keep in Mind

You can analyse your and your students' interpersonal message by scoring behaviours on the five-point scales for the Agency and Communion dimensions.
You can do this yourself or ask a colleague.

In **Activity 4.2**, you can analyse the interpersonal message communicated with behaviour in parts of your own lesson using the two dimensions of Agency and Communion.

Background Information

Observing with the Joystick Method[1]

Heleen Pennings applied a more advanced and precise method to capture teacher and class behaviour in the Interpersonal Circle. This method is called Continuous Assessment of Interpersonal Dynamics (CAID)[2] and uses a computer joystick connected to specific software to score teacher and class behaviour on video recordings from moment to moment. The researcher sits behind a screen displaying a coordinate system and a dot representing the position of the teacher or class in the Interpersonal Circle as a combination of the Agency and Communion dimensions. The screen also shows a video recording of a lesson, as depicted in Figure 4.1.

The researcher, shown in the photo, uses the joystick to map the position of the teacher or class by moving the dot through the coordinate system. The researcher constantly follows where the behaviour of the teacher or class is located on the two dimensions.

In the photo, the researcher is coding the position of the teacher, and the dot is in the upper-right quadrant. The position of the dot in the upper-right quadrant indicates that the researcher estimates that the teacher in the video has much influence and is a bit cooperative toward the students: The teacher is saying something, and the students are listening and appreciating it.

The computer records the position of the dot, and thus the scores for Agency and Communion, twice per second. The assessments of different researchers who practiced together were found to be quite consistent when independently mapping the position of the teacher or students using the joystick.

Figure 4.1 Researcher using the joystick method
Source: Still from Video in Figure 3 of Pennings et al. (2014)

The Questionnaire on Teacher Interaction (QTI)

Since graduating from the teacher training programme, Jolanda has been working at a school where every year, they administer a questionnaire to students about some teachers: the QTI. The QTI maps the perceptions of the teacher-student relationship. Jolanda administered the questionnaire to two of her classes. She also completed it herself for both classes, answering the questions by estimating each time how she thought she teaches this class. Additionally, she completed the questionnaire for her ideal teaching style. ("How would you like to teach as a teacher?")

Jolanda notices significant differences between her perception and the students' responses. For instance, she sees herself as more authoritative and less uncertain compared to the students. Also, the average answers of the students in the two classes are quite different. Jolanda wonders if it is normal for teachers to perceive themselves differently than students do. Can the results be trusted, considering that some students were absent due to illness, and a few completed the survey very quickly? And what about some students with a different cultural background than most of the students? Do they perceive her differently and do they complete the questionnaire differently? Regarding the outcomes, Jolanda is uncertain about the next steps. Should she discuss the results with the students? If she wants to appear more authoritative or less uncertain, how should she go about it?

This chapter addresses some of the questions Jolanda has, while others are addressed in Chapter 11. We will discuss mapping perceptions of students and teachers of teacher-student relationships and teacher-class relationships. This can be done using the QTI, which provides (prospective) teachers with feedback on the interpersonal climate in their classrooms. The questionnaire is based on the Interpersonal Circle for the teacher that we introduced in Chapter 3. We will discuss how this questionnaire was developed, what it measures, and the extent to which the results are reliable and valid.

Development

The QTI was created in the 1980s in the Netherlands by Hans Créton and Theo Wubbels to better assist beginning teachers in secondary education with classroom management issues. Indeed, in the supervision of these teachers, it turned out that they often had little idea of their students' perceptions of them. Understanding this perception is important to assess what the character of the relationship is and how it can be improved. Insight into this perception can be obtained, for example, by having conversations with students. However, conducting such a conversation even with one student is not always easy. Moreover, you often do not know if what you hear is the opinion of a particular student or a more widely shared perception among the students.

Background Information

Development of the Dutch Version

The QTI was created based on numerous conversations with students, teachers, school leaders, and teacher educators. The statements about teacher-student relationships collected in these conversations were categorised into the Interpersonal Circle. Many different statements (such as "This teacher is patient," or "This teacher gets angry quickly") were tested to see if students and teachers could answer the questions meaningfully and if the questions could indeed be ordered on the Interpersonal Circle. After several trial versions, a version with 77 questions was developed, distributed across the 8 sectors of the Interpersonal Circle. More recently, mostly a 24-question version is used.

As early as the 1990s, an English version was developed in the United States, consisting of 64 questions based on the original Dutch version of the QTI. A couple of years later a version reduced to 48 questions was developed in Australia. Since then, the QTI has become available in at least 40 languages, such as Turkish, Spanish, Arabic, Chinese, Bahasa Indonesia, Italian, and Malay. Over the years, many researchers have worked with the questionnaire and examined its quality. Based on all that research, it became clear that perceptions of students and teachers about their relationship could be accurately assessed in many cultures. Patterns in students' responses to different questions were also quite consistent and in line with the dimensions of the Interpersonal Circle.

Background Information

Adapting the QTI to Other Languages[3]

A crucial aspect of adapting the questionnaire to different languages is that effective versions are not created merely by translating or making slight adjustments to the questions. Instead, the process involves examining each context to identify what is characteristic of the various sectors and dimensions of the Interpersonal Circle. The English, Turkish, and Chinese versions, like the Dutch version, were developed through numerous interviews, and continuously testing and modifying the questionnaire until the eight sectors and individual questions aligned well with the circle.

A translation of a question from one language to another may yield a position of the translated question in a slightly different part of the circle than in the first language; the interpersonal meaning of literally translated questions may differ between countries or cultures. For instance, in analyses of responses from Chinese teachers and students, we found that some QTI questions ended up in a different place on the Interpersonal Circle compared to the Netherlands. A statement like "This teacher is patient" is perceived in China significantly lower on Agency and Communion than in

> the Netherlands. In other words, in China, this says more about the (lack of) "authority" of a teacher, whereas in the Netherlands, it says more about the closeness between teacher and students. Also, in one country, being strict or authoritative as a teacher may have a different connotation than in another country. What might be acceptable in Britain in terms of a teacher showing uncertainty might be unthinkable in another country, such as India. In other words, potential statements and responses are influenced by the cultural background of the respondent. While specific behaviours may have different positions on the circle in different cultures, the Interpersonal Circle with its dimensions and sectors has been proven to be valid across cultures.

Current Version

We continued to develop the QTI for a long time, and ultimately, we found that we could also get a good understanding of the perceptions of students and teachers with a much shorter version. The version of the QTI for secondary education that is currently used in the Netherlands is the one with 24 statements. Each sector of the Interpersonal Circle is measured by three statements. In Appendix 4.1 the questionnaire is included with a key indicating which question corresponds to which sector. The procedure for manually creating visual representations of the results in the Interpersonal Circle is also provided. Similarly, in Appendix 4.2 we, present the version for use in primary education, along with the processing procedure. This version consists of 16 questions, two in each sector. These questionnaires and Excel sheets to process the data are available on the website of this book (www.routledge.com/9781032914671).

The questionnaire, for both secondary and primary education, consists of statements where students indicate on a five-point scale the extent to which the statement applies to a particular teacher. Teachers can themselves indicate whether they find the statement applicable to themself in a specific class. The questionnaire comes with instructions enabling its administration in secondary education to students without additional explanation. The administration of the QTI 24-question secondary education version takes about 10 minutes, depending on the grade level. In primary education, administration can be completed in about 15 minutes. In the lower grades, oral guidance is necessary when administering the primary education version of the questionnaire. There are now also versions of the questionnaire for higher education, for online education, for one-on-one coaching, and for school leaders.

The questionnaire consists of statements that inquire about general perceptions; how a student perceives the teacher or how teachers perceive themselves *over an extended period*. Student perceptions provide information about the relationship between the teacher and the student, according to the student. Students can fill out the questionnaire after having a few lessons with a teacher because the relationship stabilises fairly quickly, and students have a pretty good idea about what to answer. In the Section on types of teacher-class relationships in Chapter 5, we will show how this relationship develops in the first four months of a teacher's lessons in a new class.

With the questionnaire, reliable data about how students perceive a teacher can be obtained by having ten students from a class complete it. Asking more students to complete the questionnaire will seldom change the overall picture. For experienced teachers in secondary education, two classes are usually sufficient to get a good idea of the teacher's overall interpersonal style. For novice teachers and students in teacher education, the differences between classes are often somewhat larger than for experienced teachers. Moreover, the level of Agency perceived by students from different classes for the same teacher is fairly consistent in secondary education. Scores on Communion, however, vary slightly more depending on which class the teacher is teaching.

It has been found that the version for primary education mainly differentiates between teachers on the Communion dimension and much less on the Agency dimension.[4] This is despite observations indicating that teachers in primary education do indeed vary in the degree to which they exhibit Agency. It seems that young children do not distinguish very much between teachers based on Agency.

Use

Teachers often use the questionnaire to gather feedback from their students about the relationship they have with a class, that is the classroom climate. In this case, you do not look at the individual questionnaires completed by each student, but at the overall picture that emerges when you combine all the responses (*the students' perception*). They can then compare the perception students have of the relationship with their own *self-perception* ("How do you think you are teaching this class?") when they also fill out the QTI about how they think they teach a specific class. Other often interesting comparisons include those with the teacher's *ideal*: "How would you like to teach as a teacher?" and the ideal of the students or what they think of their best teacher: "How would you prefer a teacher to teach?"

The results of a QTI administration then include scores per question, per sector (the average over the questions in the respective sector), and for the dimensions of Agency and Communion. Graphically, the results are often presented as a profile in the Interpersonal Circle. Figure 4.2 provides an example of such results.

In addition, the results can be presented as a point, indicating the centre of gravity in the Interpersonal Circle by plotting the Agency and Communion score, as in Figure 4.3 for the three example profiles from Figure 4.2.

When using the QTI to analyse your relationship with the class, it is important to consider the following points:

- Administering the questionnaire is voluntary for students and anonymous; you should ensure that you don't know which student filled out which questionnaire. This helps to encourage students to provide an honest completion of the QTI.
- The purpose of administering the QTI to students is to gain insight into their perception of the relationship with you, identify your strengths in the relationship with them, and recognise areas for improvement.
- Your own perception, your ideal perception, and the perception that students have of the relationship are each valuable on their own. It is not about determining who is right or wrong but about understanding where perceptions align and differ and what actions you could take based on those differences.
- As mentioned in the introduction of this book, a relationship like August has with his students, is desirable. This means aiming for relatively high scores on the QTI in the Directing, Helping, and Understanding sectors because they are associated with high student performance and motivation (refer to Chapter 11 for more details).
- The QTI captures a part of your teaching; to get a comprehensive view, you could use additional sources of information, such as video footage, conversations with students, observations by colleagues, etc.

	Your students	Yourself	Your ideal
This teacher is a good leader	2.3	3.0	4.0
This teacher is respected	2.2	3.0	4.0
This teacher acts confidently	2.7	3.0	4.0
Directing	**2.4**	**3.0**	**4.0**
This teacher is someone you can depend on	2.9	3.0	4.0
This teacher has a sense of humour	2.8	2.0	4.0
This teacher's class is pleasant	2.6	3.0	4.0
Helping	**2.8**	**2.7**	**4.0**
This teacher is patient	2.1	2.0	4.0
This teacher is understanding	3.0	2.0	4.0
This teacher is easy-going	1.5	2.0	3.0
Understanding	**2.2**	**2.0**	**3.7**
This teacher lets students get away with a lot	0.9	1.0	0.0
This teacher can be influenced by us	1.8	1.0	1.0
This teacher tolerates a lot of student behaviour	0.9	2.0	1.0
Compliant	**1.2**	**1.3**	**0.7**
This teacher's discipline is weak	0.3	0.0	0.0
This teacher is uncertain	0.8	1.0	0.0
This teacher is hesitant	0.5	1.0	0.0
Uncertain	**0.5**	**0.7**	**0.0**
This teacher is dissatisfied	0.8	1.0	0.0
This teacher is grumpy	0.7	1.0	0.0
This teacher is unhappy	0.1	0.0	0.0
Dissatisfied	**0.5**	**0.7**	**0.0**
This teacher gets angry quickly	1.1	2.0	1.0
This teacher threatens to punish students	1.0	1.0	0.0
This teacher gets angry unexpectedly	1.0	1.0	0.0
Confrontational	**1.0**	**1.3**	**0.3**
This teacher controls when students can speak	2.5	3.0	4.0
This teacher imposes silence in class	2.0	2.0	2.0
This teacher is strict	1.7	2.0	1.0
Imposing	**2.1**	**2.7**	**2.3**
Agency	**0.28**	**0.34**	**0.50**
Communion	**0.34**	**0.28**	**0.72**

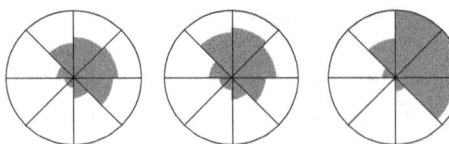

Agency and Communion run from -1 to +1
All other scores run from 0 (not at all) to 4 (very much)
Bold print figures are averages per sector and dimension.

Figure 4.2 Representation of results from the administration of the QTI in a class in secondary education. Your students: Average score of the students in your class; Yourself: Your perception of the relationship with the class; Your ideal: How you would like to see the relationship

Gaining Insight into Behaviour, Interactions, and Relationships   45

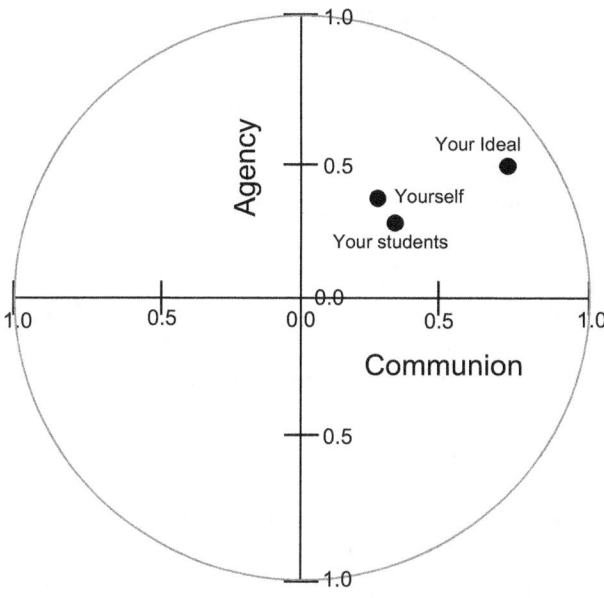

Figure 4.3 Centre of gravity of the three profiles of Figure 4.2

To Keep in Mind

- The QTI helps you investigate your own and students' perceptions of the teacher-class relationship. To get a comprehensive view of your teaching, you need additional tools.
- Administering the questionnaire should be voluntary for students and anonymous
- Your own perception, your ideal perception, and the perception that students have of the relationship are each valuable on their own.

When you have administered the QTI to one or more classes, you can analyse the results in various ways. **Activity 4.3** will guide you through this process.

Activity 4.4 gives you ideas to collect student feedback by conversations with them.

Comparison of Teacher and Students' Perceptions[5]

Students and teachers often do not share the same perception of their relationship. Only in 8 percent of cases (within the measurement's margin of error) is there complete agreement between the students' perception and the teacher's perception of the relationship. In the remaining 92 percent of cases, this is not the case. In about two-third of those cases, students' scores for Agency and Communion are lower than those of teachers, or at least one of those scores is lower, and the other is equal. These teachers believe more than the students that they determine what happens in the class and/or feel that they are more cooperative. This perception is usually closer to the teachers' ideal of the teacher-student relationship. Compared to students, they overestimate the behaviours that are positively related to student achievement and motivation. Therefore, one could say that these teachers have a more positive perception of the relationship than their students.

Figure 4.4 provides an example of the students', self-, and ideal perceptions, where the teacher's self-perception is closer to the ideal than the students' perception. In this case, one could argue that the teacher is engaging in wishful thinking.

For the remaining one third of the teachers, the opposite is true: These teachers have a more negative view of the relationship than their students, as in Figure 4.5. In other words, they have scores for their self-perception that deviate more from their ideal than the students' perception. The question is whether this last group of teachers is protecting themselves from a disappointing outcome from their students.

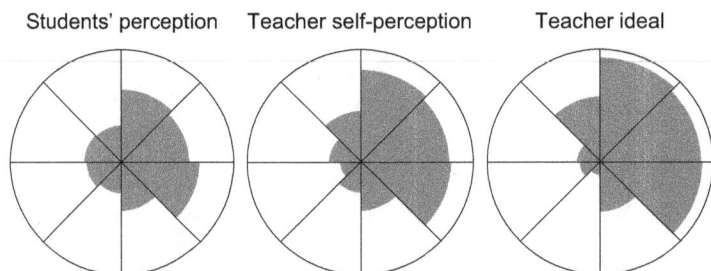

Figure 4.4 The teacher self-perception is closer to the teacher's ideal than the students' perception

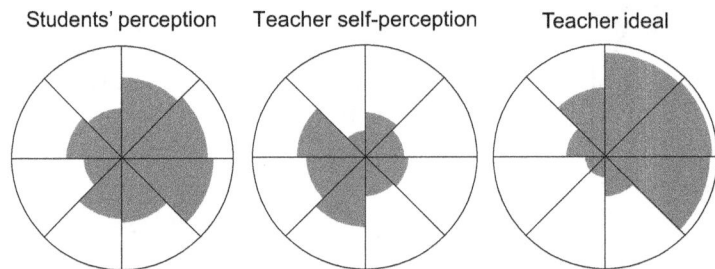

Figure 4.5 The teacher's self-perception resembles the ideal less than the students' perception

It is interesting to note that as the distance between the students' perception and the teacher's self-perception of the relationship increases, according to the students, the teacher generally scores lower on Agency and Communion. A less positive teacher-student relationship is therefore associated with a larger difference of opinion between students and teachers about the nature of the relationship.

To Keep in Mind

- Student and teacher perceptions rarely match exactly.
- Most teachers view themselves more positively than their students do.
- The better your relationship with a class, the smaller the difference between teacher and student perception usually is.

In Sum

To improve your teaching, it is crucial to carefully assess whether what you intend to convey in the classroom is actually perceived as such by the students. For this:

- You can observe your own and your students' behaviours and interactions with four simple scales representing the degree of Agency and Communion (two scales each).
- Administer the QTI to map the perceptions of your students and yourself of your teacher-class relationships; the results will provide you with feedback on the interpersonal climate in your classrooms.

Notes

1 Pennings et al. (2014).
2 Lizdek et al. (2012).
3 Wubbels et al. (2012).
4 Hendrickx et al. (2016), Zijlstra et al. (2013).
5 Wubbels et al. (2006).

5 Teacher Interpersonal Relationships and Styles

The term *relationship* refers to the patterns in the dynamics between teachers and students—how they usually interact and connect. A teacher's *interpersonal style* reflects their typical way of relating to students across different classes. These relationships can be charted using tools like the Questionnaire on Teacher Interaction (QTI, discussed in Chapter 4).

Relationships between teachers and students begin to take shape during their very first encounters. Early interactions set the tone. These connections often develop quickly to become rather stable as teachers and students get to know each other. Once the relationship is established, it shapes how students perceive the teacher's actions. For example, when the relationship is positive, the teacher's behaviour will be cast in a favourable light. That is why investing in building positive relationships is so crucial, even if it is not always an easy or seamless process.

In this chapter, we will examine the types of relationships teachers can have with individual students and entire classes, as well as the various interpersonal styles teachers bring to the classroom. We will also look at how these relationships and styles can evolve over time. In the chapters that follow, we will dive deeper into the specific behaviours that foster strong, positive relationships—and those that can create challenges.

We will begin by exploring how teacher-student interactions, relationships, and styles change on different time scales and how the nature of the relationship shapes the way behaviours are interpreted.

Changes Over Time

The way behaviours, interactions, and relationships between teachers and students evolve over time varies greatly. Teacher-student *interactions and behaviours* can shift in an instant—changing from cooperative to oppositional, or from assertive to passive, from moment to moment. For example, a teacher might ask if a student understands a concept one second and, shortly after, reprimand the same or another student for being disruptive. These rapid changes in behaviours reflect fluctuations along the dimensions of Agency and Communion.

In contrast, once established, *relationships* between teachers and students tend to be far more stable. For instance, if students perceive a teacher as authoritative, they are unlikely to suddenly view that teacher as insecure. If they do change, it is usually over weeks or months rather than within a single lesson. Significant shifts in *relationships with an individual student*

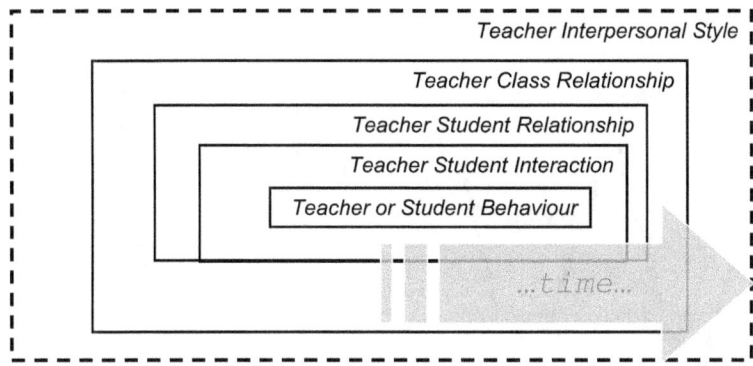

The lower the level, the faster changes over time

Figure 5.1 Changes over time for behaviours, interactions, relationships and styles

Adapted from Wubbels et al. (2023)

often result from major events—typically unpleasant ones, such as a misunderstanding that leads to frustration or anger. After such incidents, relationships often stabilise over time in a new form. Positive shifts can also occur through small but meaningful moments, such as a friendly chat during a break or a display of unexpected interest in a student's thoughts or experiences after class. These interactions can build trust and enhance the teacher-student bond.

Similarly, a *teacher's relationship with an entire class*-the interpersonal climate,-is generally steady and changes only gradually over several months. A significant incident with one student rarely alters the overall class dynamic unless it is highly visible or extreme. Shared experiences—like participating in extracurricular activities—can serve as catalysts for fostering closer connections with the class as a whole.

The most stable aspect of teacher-student dynamics is the teacher's *interpersonal style*. A teacher's interpersonal style tends to remain consistent across different classes. While minor adjustments might occur, significant changes in this style typically unfold over years, if at all, not weeks or months. Beginning teachers often experience the most rapid evolution in their interpersonal style as they gain experience and confidence in teaching (see the last section of Chapter 5).

Figure 5.1 provides a visual overview of how these changes occur across different time scales, from moment-to-moment shifts in behaviours and interactions to the gradual development of relationships and interpersonal styles.

The Relationship Colours the Meaning of Behaviour

The Interplay of Behaviour, Interactions, and Relationships

Figure 5.2 captures the interplay between exhibiting behaviour from moment to moment, the course of interactions, and the development in the relationship associated with it. All this is shown, particularly for the early days of a school year when teachers and students are just getting to know each other. During these initial lessons, the way a teacher interacts with students lays the groundwork for their future relationship.

50 *An Interpersonal Perspective on Classroom Management*

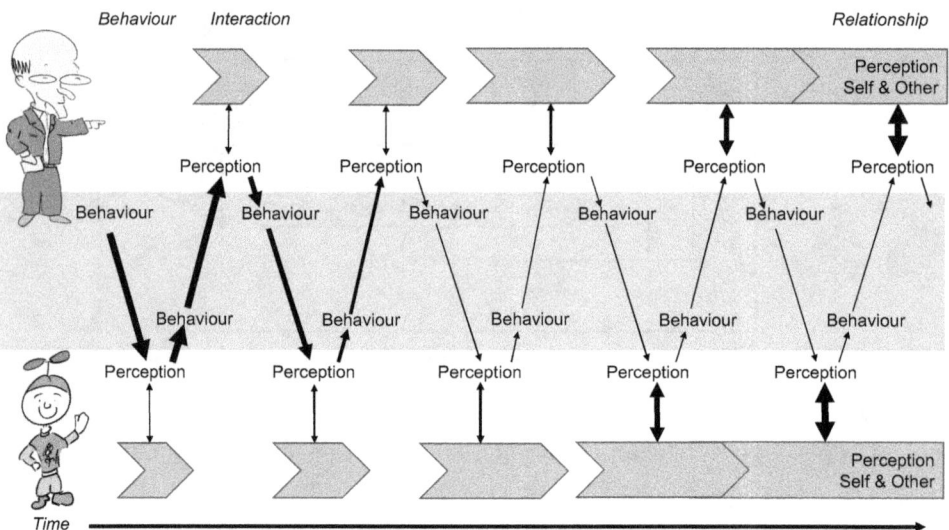

Figure 5.2 Consecutive teacher and student behaviours and perceptions of these behaviours over time and the associations with the development of the teacher-student relationship. In the figure: (1) The elongating arrows of the relationship indicate that the relationship becomes more stable. (2) The thickening of the arrows between relationship and the perception of behaviour indicates that the relationship increasingly determines how behaviour is perceived in interactions. (3) The thinning of the arrows for behaviour toward perception indicates that over time the behaviour determines the perception of behaviour less.

Relationships and Perceptions

In Arthur's first lesson with a new class, he shares personal details about himself and his family while collaborating with students to set class rules. This approach helps students perceive him as both friendly and firm. In the next lesson, when Arthur promptly corrects a student for breaking one of the rules, it reinforces their view of him as a strict but fair teacher. Over time, without needing to constantly enforce rules, Arthur's students follow them naturally because they've come to trust his authority and expectations.

In this example, we see that the perception of Arthur's relationship with students has become strict, and therefore, Arthur's behaviour is interpreted as strict without him explicitly and frequently displaying strict behaviour.

Joan, a novice teacher, in her first lesson notices that her student Ben frequently cracks jokes when she tries to quiet the class, making her feel uneasy. During a break, she talks to Ben and learns he isn't trying to undermine her—he simply enjoys chatting with his friend Carolyn. After this honest exchange, Joan approaches his behaviour differently. When Ben struggles to stay quiet in later lessons, she reacts with a playful wink, signalling understanding rather than frustration. This small shift helps reframe their relationship and how Joan interprets his behaviour.

For Joan, her conversation with Ben leads to a different interpretation of his behaviour and as a result she adapts her responses to Ben.

In both examples, we see how early interactions influence the development of relationships. These relationships colour how behaviours are interpreted, thus how students perceive the teacher's behaviour and vice versa. Therefore, the perception of behaviour depends on whether you are meeting people for the first time or have known them for a while. When students know a teacher well, they better understand whether the teacher is strict or allows more freedom in the class. Based on that, they can better assess how, or how seriously, the teacher's behaviour should be understood. A few other examples:

> A teacher always expresses appreciation for students' answers with subtle facial expressions like a slight smile or nod. Students have learned quickly that this signifies a strong form of engagement with them.
>
> A teacher always looks a bit stern when explaining something important. After a while, students no longer interpret this as anger but as a marker of seriousness.
>
> A teacher often says that whoever talks now will be sent out but never sticks to it. As a consequence, students disregard such warnings.

Background Information

Solidified History

Throughout the lessons in a new class, a teacher and students build a relationship that can also be termed a shared history. For instance, teachers may have previously expressed enthusiasm or become angry, and these instances contribute to the interpersonal perceptions of their behaviour by the students afterward. The history that a teacher and class share influences the perception they have of each other's behaviours: "solidified history."

To Keep in Mind

- Teachers and students interpret the meaning of each other's behaviour based on the relationship they have with each other. This relationship also creates expectations about behaviour.
- Invest in warm relationships with students right away; there is no evidence whatsoever that the adage "don't smile before christmas" holds.

The Role of Expectations

Relationships not only shape perceptions, but also mutual expectations. Students anticipate how a teacher will respond in specific situations, and teachers form expectations about student behaviour. Based on these expectations, recurring patterns in interactions emerge. For instance, a teacher who consistently praises good performance may disappoint students if praise is absent on occasion. Conversely, an unexpected compliment from a teacher who rarely acknowledges achievements can have a gratifying impact. When students know that a teacher promptly addresses disruptions in class, they will consider this in their behaviour. On the other hand, if they know that a teacher does not intervene, they may feel inclined to allow themselves more.

Teachers also interpret students' behaviour based on the relationship they have with each particular student.

> I think that when you have a good relationship with a student, you can say a lot, and they can say a lot without crossing certain boundaries. For example, what I just mentioned about Louis when he comes to me, stands next to me, and says something like, "Hey, Mrs.," he absolutely doesn't mean it in a mean way. I feel that immediately; there's nothing behind it. He's just seeking that contact because he needs a certain role. And he seeks it at that moment with words that makes me think: "If someone else says it, you might cross boundaries, but you're not crossing any boundaries here. At this moment, you're seeking contact in a socially awkward way, but you mean something very friendly by it".
>
> (Interview with a secondary school teacher)

Consequently, a teacher can handle two students who exhibit the same behaviour differently. For example, one student's bold greeting might be seen as an awkward attempt at connection, while the same behaviour from another student might be interpreted as defiance. The students' behaviour is interpreted based on the relationship, and the response is tailored accordingly. For the first student, the teacher may respond in a friendly manner to the bold greeting, but for the second student, the teacher may want to make it clear that such behaviour is not desirable.

Reacting differently to the same behaviour from students, goes against the often-heard advice for teachers to be consistent, meaning responding to the same student behaviour in the same way always. In our view, this needs to be nuanced because the situation should always be taken into account. When reacting to student behaviour, a teacher should consider factors such as the nature of the relationship with the specific student and the context in which the behaviour occurs. Talking among students when working in groups may warrant a different response from the teacher than talking during an exam. In Chapter 9, we further discuss consistency in teachers' actions in the context of rule enforcement.

> **To Keep in Mind**
>
> It is not always wise to be consistent. Responses from a teacher to the same student behaviour of different students may vary. After all, the same behaviour from two students can rightfully have a different meaning for a teacher, such as because of differences in the relationship with those students.

The Relational Lens

Both students and teachers interpret the behaviour of the other based on the relationship they have with each other. They look at the behaviour of the other through a relational lens—in different words— from a *relational perspective*. Because the interpretation of behaviour, and thus the response to that behaviour, depends on the relationship, focusing solely on behaviour when analysing relationships and interactions is limited in its usefulness. Behaviour alone does not convey the full picture if the context of the relationship is not known.

A strong relationship with students can serve as a buffer during challenging moments, making it easier for both teachers and students to restore 'harm' to the relationships resulting from misunderstandings and move forward. A positive relationship with a teacher often inspires better behaviour from students, underscoring the importance of fostering strong bonds.

When relationships with students are problematic, however, they can lead to cycles of unfriendly negative interactions that are hard to break. In such cases, teachers need patience and persistence to shift the dynamic, as students may take months to trust and reinterpret the teacher's positive actions considering the troubled history.

> **To Keep in Mind**
>
> Changes in your behaviour do not lead to changes in the relationship quickly. Persistence pays off.

Ultimately, focusing on behaviour alone is not enough to fully understand teacher-student interactions. The relational context provides a missing piece, helping teachers interpret behaviour more effectively and tailor their responses to build a healthier classroom dynamic.

Activity 5.1 lets you look at student behaviour from the perspective of the relationship you have with a student.

One-on-One Relationships with Students

Key Differences Between Positive and Problematic Relationships

Teachers identify three main areas where positive and problematic relationships with individual students differ:

1 Degree of Communion.
2 Location in which interactions take place.
3 Topic of conversation.[1]

On average, most problematic relationships revolve around students not conforming to what the teacher expects from them. Table 5.1 summarises these differences.

Table 5.1 Summary of differences between positive and problematic relationships

	Positive Relationship	Problematic Relationship
What does the interaction look like?	High mutual Communion predominates; characterised by warmth, mutual respect, and a sense of connection.	Typically, low on mutual Communion, marked by distance, tension, or conflict, with limited trust or mutual understanding.
Where does the interaction take place?	In the classroom but also outside of it (break times, extracurricular settings).	Primarily in the classroom, during lessons.
What is the conversation about?	A variety of topics, extending beyond academic matters, touching on shared interests, personal stories, or mutual goals.	Mostly focused on the student's misbehaviour or lack of motivation.

Communion in Positive and Problematic Relationships

In *positive relationships*, interactions between teachers and students are positioned in the right side of the Interpersonal Circle. Both teacher and student engage in cooperative, friendly, and respectful behaviours. The atmosphere is relaxed, and even when corrections are needed, they are handled smoothly and without conflict. These interactions foster a sense of mutual respect and understanding, making the classroom environment supportive and conducive to learning.

In contrast, *problematic relationships* tend to revolve on the left side of the Interpersonal Circle, where Communion is low. These interactions are often marked by rejection and unfriendliness from both the teacher and the student. The balance of Agency between teacher and student varies. For instance, a student might assert Agency by continuing to disrupt the class, or the teacher might regain control by responding sternly or enforcing rules.

In these challenging dynamics, both teacher and student frequently disapprove of each other's behaviour, creating a cycle of negative interactions. Despite their best intentions to foster a better connection, teachers often report being "pulled" toward the left side of the circle during conflicts. The next example illustrates how teacher-student relationships can become caught in a cycle of hostile reactions:

> Talking back, making remarks towards me, or non-verbal looks during class, as well as behaviour like hanging in their seats, keeping their bags on the table, and keeping on their coats. You know, those kinds of things. So, I always must ask, and that's negative attention, and then you start to feel negative. But it is behaviour that bothers me. And he knows that. But still, he lets it come to the point where I ask it every time and have to say it every time. And yes, then you notice that the relationship between me and the student is not going well. I try to turn that around and, if possible, give positive feedback.
> (Interview with a secondary school teacher)

Each interaction reinforces the negative dynamic, making it harder to establish a positive connection. However, the teacher's effort to provide positive reinforcement reflects an important strategy for breaking the cycle.

In Chapter 6, we will examine these interaction patterns in greater detail, exploring strategies for navigating and transforming such challenging dynamics into opportunities for growth and connection.

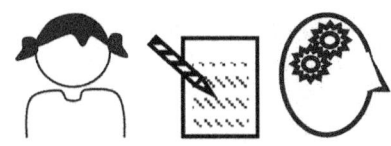

In **Activity 5.2**, you work to improve a problematic relationship with a student.

Location and Topic of Conversation

Building positive relationships with students is a powerful way to address and improve problematic classroom behaviour. The *location of interactions* and the *topics of conversation* are crucial elements in fostering these connections.

In positive teacher-student relationships, interactions extend beyond the classroom walls. Friendly, informal exchanges often occur, for example in hallways, playgrounds, during breaks, or even in the neighbourhood. These conversations are not limited to school-related matters; they might cover hobbies, vacations, shared interests, or weekend plans. These interactions create a broader relational context, helping students see their teacher as approachable and genuinely interested in them as individuals.

In contrast, problematic relationships are often confined to classroom settings and are dominated by discussions of misbehaviour or lack of motivation. Interactions are limited to lessons, and if they happen outside the classroom, they usually focus on disciplinary issues. This narrow and negative focus makes it hard to shift the dynamic.

To improve a problematic relationship, a challenging but crucial task, it is essential to break free from the cycle of negative classroom interactions. Teachers can achieve this by deliberately engaging with students *outside the lesson*: Interact with students in hallways, before or after breaks, or during school outings. These settings provide an environment where formal roles are less prominent and where problematic behaviour does not dominate interactions. In these settings, more *personal conversations* about hobbies, family, or personal interests can provide a refreshing and humanising perspective for both the teacher and the student.

Outside the classroom, teachers do not have to juggle so many things simultaneously and they are less likely to be seen purely as authority figures against whom a student should rebel. This shift in perception allows for interactions that emphasise high Communion. When students see their teacher as a reliable and approachable person in these settings, they may be more receptive to positive feedback and guidance within the classroom.

By actively seeking opportunities to connect in these informal settings and shifting the focus away from problematic behaviours, teachers can lay the groundwork for a more positive and productive relationship with their students.

To Keep in Mind

To improve the relationship with a student, you can engage in conversations with the student outside the classroom, such as in the hallway or cafeteria, preferably about topics that are not directly related to school subjects or the student's behaviour in class. This way, you can demonstrate friendliness (i.e., high Communion).

Not all problematic teacher-student relationships arise from classroom disruptions. Sometimes, the challenge lies with students who avoid forming a connection with the teacher or seem difficult to engage with for the teacher. These relationships can feel just as strained, even though the student does not openly misbehave.

In such cases, the key to improvement is the same: Persist in attempts at friendly contact in various settings. By creating opportunities for positive interaction—whether in class, during breaks, or through casual conversations—teachers can gradually break down barriers and foster trust.

When working to improve a relationship, *how* you communicate (the relationship message) is often more impactful than *what* you communicate (the content). When addressing negative situations, maintaining high Communion can steer the relationship in a positive direction. For example: If students haven't completed their homework, asking, "Is something going on that made it hard to finish your homework?" signals care and opens dialogue through high Communion. Conversely, a low-Communion response, "That will result in a failing grade for you," reinforces distance. Prioritising the relationship over the content of the message, helps teachers to transform difficult relationships into opportunities for growth and mutual understanding.

Types of Teacher-Class Relationships

Teacher-Class Relationships

As discussed earlier, all relationships in a classroom between the teacher and individual students collectively shape a certain atmosphere in the class. This teacher-class relationship plays a central role in setting the tone for your lessons. Beyond your connections with individual students, you also have a relationship with the class as a whole, and this teacher-class relationship is a part of the atmosphere in the class. A strong, positive teacher-class relationship is related to the enjoyment students have in the lessons and their motivation for the subject. Given its impact, investing in this group-level relationship is just as crucial as nurturing individual connections. While the teacher-class relationship tends to remain stable over time, it is important to remember that no two lessons are exactly alike. Students may perceive your interactions differently depending on the context of a particular lesson or their own individual experiences.

Sample Relationships

In more than 60% of classrooms globally, the teacher-class relationship according to the students is marked by high Agency and Communion from the teacher,[2] i.e., strong leadership combined with warmth. In these settings, teachers lead in a confident and friendly manner, creating an environment where students feel guided and supported. However, this classroom atmosphere is not universal. Not all classrooms experience this ideal dynamic. When we ask students about their perceptions, they often notice greater differences between teachers in Communion than in Agency. Teachers differ more in how approachable and kind they are than in how much they take charge. Both teachers and students tend to prefer classrooms with relatively high levels of Communion from both teachers and students, and in which the teacher also has relatively much Agency.[3] This creates a classroom climate characterised by a calm, pleasant and productive atmosphere where learning thrives.

Teacher Interpersonal Relationships and Styles 57

Figures 5.3–5.6 illustrate four distinct types of teacher-class relationships based on student perceptions. These figures highlight how students see the relationship with their teacher within the Interpersonal Circle. We now will elaborate on each type.

An Approachable and Authoritative Teacher

The profile in Figure 5.3 provides insight into how students perceive their relationship with this type of teacher. The circle shows more filling on the right, indicating the teacher is seen as highly approachable and friendly. There is more filling above than below revealing that the teacher is perceived as taking the lead and setting the tone in the classroom. This combination—leadership paired with warmth—is characteristic of an authoritative teaching style. Students often view this positively. The results from the QTI administered to August's students in the first chapter align with this profile. His students appreciate his structured yet warm teaching style, describing him as a leader who fosters a positive and engaging learning environment.

These teachers are natural leaders in the classroom, embodying confidence, warmth, and a passion for teaching. Their leadership feels effortless and well-balanced, creating an environment where students thrive academically and emotionally.

These teachers show enthusiasm for their profession, and their energy is contagious, inspiring students to engage actively. Their lessons are well-structured and captivating, combining clear explanations with expressive non-verbal cues. Whether through a friendly gaze, confident posture, or (in Western contexts) consistent eye contact, they communicate approachability and respect.

Students often note these teachers' sense of humour and ability to make learning enjoyable while staying focused. These teachers listen attentively, assume good intentions from students, and consider their feelings. This approach not only fosters trust but also enhances the bond between teacher and students. These teachers are highly knowledgeable yet approachable, providing sincere advice and fostering meaningful contributions from

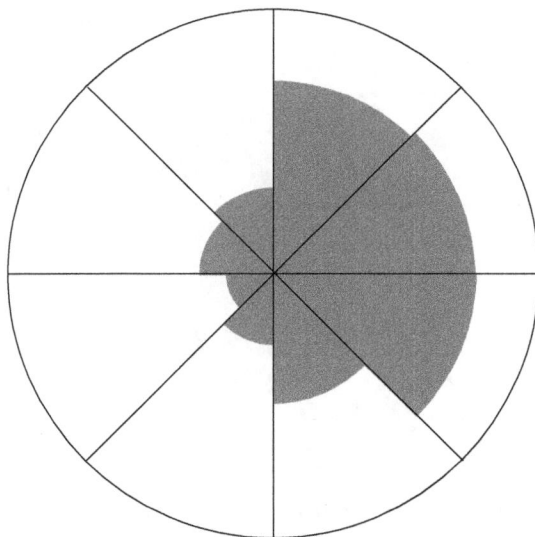

Figure 5.3 Students' perception derived from the QTI of an approachable and authoritative teacher

58 *An Interpersonal Perspective on Classroom Management*

students. They reward effort, even when answers are partially correct, by highlighting what was done well and encourage students to take on challenges, fostering a classroom atmosphere where it is safe to make mistakes and learn from them. They check regularly if students understand the material and take the time to respond thoughtfully to questions. They maintain a calm and patient demeanour, ensuring students feel supported and heard.

Students in these classrooms feel confident and motivated, often describing these teachers as their favourites, earning students' trust, respect, and admiration. They value the learning opportunities provided and appreciate the teacher's interest in their perspectives and well-being. With their blend of structure, humour, and encouragement, these teachers create a learning environment that is not only effective but also memorable.

In sum, key traits of these teachers are *highly knowledgeable and enthusiastic, clearly explaining, encouraging and motivating, humour, genuine interest, approachable, patient*.

An Approachable and Accommodating Teacher

Figure 5.4 shows how students perceive their relationship with an approachable and accommodating teacher. The circle shows more filling on the right, indicating the teacher is seen as highly approachable and empathetic. There is more filling below than above, illuminating that the students rather than the teacher determine what happens in the lesson. The results from the QTI administered to Tonia's students in the first chapter align with this profile. Her students appreciate her interest and understanding but many dislike the lack of structure in her lessons.

These teachers have a strong listening ear and show genuine understanding and trust in their students. They are willing to repeat explanations until students feel confident and ensure no one is left behind. Students feel comfortable approaching them with problems, knowing the teacher assumes their good intentions and considers their feelings.

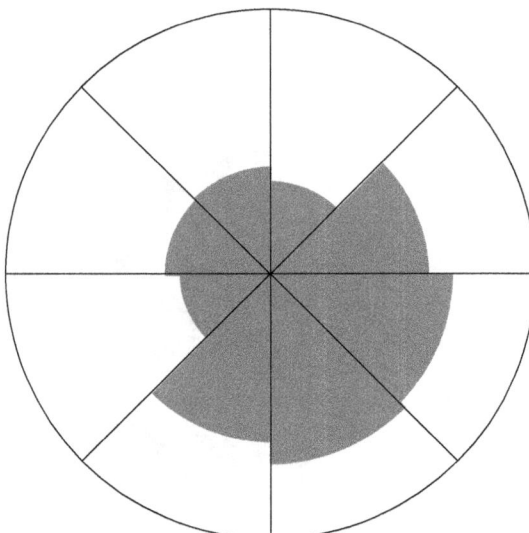

Figure 5.4 Students' perception derived from the QTI of an approachable and accommodating teacher

Teacher Interpersonal Relationships and Styles   59

Weak structure and leniency are also hallmarks of their behaviour: They aim to avoid conflict and are highly accommodating of student needs and wishes. These teachers give students significant freedom, allowing them to influence much of what happens in the lesson. Students can easily negotiate with these teachers.

When disruptions occur, these teachers often hesitate to intervene, which can lead to a noisy or unfocused classroom environment. Corrections are often phrased as gentle suggestions, which students may disregard. While generally patient, they may occasionally lose their temper unexpectedly, reflecting their internal frustration.

Their presence in the classroom is subdued, with soft or hesitant speech, minimal gestures, and limited contact. Nervous conduct, such as fidgeting, blushing, standing on one leg with knees locked or frequent use of filler words, may make them appear modest or unsure.

Students appreciate the kindness and understanding of these teachers, but many feel their teaching is too lenient. Without clear guidance or consistent structure, students may worry that they are not learning enough for staying on track.

In sum, key traits of these teachers are *genuine interest, approachable and patient, accommodating, lenient, lack of structure* and *uncertain at times*.

An Insecure and Oppositional Teacher

The profile in Figure 5.5 shows more filling on the left than on the right side of the circle: This teacher comes across as hostile to the students (low Communion). There is more filling below than above in the circle: According to the students, they, more than the teacher, determine what happens in the lesson. When Dion's students in the first chapter completed the QTI, they described a teacher-student relationship resembling this profile. His students dislike the lack of structure and hostile approach in his lessons.

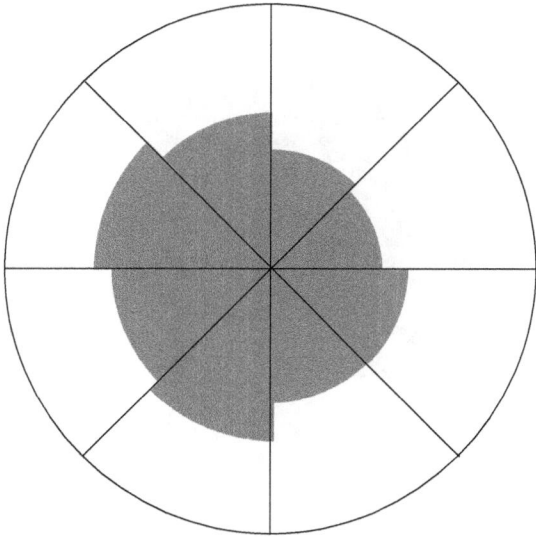

Figure 5.5 Students' perception derived from the QTI of an insecure and oppositional teacher

60 *An Interpersonal Perspective on Classroom Management*

These teachers often appear to be in a bad mood, expressing frequent irritation not just with student behaviours but also with their academic performance. Their tone tends to be sharp or even angry, and their feedback often feels more like complaints or accusations than constructive guidance.

Communication is often laced with sarcasm, cynicism, or threats of punishment. Corrections can sound accusatory, making students feel not only that their actions are wrong but that they, as individuals, are not good enough. Students often respond to corrections with complaints or even more inappropriate behaviour.

Their physical demeanour reflects their emotional state—slumped shoulders, tense posture, clenched fists, or angry facial expressions. Their gaze is fleeting, and their gestures are minimal. Their voice fluctuates between uncertainty, exasperation and outright anger. This combination of teacher's behaviours creates a classroom environment marked by tension, dissatisfaction, and lack of direction.

For students, these teachers are challenging to engage with. They often perceive the teacher as unpleasant and unapproachable, leading to frustration and disengagement. The lack of warmth and structure can prompt students to act out, escalating the tension in the classroom. Many students feel they gain little to no value from lessons with these teachers, as the focus shifts away from learning to managing hostility.

In sum, key traits of these teachers are *irritated, dissatisfied, angry, threatening, unfair, uncertain, lack of structure*.

An Authoritarian Teacher

The circle in Figure 5.6 shows more filling on the left than the right, indicating that students perceive this teacher as distant, with limited warmth or connection (low Communion). At the

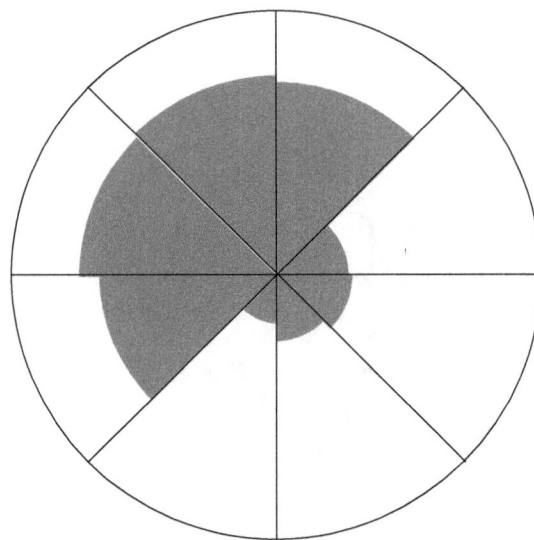

Figure 5.6 Students' perception derived from the QTI of an authoritarian teacher

same time, the significant filling above rather than below highlights a teacher who firmly controls the classroom dynamic, strongly determining what happens during lessons. When Renz' students in the first chapter completed the QTI, they described a teacher-student relationship aligning with this profile. His students appreciate his structured teaching style but fear his strict approach.

These teachers command a strong presence in the classroom, positioning themselves firmly as the leaders. Their lessons are meticulously structured, leaving little room for deviation. While they may entertain occasional student questions, these are only addressed if they seamlessly align with the teacher's planned narrative. These teachers show confidence in their expertise, expecting students to remain attentive and follow their lead without hesitation.

The pace of the lesson is entirely under their control. These teachers often anticipate student mistakes and point them out, sometimes even before they happen, making it clear they had already warned against them. Every aspect of student classroom behaviour—whether standing, talking, or collaborating—is strictly dictated by the teacher's rules.

Their demeanour is typically neutral or slightly friendly, with a loud, clear voice that commands attention without the need for shouting. Dropping strategic pauses mid-sentence adds to their authoritarianism. Their posture—upright and unwavering—complements their composed and deliberate movements, which reinforce their statements effectively. Corrections are delivered quickly with confidence. They look at the student being addressed until compliance is achieved, showing a quiet assurance that their directions will be followed.

These teachers hold students to exceptionally high, sometimes overly demanding, standards, both academically and behaviourally. While students often find their leadership style (high Agency and low Communion) rigid and unapproachable—describing them as authoritarian—they also recognise that such teachers push them to achieve and provide substantial learning opportunities. Many students are a little afraid in these teachers' classes.

In sum, key traits of these teachers are *strong presence, (too) high expectations, distant, strict, very structured*.

Undesirable Relationships

In much the same way as with relationships with individual students, a classroom climate dominated by interactions on the left side of the circle—such as those seen in the profiles of Figures 5.5 and 5.6—is far from ideal. When a teacher consistently demonstrates low Communion, creating a negative or detached atmosphere, it can stifle students' growth and development.

For instance, when a teacher exerts strong control (high Agency) but lacks warmth or cooperation (low Communion), students often become fearful and overly submissive. On the other hand, when students perceive a teacher as having both low Agency and low Communion, chaos and aggression are likely to dominate the classroom environment.

Interestingly, in a classroom of a teacher with low Agency but who is still cooperative (Figure 5.4), the atmosphere can feel more positive. While disorderly at times, the overall tone is one of tolerance and leniency rather than hostility. However, even in this more amicable setting, the lack of structure and control can limit the class's potential for effective learning.

Relationships of Beginning Teachers

For many novice teachers, stepping into the classroom for the first time brings significant challenges, particularly when it comes to asserting authority. Early in their careers, new teachers often find themselves reflecting the dynamics of profiles like those in Figures 5.4 and 5.5. Video's illustrating interactions in such undesirable environment are available in Section 5.4 of a paper to be downloaded from http://doi.org/10.1016/j.tate.2013.07.016.

Why is this so common? Much of it stems from a natural discomfort with the leadership role. Before becoming educators, these individuals often held roles of following rather than leading—whether as students themselves or in relationships with parents or coaches. This lack of experience in authoritative behaviour, combined with a tendency to identify more closely with students, can make stepping into the role of leader feel awkward or even resistant. Novice teachers often do not yet have the behavioural repertoire to show Agency.

The reluctance to take charge, however, creates a dilemma: Interactions require balance, and when one party—the teacher—does not assert leadership, the other party—students—will inevitably fill the void. This dynamic often leads to students taking control of the classroom environment, which can quickly result in disorder and mismanagement.

Fortunately, most beginning teachers adapt quickly. Through experience and reflection during their early years, they gradually grow into their leadership roles, combining authority and approachability.

A Common Challenge for Novice Teachers: Moving from Friendly Disorder to Authority

> Tom is a novice teacher working with a lively grade 7 class. Characteristic for Tom's lessons are a mix of noise and scattered attention. While the classroom isn't completely chaotic, students struggle to follow his explanations. Tom rarely calls for order, preferring to focus on his teaching, but when he does, students usually comply, but only for a short time. His habit of facing the smartboard while explaining—writing notes and projecting—means he misses much of the classroom activity behind his back.
>
> Students' engagement is minimal. Some students are preoccupied with their own conversations, make fun, or are restless. Despite this, they describe Tom as "very nice" and acknowledge his knowledge. But they also note that his lessons are hard to follow, and they don't learn as much as they could.

Tom's situation is common among new teachers. The student-teacher relationship often aligns with the profile in Figure 5.4: Low on Agency and high on Communion. The classroom atmosphere is characterised by *friendly disorder*, where the teacher is approachable but struggles to assert authority.

The Risk of Aggressive Disorder

School leadership or experienced colleagues frequently advise teachers like Tom to "be stricter" and tolerate less off-task behaviour like chatting with each other or playing with materials. They must take stronger leadership and ensure that students pay attention and participate in the lesson. The intention is to help the teacher establish greater control and ensure students focus on the lesson.

When novice teachers act on this advice, they often attempt to move upwards in the Interpersonal Circle (Figure 5.7) by adopting stricter and confrontational, less cooperative behaviour, i.e., they move *clockwise*. This transition may shift the teacher's profile to resemble Figure 5.5: Low on Agency and low on Communion. Thus, it marks a move from *friendly disorder* to *aggressive disorder*. These teachers begin correcting students more frequently, but their efforts are perceived as unconvincing or even hostile. Teachers with a teacher-student relationship with low Agency and high Communion usually have a limited behavioural repertoire on the left side of the Interpersonal Circle. Students resist the corrections, escalating into a cycle of antagonism. No longer are these teachers seen as "nice"; they become someone students describe as unpleasant, unapproachable, and even hostile.

Moving Up Counterclockwise

A more effective path for teachers like Tom is to move upward in the Interpersonal Circle *counterclockwise* (see Figure 5.7), starting from their strength, friendliness (high Communion). This approach involves building authority through positive, student-centred interactions. By focusing on building connections rather than imposing authority, teachers can achieve the same goal: A classroom where they lead the learning process effectively.

Instead of attempting to assert control with stricter rules in *whole-class settings*, teachers can introduce *individual or group work*. This provides opportunities for the teacher to strengthen individual relationships by:

— Interacting personally with students.
— Giving positive feedback and praise students' efforts and progress.
— Engaging in supportive conversations about students' work.
— Offering help and showing genuine interest in their learning.

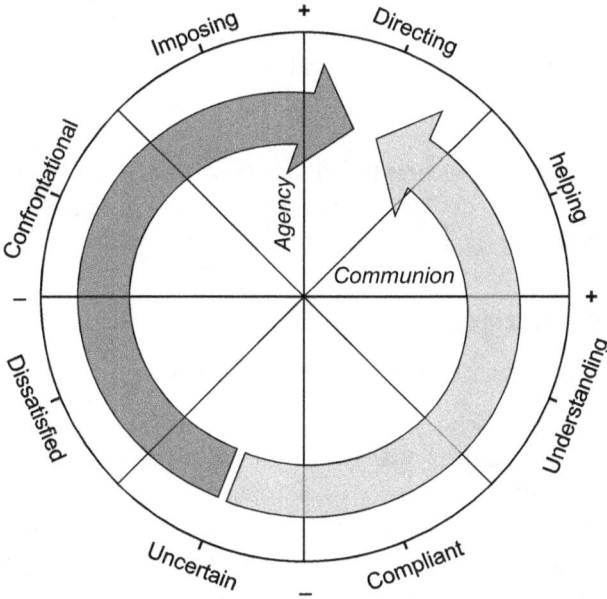

Figure 5.7 Two ways to gain authority, the dark arrow clockwise (often not productive) and the light one counterclockwise

When students feel supported and respected, their trust in the teacher grows. Over time, these improved individual relationships can influence the broader class dynamic, helping the teacher establish authority in a cooperative and constructive way.

> **To Keep in Mind**
>
> In a classroom with a poor atmosphere, resist the temptation to exhibit behaviour that you find challenging; instead, leverage your strengths. In a classroom with a positive atmosphere, practice expanding your behavioural repertoire.

Pitfalls of "Start Off Strict" Advice

A common piece of advice given to novice teachers is to *start off strict, and then loosen the reins later*, or the often-quoted adage, *don't smile until Christmas* (at the Northern hemisphere). While this guidance is well-meaning, aiming to establish authority early, it can be counterproductive for some teachers—especially those who lack a well-developed adaptive repertoire of behaviours on the left side of the Interpersonal Circle (low Communion). However, as in the case of the finding a solution for friendly disorder, teachers should as much as possible use friendliness and cooperation to build trust and rapport in the beginning of the school year. The advice to start off strict can backfire for several reasons:

Mismatch with Strengths: Teachers who naturally excel in friendliness and cooperation (high Communion) may struggle to maintain a strict demeanour.
Alienation of Students: A rigid, no-smiles approach can distance the teacher from students, preventing the formation of positive relationships. Without connection, authority feels imposed rather than earned, and students may resist.
Ineffective Corrections: Novice teachers without a strong presence in the low-Communion zone often find their corrections ignored or met with rebellion, leading to escalating frustration.

Teachers may confuse strict behaviour with confrontational behaviour when following this advice. Setting clear, consistent boundaries for behaviour and communicating them in a calm, supportive way is rather strict than confrontational. Authority does not have to mean harshness.

Development of Relationships

Changes in Relationships Throughout the School Year

The first few weeks of a new school year are a critical time for teachers and students to get acquainted and start building their relationship. This connection can set the stage for either a positive, productive dynamic or a more challenging one. You have likely heard the saying, "The first few weeks with a new class are so important, they set the tone for the rest of the year."[4] While there is truth in this, research in secondary education suggests a slightly different perspective: It is often a matter of just a few lessons, not weeks, that shape the initial

Teacher Interpersonal Relationships and Styles 65

teacher-student relationship. These early interactions set the tone regarding trust, respect, and collaboration within the classroom.

The initial relationship teachers establish with their classes in the first lessons is strongly associated with what that relationship looks like throughout the school year. The first lesson serves as a solid predictor of how interactions and dynamics will continue, often persisting in a relatively stable manner across the year.

However, this does not mean that a teacher's first impression is the definitive factor in shaping the year-long classroom climate. While it is tempting to view the connection between the first and subsequent lessons as causal, the reality is more nuanced. The consistent link between early and later teacher-student relationships underscores the importance of intentional effort from the start.

Figure 5.8 shows student perceptions of teacher-class relationships over 15 weeks using the QTI in 48 classrooms. The findings reveal two key insights:

Fluctuations within lessons: In the left part of the figure, weekly perceptions of the teacher's behaviour show noticeable variation from lesson to lesson, especially in Communion. These fluctuations suggest that day-to-day factors, such as lesson content, mood, or classroom dynamics, can temporarily impact how students view the teacher.

Overall stability in trends: When these weekly variations are averaged into trend lines (right part of the figure), the overall climate appears to remain relatively steady over time, Agency more than Communion.

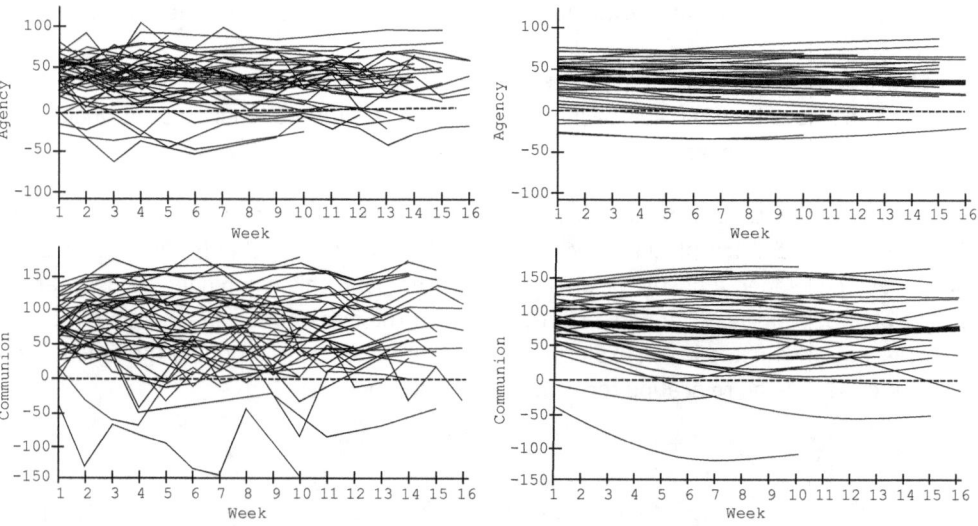

Figure 5.8 Left: raw trajectories of agency and communion in student perceptions, collected with the QTI during the first 15 weeks of the school year in 48 classes; every line represents one class. Right: The Development of Agency and Communion per Class According to the Best Fitting Statistical Model, with the Thick Line the Average Trend

Source: Mainhard et al. (2011a)

However, a clear trend emerges per teacher:

- Teachers with high Communion in their first lesson tend to maintain or slightly improve their relationship with the class throughout the year.
- Teachers who start with lower levels of Communion often see a continued decline, with the relationship deteriorating further as the year progresses.

This data highlights the critical importance of building strong, positive relationships from the outset. Teachers who invest in creating a climate of warmth, cooperation, and mutual understanding set the stage for sustained success, while those who struggle early may find it harder to recover. A shaky start with a class can cast a long shadow over the classroom atmosphere, making recovery difficult. For early career teachers, the dynamics can vary widely between classes. A fresh start in a different group, ideally with structured behavioural support, can make a significant difference.

The key to effective teacher-student relationships lies in fostering a positive relationship with students from the outset—one characterised by high Agency and high Communion. Establishing this combination during the first lessons can set the tone for the rest of the year. In Chapter 10, we outline several strategies to help teachers create strong connections right from the beginning of a lesson, including the very first one.

A good starting point is to use simple, consistent lesson structures in those critical early days. For example:

- Set clear and predictable expectations, such as assigning and reviewing homework regularly.
- Clearly outline the lesson's objectives at the start.
- Use consistent and fair approaches to interactions with students so they understand what to expect from you.

Since relationships tend to persist, it is crucial to consider the potential impact of a negative class climate when placing teacher trainees in internship schools. Once their classrooms have developed a hostile or disruptive environment, this can hinder trainees' ability to develop essential classroom management skills. If the classroom climate is untenable for a teacher in training, it is worth exploring alternatives—such as reassigning the teacher to a different class or even relocating their internship placement.

> **To Keep in Mind**
>
> It pays off to practice extensively for the start of your first lesson in a new class, ensuring that you create an impression that is high on both Agency and Communion.

Changes in Relationships as a Result of Marked Teacher Behaviour[5]

A teacher's behaviour, particularly when it exhibits extreme intensity in the Communion dimension, can have a noticeable ripple effect on the classroom atmosphere, shaping interactions in subsequent lessons. For instance, when a teacher displays in a lesson *strong oppositional behaviour*, such as shouting, using sarcasm, or angrily punishing students, the immediate result is a shift in the classroom atmosphere. According to QTI data from students, the class perceives *a slight reduction in the teacher's Agency* in the lesson following the outburst.

Interestingly, this reduction in Agency tends to resolve within a week if the oppositional behaviour is not repeated. However, when such behaviour becomes a pattern, the consequences deepen. Persistent displays of anger lead to a continued decline in the teacher's Agency, and over time, *Communion also erodes*.

Ironically, these angry outbursts—intended to assert control and authority—often achieve the opposite. Rather than gaining influence, the teacher's leadership diminishes, leaving the classroom atmosphere strained. Repeated teacher angry outbursts, though tempting in moments of frustration, are counterproductive, eroding the very authority they aim to establish.

> **To Keep in Mind**
>
> Displaying friendly, helping, supportive, and understanding behaviour (interpersonal support) can help improve the classroom atmosphere on the Communion dimension, while intense oppositional behaviour can worsen the atmosphere on both Agency and Communion.

In contrast, *supportive behaviour*, characterised by high Communion, has a modest but positive impact. When teachers show genuine care and encouragement during a lesson, students perceive an improvement in Communion, which extends into the next week. However, this supportive approach does not seem to influence the perception of Agency directly.

Teacher's Interpersonal Style

Teacher-Student Relationships in Different Classes

Students often perceive a teacher's relationship with their class in a remarkably consistent way across different groups. Experienced teachers tend to foster a similar atmosphere in their classes, which reflects their interpersonal style. While students usually see uniformity in their teacher's approach, teachers themselves often perceive greater variation.[6] For instance, they might describe one class as their "best" class, with a positive and well-functioning atmosphere, and another as their "worst," where interactions feel more challenging. This difference in perception can be attributed to contrasting frames of reference. Teachers compare the atmosphere across their own classes, while students compare their experiences with various teachers.

However, even for experienced teachers, some variation in relationships between classes is visible. While the Agency dimension tends to remain consistent across all their classes, the Communion dimension may fluctuate a bit more.

For novice teachers, however, the variation between classes can be much more pronounced. Students often perceive a clear divide between the teacher's "best" and "worst"

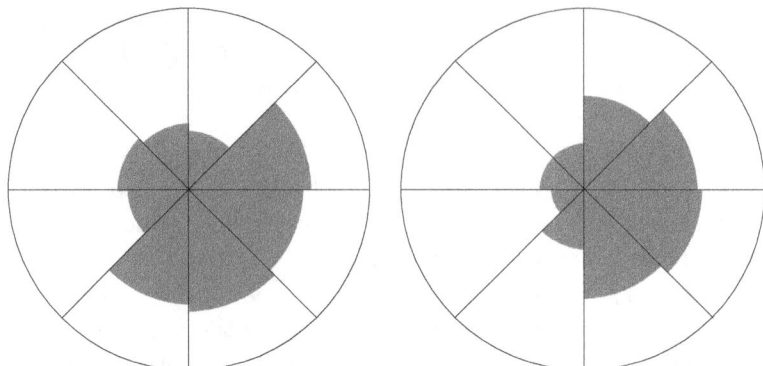

Figure 5.9 Perceptions gathered with the QTI from students in two different classes of a novice teacher

classes, with significant differences in the overall classroom climate. Figure 5.9 illustrates this dynamic with profiles from two classes taught by the same novice teacher. Both profiles indicate high Communion, showing that the teacher maintains warmth and connection in both groups. However, the left profile reflects a disorderly classroom atmosphere, while the right shows a more orderly environment.

This example underscores that while a novice teacher's interpersonal style provides a foundation, the dynamics of each class can still influence how it is expressed.

Variability Across Teachers in Teacher-Student Relationships

Although experienced teachers typically create a similar atmosphere across their classes, the differences between teachers are more striking. Every teacher brings a unique *interpersonal style* to the classroom, and this individuality plays a significant role in shaping relationships with students. This raises an intriguing question: What has the greatest influence on the classroom climate—the teacher, the students, or their interactions?

Research suggests that classroom atmosphere is primarily shaped by the *teacher* and their *interactions with students*, far more than by the characteristics of the class itself.[7] This contests the notion of "challenging classes" as a defining factor. Instead, the focus shifts to how teachers manage and engage with their students.

> **To Keep in Mind**
>
> Teachers play the central role in shaping the classroom atmosphere.

The Evolution of a Teacher's Interpersonal Style

Figure 5.10 illustrates the development of teachers' interpersonal styles throughout their careers on Agency and Communion as perceived by students, teachers, and in comparison, to teacher ideals.

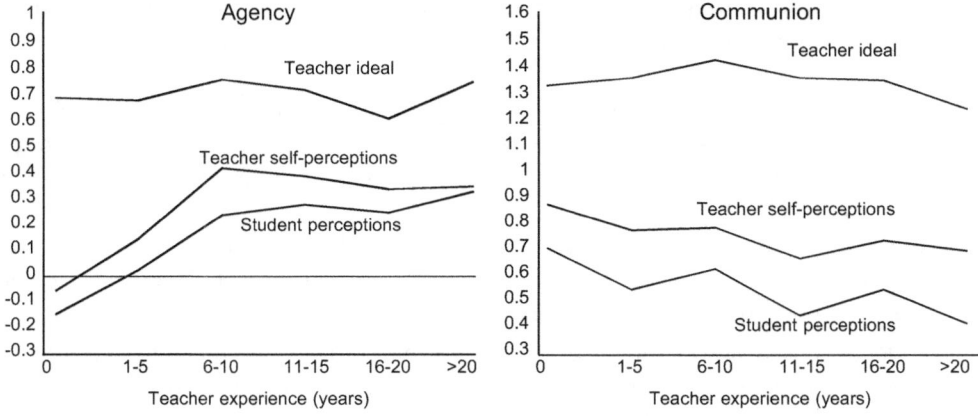

Figure 5.10 Interpersonal teacher style across the teaching career

Source: Brekelmans et al. (2005)

Agency: Teachers tend to experience significant growth in Agency during their first 10 years. In this period, they refine their ability to manage and lead the classroom effectively. After the initial decade, growth continues, albeit more gradually.

Communion: In contrast, many teachers start their careers with high levels of Communion, showing strong support and warmth toward students. However, over time, perceptions of Communion often decline slightly. This trend may reflect the widening gap between teachers' age and experiences compared to those of their students, which can make fostering close relationships more challenging.

While these patterns provide a general roadmap, individual teachers can deviate significantly. Some novice teachers demonstrate strong Agency from the outset, while others may struggle for years. Similarly, some experienced teachers maintain high levels of Communion even after teaching for 30 years, while others may see a decline.

Figure 5.10 highlights an interesting and persistent phenomenon, *the perception gap* between how teachers see their relationship with students and how students experience it. This gap exists on both dimensions of the teacher-student relationship—Agency and Communion.

Experience does not close the gap: One might assume that experienced teachers would better gauge how they come across to students than novice teachers. Surprisingly, this is not the case. The perception gap remains for most of a teacher's career, with the exception of Agency, where highly experienced teachers show a bit better alignment with student perceptions.[8]

The ideal vs. reality: Teachers' aspirations for their relationships often outpace what they or their students perceive to be the reality. Interestingly, the gap between a teacher's ideal and actual Communion tends to widen in the first ten years of their career, suggesting that they may become increasingly aware of the challenges in meeting their relational goals.

To better understand how teachers evolve in their interpersonal style, Figure 5.11 maps their development on the two dimensions collectively across different career stages.

> *Student teachers*: The centre of gravity for most teachers in training lies in the *understanding sector* of the Interpersonal Circle, where high Communion combines with medium low Agency. Novices often prioritise being approachable and supportive, sometimes at the expense of authority.
>
> *Novice teachers*: The centre of gravity for most novice teachers lies in the *helping sector*, where high Communion combines with medium high Agency. Novices have already learned to take the lead more than student teachers.
>
> *Experienced teachers*: For the majority, the centre of gravity is in the *helping sector* as they gain confidence and skills, leading to a better combination of high Communion and increasing Agency. Some teachers have a centre of gravity in the imposing sector.
>
> *Veteran teachers*: Over time, the shift continues *upward and slightly leftward*. This reflects a gradual increase in Agency as teachers assert more control and influence in their classrooms, coupled with a slight decrease in Communion. This leftward move could indicate the influence of age and experience, as teachers manage a growing generational and experiential gap with their students.

Background Information

Data for Teacher Development

The insights on career development are based on both cross-sectional and longitudinal research, spanning generations of teachers. Some studies have followed educators throughout their entire careers, offering a robust view of how interpersonal styles evolve. For example, teachers who began participating in Créton and Wubbels' doctoral research (1984) continued to provide data through the QTI until retirement, revealing stable trends over decades.

To Keep in Mind

It is important to:

- Recognise the gap between ideal and actual relationships.
- Monitor your Agency (specifically for novice teachers) and Communion (specifically for seasoned teachers).
- Seek student feedback to better align your perceptions with those of your students.

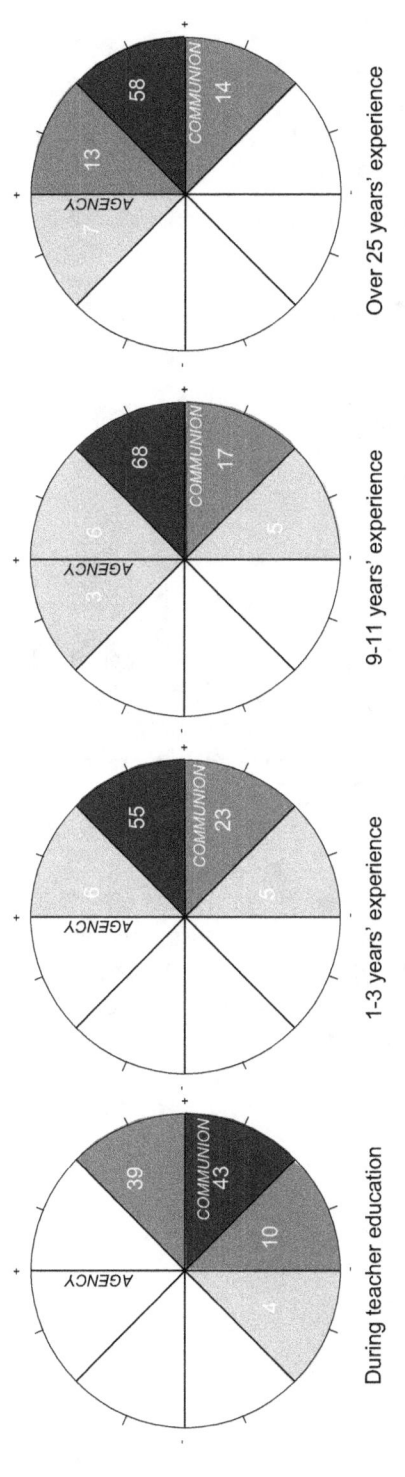

Figure 5.11 Frequency (as a percentage of the total number of teachers) of the position of the centre of gravity of teacher profiles in four stages of the career

Source: Brekelmans (2010)

In Sum

Teacher-student interactions vary from moment to moment; teacher-student relationships and teacher interpersonal style change over longer periods of time.

The relationship of teachers with their students and their shared history colour the perceptions they have of one-another's behaviours in the moment.

Interactions with individual students in positive relationships are characterised by:

- High levels of Communion.
- Encounters inside and outside the classroom.
- A variety of conversation topics, academic, student personal interests, etc.

Interactions with individual students in more problematic relationships are characterised by:

- Low levels of Communion.
- Encounters mainly within the classroom.
- Talk focused on the student's problematic behaviour.

Teachers in favourable teacher-student relationships are perceived by their students high on Communion and Agency—approachable and authoritative. In unfavourable relationships, teachers are viewed as low on Communion and Agency—insecure and oppositional.

When teachers who are seen by their students as approachable and accommodating try to gain more Agency, they should avoid becoming oppositional and overly stern. Instead, they should gain Agency via the right side of the Interpersonal Circle: Showing higher Agency while maintaining high Communion.

Relationships of novice teachers with their students often differ in different classes, whereas experienced teachers' relationship vary less between classes.

Teacher-student relationships quickly stabilise in the beginning of the school year. So, being perceived in the first lesson as high on Agency and Communion is crucial.

Notes

1 Claessens (2016).
2 Maulana et al. (2012).
3 Wubbels et al. (1985).
4 https://classteaching.wordpress.com/2017/08/22/getting-off-to-the-best-start-with-a-new-class/
5 Mainhard et al. (2011b).
6 Créton and Wubbels (1984).
7 Brekelmans (1989).
8 Brekelmans et al. (2005).

6 Complementarity in Interactions

Interactions in the classroom are chains of behaviours where teacher and student actions mutually influence each other. These interactions, often subtle and continuously, shape the quality of relationships and the classroom atmosphere. In Chapter 3, we explored an example of such chains where student disruption and the teacher's reactions created *a reinforcing cycle*. As students became more restless, the teacher's actions mirrored and intensified the chaos, which in turn heightened the students' restlessness. This feedback loop exemplifies how interactions can escalate, creating situations where effective learning suffers.

Mutual influence can lead to undesirable outcomes. For instance, when students whisper, a teacher might respond by speaking louder. This can prompt students to raise their voices further, resulting in a rapidly escalating noise level. Over time, such dynamics may result in a breakdown of classroom order and mutual trust, with both parties blaming each other:

- Teachers perceive inattentiveness as the reason for poor student performance.
- Students attribute their lack of understanding to the teacher's inability to manage the classroom and explain effectively.

On the other hand, mutual influence can foster positive environments as well. When teachers warmly greet students, this may elicit friendly, cooperative student behaviours in return. This reinforces the teacher's approach, creating a virtuous cycle of positive interactions that benefit the classroom atmosphere.

This chapter delves into the concept of *complementarity* and its significance in understanding such chains of behaviours that unfold in the classroom. The understanding of complementarity is not just theoretical—it is a practical tool for building stronger relationships and navigating interactions with students, helping to ultimately create a positive and cohesive classroom environment.

Two Complementarity Patterns

Complementarity in interactions explains how people are *likely* to respond to each other's behaviour. It is about patterns of behaviour that often occur in response to specific actions—essentially, how we intuitively react to one another. While these responses are predictable to a degree, they are not set in stone; non-complementary reactions can and do happen. In fact,

74 An Interpersonal Perspective on Classroom Management

as we will explore in the last section of Chapter 6 on professional teacher behaviour, there are times when deliberately breaking the cycle of complementarity can be a powerful and effective teaching strategy.

At its core, complementarity stems from basic human needs: The drive for connection, emotional security, validation, and acceptance. The complementarity principles are fundamental to creating social cohesion and fostering harmonious relationships.[1]

When it comes to the behaviours outlined in the *Interpersonal Circle*, each of the dimensions Communion and Agency has its own unique patterns of complementarity, summarised in Figure 6.1, which we will explore in detail in the following sections.[2]

Complementarity in Communion

Mirroring

Along the Communion dimension, the level of Communion of teachers and students tends to *mirror each other*. As shown by the elliptical arrows on the right side of Figure 6.1, when one person demonstrates high Communion—such as friendliness or warmth—the other is likely to respond in kind. *High Communion tends to evoke high Communion*. A teacher who greets students warmly often receives similar kindness in return. Likewise, when a student shows a respectful and kind attitude, teachers are inclined to respond friendly.

Similarly, low Communion behaviours—hostility, anger, or coldness—tend to elicit equally low Communion responses as illustrated by the elliptical arrow on the left of Figure 6.1. *Low*

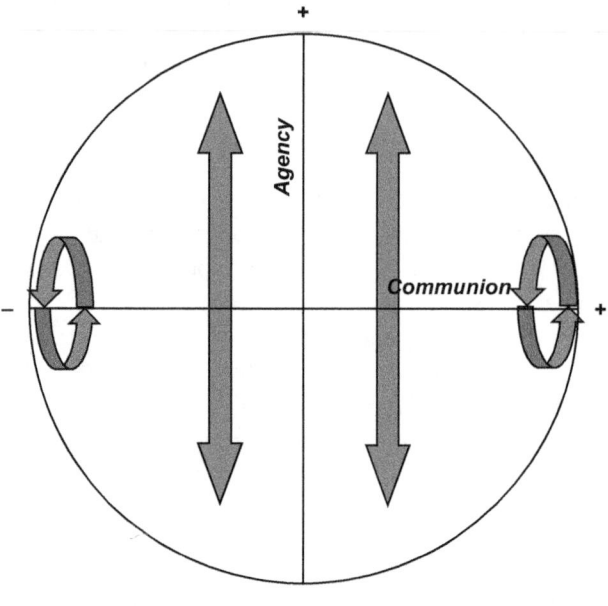

Figure 6.1 Complementarity: communion often elicits the similarly communal behaviour from the other (mirroring). Agency often elicits opposite behaviour from the other (reciprocity)

Communion evokes low Communion. A hostile reaction from a teacher often provokes anger or fear in students. Likewise, a disruptive student may frequently draw an angry response from the teacher.

This tendency to reflect similar levels of Communion is sometimes referred to as *correspondence*[3] or *symmetry*.[4]

Again, complementarity is not a rigid rule or law; it is about likelihood, not certainty. Also, personal and cultural contexts can all influence the behaviour people show, leading to variations in interaction patterns. For example, in some cultures it is common for students to not react hostile when the teacher is hostile due to cultural factors such as respect for authority and elderly. A warm, positive reaction from students may nonetheless be rather unlikely in such a situation, while, for example, fear or uncertainty may be the result of hostile teacher behaviour (indicating low Communion).

Building Bridges or Barriers?

Complementarity can drive interactions in two vastly different directions:

Positive reinforcement: High Communion from both teacher and students creates a cycle of friendly, cooperative behaviours. This fosters a pleasant, productive classroom atmosphere, benefiting everyone involved.

Negative escalation: Low Communion interactions, on the other hand, can spiral into hostility and increasing emotional distance, creating an environment that feels adversarial or even combative.

To Keep in Mind

Displaying high Communion can be used to create a friendly atmosphere in your class. With low Communion, you run the risk of creating an unpleasant atmosphere.

Cultural Nuances in Communion Complementarity

The expression of symmetry in Communion may differ across cultures. *Complementarity is about the interpersonal meaning people attach to behaviour*, not so much about specific behaviours (such as frowning or raising one's voice) per se. For example, in some Asian cultures, students might exhibit stronger reciprocity to high Communion from teachers, reflecting deep cultural respect for educators. Conversely, when teachers express anger, students may refrain from responding in kind openly due to cultural norms emphasising deference and restraint.[5] While similar processes of complementarity may occur, their expression may be modified by cultural conventions. For example, some teacher behaviours are perceived as clearly low in Communion in some cultures, while in other cultures, similar behaviour is perceived as more neutral. Frequent smiles in Western classrooms convey teacher Communion, in other cultural contexts frequent smiles may also convey uncertainty (low Agency and Communion).[6]

Understanding cultural differences in these dynamics and the interpersonal meaning people attach to certain behaviour can help teachers navigate interpersonal relationships in diverse classroom settings, fostering positive environments regardless of cultural boundaries.

It is important to recognise complementarity in interactions. In **Activity 6.1**, you can practice recognising complementarity on Communion in your lessons.

Complementarity in Agency

Reciprocity

The straight arrows in the centre of Figure 6.1 represent the dynamic of reciprocity along the Agency dimension, where one person's behaviour often *elicits the opposite response* from the other.[7] For example: When a teacher displays high Agency through assertive behaviour, students are likely to respond with low Agency, exhibiting passivity or obedience. They exert minimal influence on the classroom dynamic, often leaving the teacher in full control. Conversely, if a teacher shows low Agency by adopting a passive stance, students often step in to fill the void, becoming more active and taking the initiative.

While this reciprocal dynamic can foster engagement when managed intentionally, it can also create undesirable situations:

High teacher Agency/low student Agency: When a teacher dominates the classroom, students may disengage, leading to passive participation. Teachers in Western cultures then may blame students for being uninterested, saying, "They just sit there and don't participate," while students might counter with, "The teacher talks nonstop and never involves us." However, in Asian countries this might be a normal and acceptable situation.

Low teacher Agency/high student Agency: While this can encourage active learning when guided properly, it can devolve into chaos if the teacher fails to assert enough control to ensure structure and clarity.

Understanding and leveraging the principle of reciprocity can help teachers create a balanced classroom dynamic where leadership and student initiative coexist harmoniously.

To Keep in Mind

With high Agency, you can make students compliant; with low Agency, you allow or encourage them to take initiative, but this can also introduce chaos.

Cultural Nuances in Agency Complementarity

The principle of reciprocity on the Agency dimension, though globally observed,[8] may manifest differently across cultures:

- In *Western contexts*, low teacher Agency often prompts students to adopt higher Agency, taking charge or showing initiative. This dynamic aligns with a cultural emphasis on individualism and student autonomy.
- In *East-Asian contexts*, where Confucian values prioritise harmony and respect for authority,[9] reciprocity may play out differently. Instances of low teacher Agency may be more unexpected and infrequent and therefore, if they occur, send a different message to the students. A teacher displaying low Agency may not evoke the same level of student initiative seen in Western classrooms. Similarly, high teacher Agency may elicit complementary responses of stronger student passivity due to cultural norms that emphasise deference to authority.

These cultural differences suggest that teachers may need to adjust their strategies based on the cultural context. For instance, teachers in Western classrooms might need to balance high Agency with opportunities for student involvement to prevent passivity. Teachers in Asian settings might use smaller variations in Agency to have a similar effect as larger variations in other cultures.

It is important to recognise complementarity in interactions. In **Activity 6.2**, you can practice recognising complementarity on Agency in your lessons.

Complementarity in the Combination of Agency and Communion

So far, we have explored complementarity within the individual dimensions of Agency and Communion. However, interpersonal behaviour always involves a *combination* of the two. For instance, corrective or angry teacher behaviour located in the upper-left corner of the interpersonal model combines moderately high Agency with low Communion. The complementary student response to this behaviour is found mirrored in the Communion axis of the model: A mix of moderately low Agency and low Communion. This could manifest as dissatisfied or uncertain student behaviour.

In practice, this dynamic means:

- A student receiving corrections may respond with dissatisfaction.
- A grumbling teacher moderately low on Agency may provoke irritation from students.

This reciprocal dynamic underscores the importance of being mindful of the combined Agency and Communion messages you send.

Specific Combinations of Agency and Communion

Complementarity in behaviour plays out through specific combinations of Agency and Communion. Next, we examine five key combinations (illustrated in Figures 6.2–6.6) to understand how these dynamics influence teacher-student interactions.

78 An Interpersonal Perspective on Classroom Management

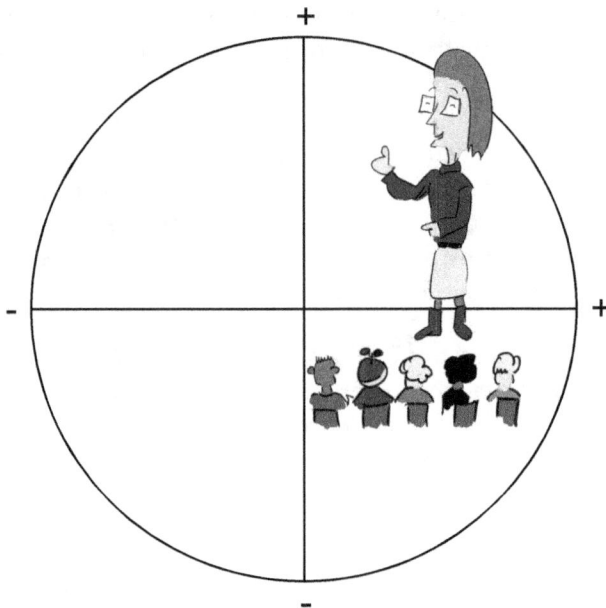

Figure 6.2 Complementary response of students on a teacher whose behaviour is moderately high on both agency and communion

> *Moderately high teacher Agency and Communion* (Figure 6.2): The teacher demonstrates moderately high Agency and Communion, such as kindly but clearly directing students. The complementary response from students is moderately high Communion paired with moderately low Agency–they comply kindly and follow the teacher's lead. For example, a teacher says, "Please take out your notebooks and start the activity," with a warm tone and confident posture, prompting students to cooperate willingly.
>
> *Moderately low teacher Agency and high Communion* (Figure 6.3): When teachers take a more passive role with high Communion–such as responding warmly to students' questions or requests–students may take the lead with moderately high Agency and high Communion. For example, a student asks for clarification during a lesson, and the teacher listens attentively to provide a thoughtful response. This can also be seen when students explain something to other students, and the teacher listens. This encourages a reciprocal flow of ideas, reinforcing a collaborative learning environment.

Not all forms of complementarity in the Interpersonal Circle make positive outcomes in the classroom more likely. On the left side of the circle, we encounter interactions that can disrupt a positive classroom dynamic and even escalate conflicts.

> *Moderately high teacher Agency and low Communion* (Figure 6.4): When a teacher displays behaviour characterised by control with little warmth (being confrontational or hostile), it may prompt students to respond with grumbling or passive dissatisfaction– low on both Agency and Communion. For example, a teacher sharply corrects students without showing understanding. Students may comply outwardly but grumble or disengage internally, creating a tense atmosphere.

Complementarity in Interactions 79

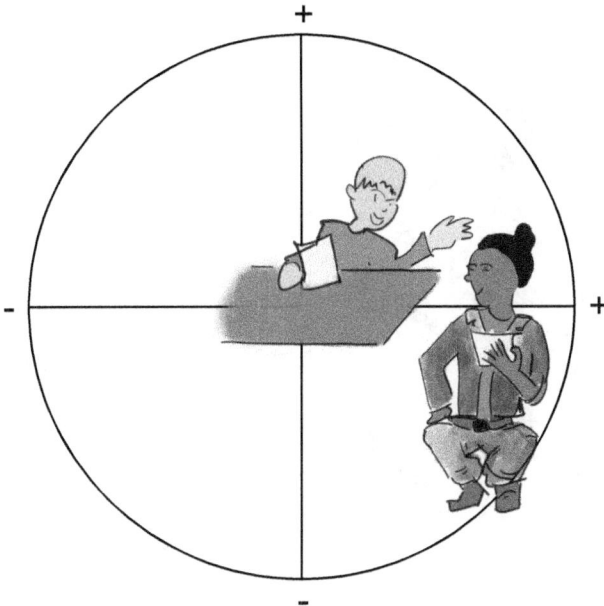

Figure 6.3 Complementary response of a teacher on a student whose behaviour is moderately high on both agency and communion

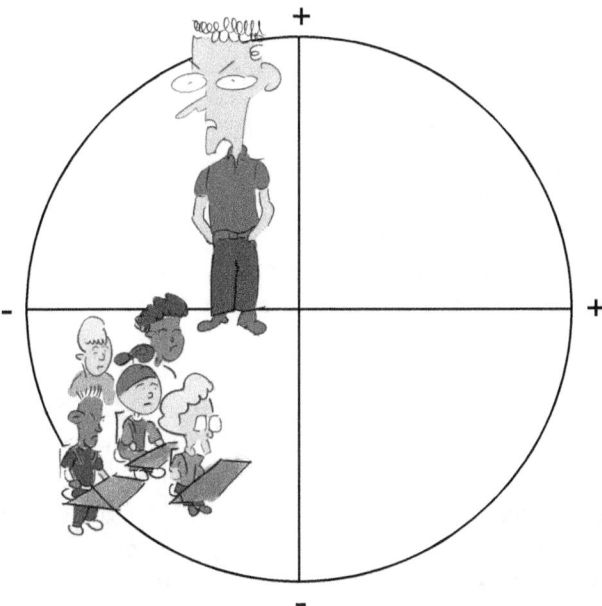

Figure 6.4 Complementary response of students on a teacher whose behaviour is moderately high on agency and low on communion

80 An Interpersonal Perspective on Classroom Management

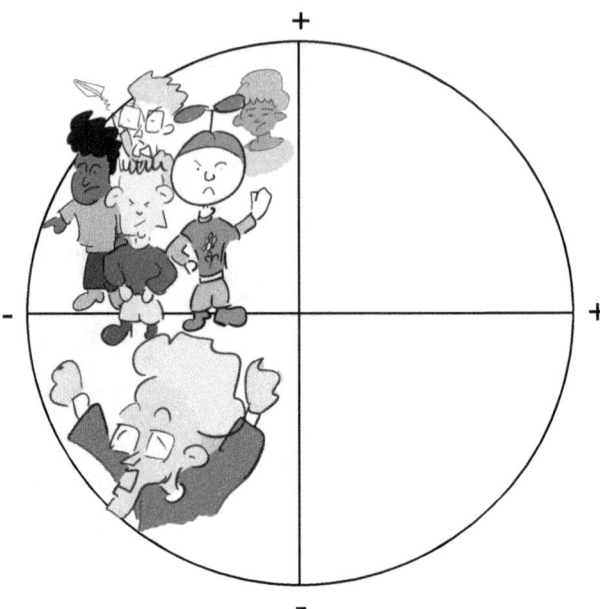

Figure 6.5 Complementary response of students on a teacher whose behaviour is moderately low on both agency and communion

> *Low teacher Agency and low Communion* (Figure 6.5): When a teacher exhibits disengagement and dissatisfaction, students may respond actively but negatively, falling into the upper-left quadrant of the circle, where they, eventually, may oppose the teacher's authority. For example, a teacher shows visible uncertainty and lack of leadership, leading students to act out or challenge the teacher.
>
> *Competition over Agency* (Figure 6.6): If there is competition over Agency, students may *not* respond in complementary ways to the teacher. If a teacher combines moderately high Agency with moderately low Communion such as shouting in class, in Western contexts, students might respond with complementary low Communion but matching (moderately) high Agency–openly questioning the teacher's authority or ignoring instructions. For example, a teacher threatens punishment in a commanding tone, and a student talks back, creating a standoff over who has control.

In this last scenario, teacher and students enter a power struggle, with intensifying behaviours threatening to derail the learning environment. When escalation seems likely, teachers might increase Agency and decrease Communion even further: This involves stricter enforcement or even punitive actions (e.g., detentions or referrals). While sometimes effective, such an approach risks exacerbating hostility if not carefully managed. However, a more empathetic response could help de-escalate tensions. Shifting to high Communion and demonstrating care and respect may encourage students to step back from confrontation.

Having follow-up conversations with students after class may be essential to restore the relationship and foster mutual respect. In extreme cases, seeking assistance from school leadership might be helpful.

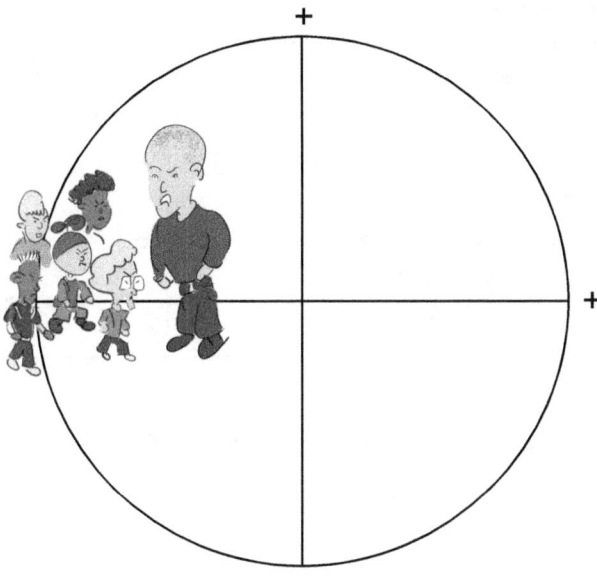

Figure 6.6 Response of students on a teacher whose behaviour is moderately high on agency and low on communion; on communion the students respond complementary but on agency the students react non-complementary

Demonstrating high Agency in combination with high Communion is of great importance for creating and maintaining positive relationships with your students. In **Activity 6.3**, you can work on this.

Strictness and Confrontation

There is an important *distinction between strict and confrontational behaviour*–a distinction that some teachers overlook. While both involve high levels of Agency, their differing levels of Communion can significantly impact student responses and well-being.

Strict behaviour is characterised by high Agency and moderately low Communion. This approach often prompts students to withdraw or murmur, rather than openly resist. While the atmosphere may become slightly tense, the classroom order generally remains intact. The teacher may strictly emphasise rules, however without threatening consequences.

Confrontational behaviour, on the other hand, combines moderately high Agency with low Communion. This type of intervention risks eliciting oppositional responses from students, escalating conflict and potentially undermining classroom order. The teacher may use threats or may shout and more freely show frustration with students.

Understanding this distinction through the lens of complementarity helps explain why strict behaviour is often more effective than confrontational behaviour. Confrontational behaviour, especially in its more intensive forms—perceived as overly hostile or aggressive—can provoke direct opposition, amplifying any existing disorder or hostility in the classroom. However, strictness, when applied without hostility, creates an environment where students are less likely to challenge authority, also because it conveys higher levels of Agency than confrontational behaviour.

To Keep in Mind

Teacher strict behaviour might evoke student (disengaged) silence. Confrontational behaviour might elicit student opposition.

Background Information

Complementarity Visualised with the Joystick Method[10]

The graphs in Figure 6.7 have been generated using the joystick method described in Chapter 4. They represent the scores of a teacher and a class on Agency and Communion during the first 10 minutes of a lesson. The solid line represents the teacher, and the dashed line represents the class.

It is clear that there is complementarity: When the teacher's Agency increases, that of the students decreases, and vice versa. When the teacher becomes higher on Communion, so do the students.

The question is, who takes the initiative for changes in the degree of Communion and Agency? Is it the teacher, and the students follow, or is it the other way around? It turns out that both cases occur approximately equally. Interestingly, in classrooms with a positive classroom atmosphere, teachers are slightly more likely to take the lead in adjusting the degree of Agency than in classes with a less favourable atmosphere.

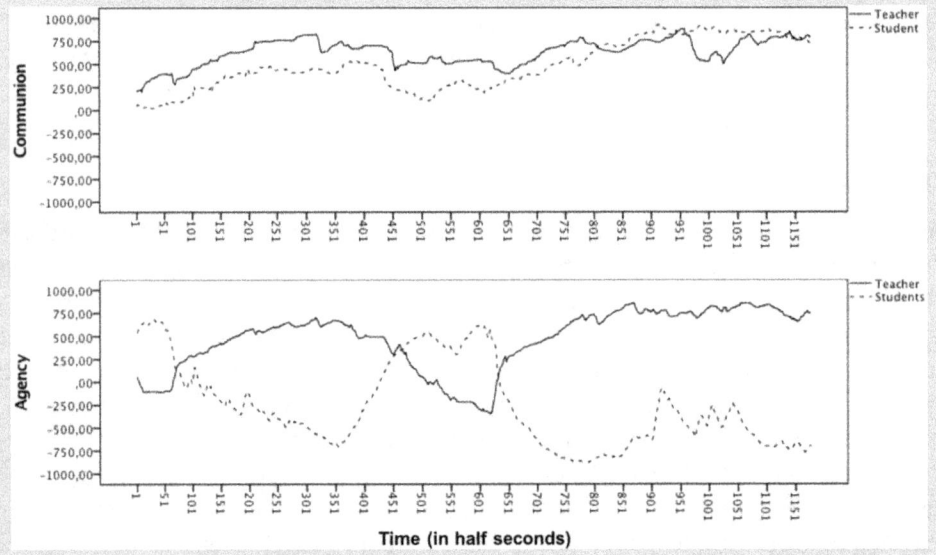

Figure 6.7 Graphs depicting the levels of agency and communion of teachers and class generated with the joystick method

Source: Pennings et al. (2018)

In **Activity 6.4**, you can investigate whether there is complementarity by drawing the interaction in the Interpersonal Circle.

Professional Teacher Behaviour and Complementarity

Complementary responding can be an effective strategy for teachers, fostering a positive and productive classroom atmosphere. Using complementarity on the high Communion side of the circle—characterised by friendliness and helpfulness—is particularly functional in promoting strong interpersonal connections and student cooperation. As we have illustrated in earlier examples, when teachers consistently display such behaviour, it encourages students to mirror positively, making harmonious relationships like those of August and Tonia in Chapter 1 achievable.

That said, especially in negative situations it is equally professional for teachers to respond *non-complementarily*. This involves deliberately resisting the reflex to respond in a complementary manner and instead breaking a negative complementary pattern. By doing so, teachers can address situations that require a shift in dynamics, such as managing disruptions or redirecting unproductive behaviours, while maintaining or establishing their authority in the classroom.

There are two types of adopting a *non-complementary* approach that can lead to a more positive interaction and improved relationships.

Handling Student Behaviour with High Communion

When students display challenging or defiant behaviour, teachers must be able to resist the inclination to respond negatively, that is, in kind on the Communion dimension. Instead, they should be able to adopt a non-complementary response of kindness and understanding. For example, if a student makes an unpleasant remark, the teacher might respond not with blame or punishment but by calmly and kindly asking the student to elaborate on the comment. This requires setting aside irritation and consistently responding with friendliness and openness, thereby nudging interactions towards the right side of the Interpersonal Circle. This can be referred to as a positive interpersonal bid by the teacher.

Table 6.1 provides some responses from teachers to student misbehaviour that, by using appropriate non-verbal behaviour (smiling, speaking softly, etc.), can be high on Communion and thus non-complementary, potentially moving the student towards the friendly side of the circle.

These responses illustrate the use of communication to maintain moderate Agency to uphold classroom structure and rules while demonstrating high Communion to foster respect and rapport with students.

It is worth noting that this strategy may be more effective and culturally appropriate in Western contexts, where fostering open and communicative teacher-student relationships is often emphasised. In other contexts, where different norms and expectations shape teacher-student dynamics, other behaviour communicating Communion maybe more appropriate, and thus this approach may vary.

84 *An Interpersonal Perspective on Classroom Management*

Table 6.1 Examples of teacher responses to student misbehaviour that are high on communion

Student behaviour	Teacher's response	Comment
Mary grumbles when asked to start the lesson.	"Mary, why don't you start reading on page 86? Maybe we can make sense of it together."	This response avoids direct confrontation while gently redirecting Mary's energy towards the task at hand. By offering support ("make sense of it together"), the teacher fosters a collaborative environment.
Fiona talks to her neighbour during instructions.	You ignore it for a moment and, when everyone is working, walk by to say: "Fiona, I understand it's fun with Aya next to you, but try to pay attention during the explanation. It will really help later when you must do homework."	The teacher strategically delays addressing the behaviour to avoid disrupting the instructions and then uses a private, low-stakes interaction. By acknowledging Fiona's social connection ("fun with Aya") and framing the correction in terms of helping her succeed ("really help later"), the teacher maintains high Communion while subtly asserting control (Agency).
Julia talks through a difficult concept explanation.	"Julia, can you pay attention, or do you want me to stop, and the rest of the class might get upset with you?"	This response introduces mild social accountability by framing Julia's behaviour as potentially disruptive to her peers. The teacher asserts their authority while giving Julia the opportunity to make a positive choice.
Nina makes a loud inappropriate joke in response to something you say.	"Come on, Nina, I know you like to have a good time in class, but I don't find this joke very successful, and I know you can make better jokes than this."	The teacher acknowledges Nina's sense of humour while subtly critiquing the inappropriate nature of her comment. By expressing confidence in Nina's ability to do better, the teacher redirects her behaviour without harshness.

Teachers with strong positive relationships with their students are better positioned to manage challenging behaviours without resorting to hostile reactions. By maintaining a foundation of trust and respect, they can employ strategies that de-escalate tensions and foster positive interactions. However, this approach is not foolproof, especially in cases involving students with persistent behaviour issues (see the last section of Chapter 9) or when patterns of interaction are heavily ingrained in existing relational dynamics.

In such scenarios, teachers might explore entirely different approaches to reshape the interaction dynamics such as working in groups instead of a whole class. We will return to these interventions at the end of this chapter.

To encourage positive student behaviour, non-complementary behaviour can be useful. In **Activity 6.5**, you can practice displaying friendly behaviour in response to undesirable student behaviour.

Complementarity in Interactions 85

Encouraging Student Initiative Through Low-Agency Behaviour

On the Agency dimension, fostering student initiative can require teachers to consciously step back. While their reflex may be to fill silence or take control, effective teaching sometimes means suppressing that impulse. By deliberately displaying low-Agency behaviour, teachers can create space for students to step up and take the lead.

For example, when students are unresponsive to a question, instead of repeating the question or answering it yourself, try sitting down, stepping back, or waiting calmly. This shift in body language and positioning communicates patience and trust, inviting students to assume a more active role in the interaction.

> **To Keep in Mind**
>
> – A positive interpersonal bid—not responding in a complementary way to negative student behaviour on the left side of the Interpersonal Circle can help maintain a good atmosphere.
> – To make students active, teacher behaviour low on Agency can be a good trigger.

To create a friendly atmosphere in your lessons, you can intently use the complementarity principles. This is the topic of **Activity 6.6**.

Difficulties in Changing Interactions and Relationships

Escalated interactions in the classroom often arise from mutually reinforcing, complementary responses between teachers and students. Once the pattern is established, pinpointing the starting point or assigning blame is unproductive. Even if it were possible to find the starting point or identify the culprit, it still would not help improve the situation. Instead, professional responses focus on how to break negative complementarity and de-escalate the situation.

In the following chapters, we will provide various concrete examples of professionally responding to student behaviour. However, in established undesirable classroom dynamics, changing your behaviour may not yield immediate results. Established dynamics are highly resistant to attempts to change them. For instance, passive students may not immediately respond to the teacher adopting low-Agency behaviours, such as waiting quietly after asking a question. Patience and repetition are key: Stay consistent in your new approach and give students time to adjust. You might discuss your behavioural changes with students, explaining the rationale behind them. This transparency can help build trust and create a foundation for improved interactions.

Extremely negatively escalated dynamics may ask for more drastic measures. When for example disorder has become "normal," you can:

- Shift from whole-class instruction to group or individual work to diffuse tension and create opportunities for positive, one-on-one interactions; this setup allows you to show high Communion in personal conversations with students, thus rebuilding trust with individual students.
- Modify seating arrangements.
- Reinforce positive student behaviour by acknowledging and rewarding student achievements, such as giving deserved high grades for completed work.
- When whole-class teaching is necessary, avoid asking students to respond to questions.
- Ask support from the school leadership.
- For students with more profound behaviour challenges, develop individualised strategies or consult with school counsellors and psychologists.

To Keep in Mind

To break established negative interaction dynamics:

- Avoid blame.
- Respond non-complementary to negative student behaviour.
- Rearrange your teaching setup.
- Persist.
- Communicate about your approach.
- Seek support from others.

In Sum

To recognise complementarity is key for understanding the chains of teacher and student behaviours that unfold in the classroom. The principles are:

- Communion elicits similar communal behaviour from the other.
- Agency elicits opposite behaviour from the other.

You can use the complementarity principles for creating positive relationships with your students:

- Behaving complementary on high Communion.
- Avoiding complementarity on low Communion.
- Employing high Agency when you need students to comply.
- Employing low Agency to encourage students' initiative.

Notes

1 Chuang (2005).
2 These principles go back to the work of the anthropologist Gregory Bateson in New Guinea (1958).
3 Kiesler (1983).
4 E.g., Watzlawick et al. (1967).
5 Maulana personal communication.
6 Sun et al. (2019).
7 Kiesler (1983).
8 Horowitz and Strack (2010).
9 Chen and Starosta (2003).
10 Pennings et al. (2018).

7 Non-verbal Communication in Interactions

The level of Agency and Communion in interpersonal messages is mostly communicated through non-verbal behaviour. This includes *body posture, facial expressions, gestures, whether or not eye contact is made, physical proximity to others, how someone utilises the available space in the presence of others, and the non-linguistic aspects of speech such as volume, intonation, pauses, and pitch*. These are also referred to as "channels" for non-verbal behaviour. This chapter explores the specific interpersonal meaning of non-verbal cues for the Agency and Communion dimensions of the Interpersonal Circle. We also include a discussion of some variations in interpersonal meaning across cultures and the significance of these variations for communicating effectively in multicultural classrooms. Finally, attention is given to the alignment between verbal and non-verbal behaviours and how to train yourself in communicating non-verbally effectively.

Communicating Communion Through Non-verbal Cues

To foster positive interactions with students, teachers should aim to convey high Communion through their behaviour and minimise instances of low Communion as much as possible (but please check the section on redirecting student behaviour in Chapter 8). Among the tools at a teacher's disposal, non-verbal communication plays a pivotal role in signalling Communion and reinforcing desired student behaviours.

In Western cultures, teachers can establish high Communion non-verbally through various channels:[1]

- *Physical distance*: Standing close to students creates a sense of positive connection when combined with a positive facial expression and/or positive tone of voice.
- *Eye contact*: Looking directly at students signals attentiveness.
- *Body orientation*: Facing students frontally shows engagement and openness.
- *Posture*: Adopting an open posture (e.g., uncrossed arms) conveys approachability.
- *Leaning forward*: Demonstrates interest and attentiveness when combined with a positive facial expression and/or positive tone of voice.
- *Facial expressions*: A warm smile communicates friendliness.
- *Voice tone*: Gentle, clear tones reinforce approachability and support, especially in one-on-one situations.

DOI: 10.4324/9781003563464-7

Figure 7.1 Communicating communion with non-verbal behaviour

The combination of physical distance from the student, facial expressions, and voice usage is particularly important.

Figure 7.1 provides a visual example of a teacher demonstrating high Communion: standing close to a student, making eye contact, and leaning forward. Because she pairs this with a smile, this combination signals attention and support, likely encouraging a student to feel valued and seek help confidently. However, the same posture with an angry expression will alarm the student, leading them to feel anxious or defensive.

We now delve into some of the channels of non-verbal behaviours.

Eye Contact

Making *eye contact* with an authority figure (like a teacher) and vice versa during a conversation is considered respectful in some cultures, but not in others.[2] For example:

- *Western Cultures*: Maintaining eye contact with a teacher is seen as respectful and a sign of paying attention and engagement.
- *Asian and Middle Eastern Cultures*: Direct eye contact, particularly with an authority figure, may be interpreted as disrespectful or confrontational. Lowering one's gaze is often a gesture of respect.
- *Chinese Classrooms*: Eye contact can even serve as a subtle warning rather than a positive affirmation, indicating potential disapproval.[3]

Physical Distance and Touching

The physical distance people find comfortable during conversations varies widely across cultures and regions. This comfort zone generally expands as one moves further from the equator.[4] For example:

- *Arab and Latin cultures*: People tend to stand relatively close together during interactions, emphasising warmth and connection.
- *North American and North-Western European cultures*: A greater space is preferred, with close proximity sometimes considered intrusive.
- *Latin America*: Touch—the most direct way of reducing physical distance—often conveys friendliness, while in *Asian cultures*, it might be deemed inappropriate or disrespectful.

The interpretation of touching depends heavily on context and accompanying non-verbal cues:

- *Positive effects*: A light touch can provide reassurance, foster connection, and signal support.
- *Negative effects*: The same touch, paired with an angry expression, might be perceived as invasive or even aggressive.
- *In classroom* and other professional settings, touching interaction partners may not be appropriate, depending on the cultural context.

Touching can also provoke discomfort if perceived as overly intimate. This discomfort is influenced by:

- *Cultural norms*: For instance, students in some cultures might see close physical proximity from teachers as overly forward or inappropriate.
- *Age dynamics*: Younger children in primary education might be more comfortable with close teacher proximity, whereas older students in secondary education may find it inappropriate.
- *Gender considerations*: Male teachers, for example, may need to be more cautious to avoid any actions that could be misconstrued, such as touching a female student.

Facial Expressions

The human face, with its intricate, dedicated network of small muscles, plays a critical role in communication. Facial expressions convey a range of emotions and levels of Communion, either fostering connection or creating distance.

Figure 7.2 highlights facial expressions:

- *Low Communion* (four faces on the left): Frowns, narrow eyes, or tight lips signal hostility or disinterest and should generally be avoided. Anger is an extreme variant of this. For teachers in Western classrooms, this is almost never functional because students perceive it as a sign of losing self-control and thus not only as low Communion but also as a loss of Agency in the class. Contempt is even less functional because it is an expression that is easily perceived as a very negative emotion directed at the student as a person.
- *High Communion* (face on the right): A relaxed expression, open eyes, and a warm smile foster trust and approachability.

Key facial elements contributing to Communion include:[5]

- *Eyebrows*: Raised brows often indicate interest or friendliness, while furrowed brows suggest disapproval.

Non-verbal Communication in Interactions 91

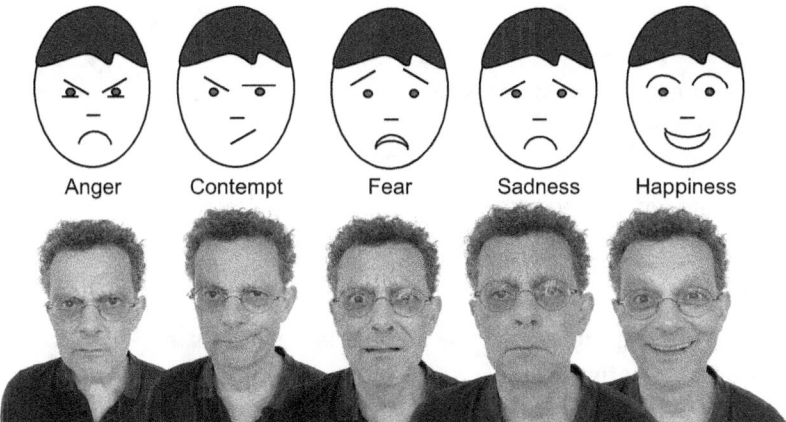

Figure 7.2 Expressions of emotions through different facial expressions

- *Eyes*: Direct eye contact, when culturally appropriate, conveys attentiveness; soft, open eyes are inviting.
- *Mouth*: A slight, genuine smile communicates warmth and receptiveness.

Facial expressions, especially smiling to convey connection with others and happiness, are often considered universal. However, the rules governing how and when to use these expressions can vary across cultures. For instance, some *Asians* use friendly or smiling expressions in response to a range of emotional states—not just happiness. This practice can seem unusual or puzzling to *Westerners*, who typically associate smiles exclusively with positive emotions. Conversely, Western facial expressions might appear overly direct or intense to individuals from Asian cultures.[6] This cultural variation can lead to misunderstandings in interpreting facial expressions, also in multicultural classrooms.

Exactly because conveying high or low Communion through facial expressions is so nuanced, facial expressions are powerful non-verbal behaviours. As a teacher, with your facial expression, you can convey a lot about how you relate to students and what you think of their actions. Smiling at the right times and in appropriate contexts, in particular, is important for conveying a positive and close interpersonal message to students.

As a teacher, it is very useful to be able to use certain facial expressions intentionally and to "control" them well. Especially with younger students, it sometimes helps to emphasise facial expressions a bit more to make clear what you think of certain behaviours or performances.

The Voice

Beyond facial expressions and physical distance, the voice plays a powerful role in communicating Communion. Elements such as volume, intonation, and the use of pauses significantly influence the message conveyed. For instance:

- *Anger or frustration* is often signalled by raising your voice or shouting.
- *Friendliness and warmth* are conveyed through varied intonation—alternating between high and low pitch—a moderate speaking pace, and a soft yet audible tone. Clear articulation further reinforces a positive and approachable demeanour.

To Keep in Mind

For communicating Communion, the combination of physical distance from the student, facial expressions, and voice usage is particularly important.

It is important to be able to express non-verbally interpersonal messages as you intend. You practice this in **Activity 7.1**.

Communicating Agency with Non-verbal Cues

To effectively convey high Agency, a teacher should focus on *emphasis*, *calmness*, and *space* and *posture*. Through these elements, you can show confidence and authority.

Emphasis

Behaviours that emphasise a point you make—such as purposeful gestures or varied intonation—are often perceived as influential. Strategic pauses, or "meaningful silences," can also draw attention to key points. Speaking with emphasis and employing powerful gestures naturally commands the attention of students, projecting high Agency. Especially with younger children, seemingly exaggerated emphasis can be vital to hold their attention.

A loud speaking volume which is well audible in the entire classroom is often associated with emphasis and thus high Agency, although cultural expectations play a role here. In cultures where teachers are traditionally loud, volume may not correlate as strongly with Agency. Conversely, when students are working independently, teachers may intentionally reduce emphasis, speaking softly and using fewer gestures to shift focus away from themselves.

Calmness

Accentuating voice or gestures can help emphasise a message, but it is important to strike a balance—overdoing it may come across as restless, undermining the perception of high Agency. Calm, non-verbal behaviour often enhances the impression of control and authority, reinforcing a teacher's Agency.

A calm demeanour projects confidence and authority without appearing overly domineering. It signals that teachers feel secure in their role and trust their ability to manage the classroom effectively. Calm teachers convey that their leadership is natural, not forced.

While calmness is key, maintaining a sense of control and awareness is equally important. Many teachers intuitively adopt positions or postures that allow them to oversee the class while appearing relaxed. For instance, in Western cultures, the "classic" posture of sitting on a desk at the front of the class, as shown in Figure 7.3, strikes this balance. This pose, often dramatised in Hollywood films, combines approachability with authority.

However, cultural expectations play a role. In Asian classrooms, sitting on a table may be perceived as inappropriate or even disrespectful, reflecting poorly on the teacher's professionalism.[7]

Non-verbal Communication in Interactions 93

Figure 7.3 Agency: A teacher combining calmness and overview by sitting on a table

The way a teacher speaks—including the use of pauses, pacing, and gestures—can influence how calm and composed they appear. Teachers who incorporate deliberate pauses and measured gestures signal confidence and ease. Their calm behaviour shows they do not feel threatened or pressured, reinforcing their natural Agency.

By mastering calmness while maintaining oversight, teachers can establish authority that feels both confident and approachable.

Use of Space and Posture

Traditionally, controlling space is a clear symbol of authority and Agency. Whether it is the head of the table or a throne that elevates a leader above others, spatial dominance often reflects status. In the classroom, teachers can use the space strategically to project Agency while also fostering engagement. Moving intentionally around the classroom and using its full space can signal Agency as well. However, maintaining an optimal position is key—it should allow the teacher to oversee the entire room. In a similar vein, being visible for all students signals Agency too.

Adopting an expansive posture—broad shoulders, open stance—can communicate high Agency. However, if a teacher has a relationship with students where their Agency is perceived as relatively low, this posture may come across as forced or compensatory rather than natural. Body language that appears overly assertive can indicate intent rather than inspire perception of authority.

Sometimes, it is effective for a teacher to adopt a less visible, more modest posture. This approach, which reduces the teacher's Agency, can encourage students to take initiative,

Figure 7.4 Low agency: A teacher squatting.

such as leading a discussion or asking questions. For example, when teachers crouch down—illustrated in Figure 7.4—while assisting students with their work, they create a sense of equality. This positioning helps foster a connection, making it easier for students to engage and share their thoughts.

> **To Keep in Mind**
>
> To effectively convey high Agency, a teacher should focus on:
>
> - Emphasis.
> - Calmness.
> - Visibility.
> - Audibility.
> - Space and posture.

In **Activity 7.2**, you will collaborate with colleagues to explore how you can demonstrate non-verbal high and low Agency.

Combination of Non-verbal Behaviours

This chapter has explored the numerous ways teachers can communicate Agency and Communion through non-verbal behaviours. While it is valuable to understand how individual actions with one channel—such as gestures, posture, or vocal tone—convey specific interpersonal messages, it is essential to remember that students interpret these together, as part of a larger whole.

The interpersonal meaning students derive comes from the *entirety of the teacher's behaviour*, encompassing both verbal and non-verbal elements. This holistic interpretation means that no single behaviour acts in isolation; rather, multiple behaviours together shape how students perceive their teacher's Agency and Communion.

Figure 7.5 illustrates how the interplay of behaviours can lead to perceptions of either low or high Agency, highlighting the importance of intentional communication for effective classroom management and engagement.

In **Activity 7.3**, you will examine the interpersonal messages that can be derived from non-verbal behaviour. You will place teachers in the Interpersonal Circle based on their facial expressions.

Figure 7.5 Combinations of non-verbal behaviours leading to high agency (left) and low agency (right). Left: Speaking almost continuously with a reasonably high volume, scanning the class with the head, and maintaining some distance from the students. Right: whispering, bending the head toward the student, and being close to the student.

Non-verbal Cues in Multicultural Classrooms

As many classrooms are increasingly multicultural, the interpretation of non-verbal behaviours can vary widely among students, even within the same country or class. Behaviours that are typical or acceptable in one cultural context may hold a different meaning in another. This diversity highlights the need for teachers to be aware of cultural nuances, particularly in areas such as *eye contact*, *physical distance*, and *gestures*.

> *Eye contact*: In some cultures, maintaining eye contact conveys respect and attentiveness, while in others, it can be seen as confrontational or disrespectful.
> *Physical distance*: Comfort levels regarding proximity can differ; standing close might be friendly in one culture but intrusive in another.
> *Gestures*: The meaning of specific gestures can vary widely across cultures. For instance, the "thumbs up" gesture, which means "good" or "okay" in many *Western* cultures, may be offensive in some *Middle Eastern* countries. A head nod might signify agreement in some cultures but disagreement in others. The frequency and intensity of gestures can also differ. *South Europeans* and *Latin Americans*, for example, are known for their expressive gestures, while *North Europeans* and *East Asians* typically use fewer, more subdued movements.

Understanding these cultural nuances is essential, especially in diverse settings, to avoid misinterpretation and to foster effective communication and relationships. You must recognise and adapt your behavioural style to fit the cultural expectations and interpersonal preferences of your diverse classrooms.

In the United States, in urban classrooms, teachers often successfully connect with their students employing an *assertive communication style*. These teachers:

- Correct quickly and explicitly, ensuring clarity.
- Set high and clear expectations, providing structure and goals.
- Demonstrate high Communion, showing warmth and attentiveness.

Their blend of firmness and care has earned these teachers the label of *warm demanders*.[8] Their approach resonates well with many Black students in urban schools, aligning with cultural norms that value both respect and relationship-building. However, this assertive style might not be universally effective. In other parts of the United States—or in schools with different cultural compositions—it could conflict with what students are accustomed to or prefer.

Aligning Verbal and Non-verbal Messages

Effective communication hinges on congruence between what you say and how you say it. When verbal and non-verbal cues align, the message becomes clear and trustworthy. Consider these examples:

- A teacher says, "That's kind of you" with a warm smile and relaxed posture. The message is most likely perceived as high on Communion.

- The same sentence, spoken with a stern expression and intensely looking to the student, sends another message, likely interpreted as less friendly or even sarcastic.

When verbal and non-verbal signals conflict, the *non-verbal message typically prevails*.[9] Students are more likely to trust what they see over what is said, particularly when the two are misaligned. An exception to this rule occurs with very young children, who may focus more on the content of what is said than on accompanying non-verbal cues.[10] This discrepancy can lead to confusion in early education settings, emphasising the need for clarity. Thus, especially with young children irony and sarcasm are ill-advised.

Stress or strong emotions like frustration can make it challenging to maintain control over non-verbal communication. Shouting, for instance, may betray frustration rather than convey control and authority, as seen when a teacher yells, "I'm in charge here!" in a noisy classroom. Such behaviour is likely to be perceived as desperation rather than genuine control.

To project confidence and professionalism, you should practice aligning verbal and non-verbal communication, particularly in high-pressure situations. For example:

- Use calm, deliberate movements to project confidence, even if you feel anxious or frustrated.
- Practice maintaining a neutral or serious facial expression as opposed to an angry expression, to avoid unintentionally conveying frustration or anger. This may include reappraising your emotions, as will be discussed in the beginning of Chapter 9.

Developing the ability to intentionally use and control non-verbal cues is an invaluable skill for teachers: a key aspect of teacher professionalism. It requires self-awareness and practice to ensure that your actions reinforce your words, creating clear, consistent, and effective communication with your students. This alignment is essential for building trust, maintaining authority, and fostering a productive classroom atmosphere.

Activity 7.4 helps you investigate if verbal and non-verbal behaviour are congruent.

To Keep in Mind

Navigate non-verbal cues thoughtfully by

- Cultural awareness: For example, adjust proximity and gestures to align with students' cultural norms.
- Respect for personal space: Avoid encroaching on students' personal space, particularly in older age groups or mixed-gender interactions.
- Mindful facial expressions: Use expressions that convey high Communion, avoiding those that might unintentionally signal frustration or indifference.

In Sum

The level of Agency and Communion in interpersonal messages is to an important extent communicated through non-verbal behaviour. Pay attention to:

- Body posture.
- Facial expressions.
- Gestures.
- Whether or not eye contact is made.
- Physical proximity to others.
- How you utilise the available space in the presence of others.
- The non-linguistic aspects of speech such as volume, intonation, pauses, and pitch.

High Communion is communicated through close physical distance, smiling and a friendly voice and low Communion through distance, angry or dissatisfied facial expressions and voice.

High Agency is communicated through speaking with a reasonably high volume, scanning the class with your head, standing up straight and maintaining some distance from the students. Low Agency is communicated through speaking softly, bending your head towards the student, and being close to the student.

You should be aware of differences in meaning of non-verbal behaviours in different cultures and contexts.

Effective communication hinges on congruence between what you say and how you say it.

Notes

1. Andersen (1979); Andersen and Andersen (1982).
2. Burgoon et al. (2022).
3. Liu personal communication.
4. Gifford (2010).
5. Ekman and Friesen (2003).
6. Gifford (2010).
7. Maulana personal communication; https://manajemenmudah.blogspot.com/2021/11/1-duduk-di-atas-meja-ketika-mengajar.html
8. Bondy and Ross (2008), Polderdijk et al. (2025).
9. Watzlawick et al. (1967).
10. Woolfolk and Brooks (1985).

8 Maintaining, Directing, and Redirecting Student Behaviour

On her first day teaching her class in the early years, the teacher begins with a warm welcome and an introduction while students are sitting in a circle. With a smile, she says, "I'm excited to get to know all of you! My name is Ms. Taylor, and I'd love to hear each of your names too."

Immediately, students eagerly call out their names. Ms. Taylor gently raises her hand and says, "Hold on a moment—I can't hear all your wonderful names like this. Let's take turns. When I point to you, it'll be your turn to share."

She points to one student, who proudly announces her name while the others listen. "Great! Thank you," Ms. Taylor says encouragingly, before pointing to the next student. "And you?" The introductions continue around the circle, each student sharing their name one by one, as Ms. Taylor nods and smiles, setting a tone of respect and order for the classroom.

Undesirable student behaviour, particularly disruptions, can be a significant source of stress for teachers, especially those just starting out. How can you ensure students stay engaged and participate actively in the lesson?

In the previous example, the teacher effectively handles disruptive behaviour by employing a sequence of strategies:

- *Redirecting* the undesirable behaviour with a clear cue: "Hold on a moment."
- *Directing* the desired behaviour by setting a simple rule: Let's take turns. "When I point to you, it'll be your turn to share."
- *Maintaining* the desired behaviour through positive reinforcement: "Great! Thank you."

These three types of teacher behaviours play a crucial role in creating a focused and interactive classroom environment. While redirecting and maintaining respond to what students are doing in the moment, directing aims to set expectations proactively, reducing the likelihood of disruptions before they occur.

The old saying, *Prevention is better than cure*, holds particularly true in the classroom. Investing time in building strong, positive relationships with your students is one of the most effective ways to prevent undesirable behaviour. When students feel respected, understood, and part of a supportive environment, they are naturally more inclined to participate positively.

DOI: 10.4324/9781003563464-8

In this chapter, we will explore strategies to maintain and direct desirable student behaviour. Because disruptions cannot always be avoided, we will also address techniques for redirecting undesirable behaviour effectively when it arises. By mastering these approaches, teachers can create classrooms where participation flourishes, and challenges are managed constructively.

Maintaining Desired Student Behaviour

The Role of Rewards and Appreciation

Rewards and appreciation are powerful tools for fostering a positive classroom environment. These actions reflect a combination of high Communion and some to significant Agency–a position in the upper-right quadrant of the Interpersonal Circle Teacher (see Figure 3.2). When teachers reward students, they invite a complementary response: collaborative behaviour from students (see Figure 3.4). This mutual reinforcement creates a positive feedback loop, enhancing the classroom atmosphere and motivating students to engage (as illustrated in Figure 6.2).

Rewarding and appreciating desired behaviour send a clear message: *I see you, and you matter. What you're doing is valuable. I recognise you and your potential.* These affirmations resonate with everyone, including students. Simple statements like the following can instil self-confidence and build trust:

— "Good morning, glad to have you back."
— "You're on the right track."
— "Great effort."
— "I can see you are committed to this."

When students feel recognised and their effort is appreciated, they are more likely to repeat and sustain the desired behaviour. This positive reinforcement fosters trust, which enhances participation and cooperation, ultimately improving the classroom climate.[1] Rewarding students does not just maintain desired behaviour; it accelerates the learning process. Conversely, relying heavily on punishment tends to slow learning and create resistance.

Every student, no matter their challenges, displays positive behaviours worth rewarding. Actively seeking these behaviours—especially in students with whom you might have strained interactions—can help strengthen the teacher-student relationship, foster a sense of belonging and trust and encourage the repetition and reinforcement of those desired behaviours. Note that behaviours that are normal or even somewhat disappointing for one student may be a great achievement for another.

Principles of Rewarding Behaviour

Creating and sustaining a friendly classroom environment is fundamental for effective teaching. To achieve this, educators must have a broad repertoire of strategies for maintaining desired student behaviour. These strategies range from small gestures that communicate Communion like nodding, smiling, or giving a thumbs-up to behaviour that communicates

Maintaining, Directing, and Redirecting Student Behaviour

high Communion; in Chapter 7, we introduced which non-verbal cues can be employed to communicate Communion.

By employing verbal and non-verbal behaviours that convey Communion, teachers not only sustain but can also reinforce desired conduct, contributing to a positive and productive classroom atmosphere. Even actions or behaviours considered routine—like taking a seat, retrieving materials, participating in discussions, or starting an assignment—benefit from appreciation. Recognising these "ordinary" behaviours can improve the overall classroom dynamic.

To build a positive relationship, it is important to sustain or reinforce desired behaviour. However, it is not effective to reward arbitrarily—in fact, it can be counterproductive. For rewards to be effective, they must be:

- *Genuine*: Reflect sincere appreciation for behaviour or effort.
- *Fair*: Proportionate to the action or achievement. Small rewards can work wonders!
- *Timely*: Delivered immediately after the behaviour to strengthen the effect.
- *Tailored*: Aligned to the age, preferences, culture and individual needs of students.

Young children may respond well to tangible rewards like stickers, drawing a star in their notebook, or a pat on the shoulder, whereas older students might appreciate verbal recognition or privileges. Even within the same age group, individual differences matter: Some students value quiet praise, while others thrive on public acknowledgement. A smile will work for most students.

To become aware of the rewards you use in your teaching, you can ask a colleague to observe this in a lesson (**Activity 8.1**).

In **Activity 8.2**, you reward colleagues for providing a right answer and you practice rewarding students in your lessons.

To Keep in Mind

Genuine, fair, timely and tailored rewards are integral to sustaining a positive, engaged, and cooperative classroom environment. By consciously using rewards, you can transform challenging situations into opportunities for connection.

> **Background Information**
>
> ### Active Listening
>
> Active listening, situated in the Understanding sector of the Interpersonal Circle, plays a vital role in maintaining and reinforcing desired student behaviour. By showing students they are truly heard, teachers communicate appreciation and acknowledgement, which makes students feel valued.
>
> Active listening can be expressed through a combination of non-verbal and verbal behaviours:
>
> - Displaying non-verbal signals such as nodding, calmness, an open posture, and, in Western cultures, making eye contact.
> - Allowing the student to finish speaking and postponing your judgement or opinion.
> - Affirming student utterances: simple words like "yes" or "I see."
> - Paraphrasing, i.e., restating the essence of the student's point in your own words— e.g., "So, you're saying that..."
> - Summarising what the student said.
> - Asking open-ended questions, e.g., "What made you feel that way?"
> - Asking follow-up questions delves into specifics, e.g., "Can you tell me more about that?"
>
> By mastering active listening, you can contribute to a classroom dynamic where every student feels heard, valued, and motivated.

Key Strategies for Maintaining Positive Student Behaviour

You can maintain behaviour in various ways.

Praise and compliments: Explicitly recognising and appreciating positive behaviour solidifies and encourages its repetition. Compliments can be linked to specific actions, such as completing assignments, behaving respectfully, achieving good grades, actively participating in lessons. For example, phrases like "Great job finishing that assignment on time," or "I appreciate how well you stay focused today" reinforce desirable behaviours and motivate students.

Encouragement: Even teacher actions not directly tied to verbal praise can encourage positive behaviour. For instance, checking homework completion sends a clear message that it is valued, actively observing group work signals that their efforts are recognised. These actions remind students of the importance of their work and behaviour, reinforcing a sense of accountability and motivation.

Feedback and grades: Feedback and grades are impactful tools for maintaining desired behaviour in education, potentially combining high Communion with high Agency. High grades reward students' hard work and foster motivation. They communicate trust and value in the student's abilities. When grades are low, providing specific, constructive feedback and highlighting positives despite the low grade can help prevent alienation and encourage improvement. For instance: "This essay shows creativity, the next step could be focusing on structure to make your ideas even clearer. Let's work on this together."

Grading, however, carries risks. Low grades, particularly without context or constructive feedback, can communicate low Communion and thus strain teacher-student interactions. The effort of students who worked hard goes unrecognised, while those who did not prepare remain disengaged because they receive exactly what they likely expected. For some students, this might (further) diminish their motivation. However, performance-oriented students may interpret low grades as a challenge to improve. Therefore, when having to give low grades, providing helpful feedback is essential to help restore the relationship.

> **To Keep in Mind**
> - Assigning grades carries interpersonal significance: grading itself generally implies Agency; giving high grades rewards students, while low grades might create distance.
> - Ensure that high grades feel earned.
> - To mitigate potential relationship strain of low grades, provide helpful feedback alongside.
> - Recognise that students respond differently to feedback and grades. Tailor your approach to what motivates them.

Teaching requires creative and diverse ways to reward and reinforce desired student behaviours. Beyond praise, compliments, encouragement and grading, and feedback, various teacher behaviours can convey high Communion. Table 8.1 provides an overview of ways to reward ordered in five categories: interactive, tangible, activity-based, social, and exchange rewards.

Rewards vary not only in type but also in their intensity and significance. For instance, remembering a student's birthday is generally more meaningful than simply using their name in class. Adjusting the intensity of rewards ensures that the student effort required for the behaviour aligns with the reward's perceived value. It is useful for teachers to have access to rewards with a variety of intensity to be exemplified in a hierarchy of rewards. You must be able "to climb this appreciation ladder" to align your reward with the character of the behaviour to be rewarded. To maintain the lesson flow, it is especially helpful to be able to reward students with a low intensity (a nod, a smile, etc.) repeatedly during a lesson. When students behave exceptionally well, a more intense verbal reward might be appropriate. Do what is needed, but not more than is necessary.

> **To Keep in Mind**
> - To have a broad repertoire in expressing appreciation and giving rewards is an essential element of a teacher's professionality.
> - Do not forget low-intensity rewards.

104 An Interpersonal Perspective on Classroom Management

Table 8.1 Overview of rewards

Interactive rewards

Non-verbal (in Western contexts)

- Thumbs-up
- Nodding or another head movement
- Wink
- Applause
- Smile
- Laugh
- Pat on the shoulder
- .....

Verbal

- Name the behaviour to be rewarded ("You are well on your way")
- Compliment: Okay, yes, well done, excellent
- Repeat a student answer for everyone
- Write the student answer on the board
- Ask other students to repeat a student answer
- Come back later to a correct student comment
- .....

Tangible rewards

Sticker, smiley, healthy edible treat, certificates, etc.

Activity-based rewards

- Giving students confidence by letting them do something (experiment, role as referee, etc.)
- Having a student pass out or collect materials
- Giving students leadership roles in the class (e.g., line leader, helper)
- Letting a student tell a story
- Reading to the students
- Caring for plants

- Telling a joke
- Allowing students to choose a favourite activity after completing work
- Letting students help the teacher or other students
- Having students show something they are good at
- ....

Social rewards

- A chat for example about hobbies, sports, music, home
- Listening, showing interest, paying attention
- Showing trust or confidence
- Giving feedback
- Offering praise in front of peers
- Awarding the student of the week (provided it is clear that anyone can win)
- Going and watch student extra-curricular activities

- Favourable note
- Allowing free sitting
- Knowing and paying attention to students' birthday
- Mentioning someone's name in a positive context
- Providing success experiences
- ....

Exchange rewards

In this approach, a student receives something to accumulate points for an eventual tangible or activity reward. For instance, it could be a mark on a checklist, a dot next to their name, or a sticker. These accumulated points can be exchanged for a reward once the required points have been collected. This is also called *token economy*.

Activity 8.3 prompts you to explore rewarding desired (and not undesired) student behaviour, thinking about the intensity of rewards you would want to use and creating a hierarchy of rewards.

Pitfalls in Rewarding Student Behaviour

While rewarding desired behaviour is an effective strategy for maintaining positive classroom interactions, certain pitfalls can undermine its success. Being aware of these potential issues can help you apply rewards thoughtfully and avoid unintended consequences.

> *Negating compliments with "but"*: A common mistake is following a compliment with a contradictory statement introduced by "but."[2] For example: "You did well on the test, but make sure next time you..." This structure diminishes the positive impact of the initial compliment, making it feel insincere or conditional. To maintain a high level of Communion, you better separate feedback from praise. For instance: "You did well on the test. Let's talk about how we can prepare for the next one to make it even better." You can also separate feedback from praise by delivering them at different times.
>
> *Undermining intrinsic motivation*: Research by Ryan and Deci[3] highlights that rewards can sometimes shift a student's focus from the intrinsic value of an activity to the external reward. For example: A child in a Montessori classroom chooses an activity because it is enjoyable. When a teacher says, "How nice that you're doing that," the child may start to associate the activity with gaining approval rather than personal enjoyment. Over time, this can lead to a dependency on external rewards and reduce spontaneous engagement. If the reward is removed, the student might no longer find the activity appealing. So, it is wise to use rewards sparingly for activities students already enjoy.[4] You also might emphasise how the task aligns with students' interests or strengths, thus focusing on intrinsic motivation. Additionally, low-intensity rewards may help prevent student motivation from shifting towards more extrinsic forms.
>
> *Rewarding undesirable behaviour*: Teachers can inadvertently reinforce undesirable behaviours by giving them attention. For example, telling talkative students to be quiet can reward them with the teacher's focus, and might lead to repeated disruptions. Keep in mind that for young adolescents, defying the teacher often becomes more appealing and seen as "cool." Responding to an inappropriate joke might encourage similar behaviour in the future. This also can be an unintended consequence of behaviour redirection, which we will discuss further in the next section.

Material Reward Systems (Token Economies) in Primary Education

One popular method, especially in primary education, involves material rewards, such as stickers, points, or tokens. Apps like Working4 (https://pecsusa.com/shop/working4/#tab-description) are designed to facilitate this. Based on the principles of behaviourist psychology, token economies operate under the premise that rewarded behaviours increase and ignored behaviours diminish.

While the principles are straightforward, ensuring that rewards effectively shape behaviour requires careful planning:

– *Define target behaviours clearly*: Make sure students know what actions are being rewarded.

- *Select appropriate rewards*: Tailor rewards to individual preferences and age-appropriate needs.
- *Establish transparent rules and procedures*: Clearly communicate how the reward system works and the criteria for earning rewards.

It is equally important to be mindful of *individual differences*. Not all tools available support this. Some students may struggle to meet certain behavioural expectations. Insisting on unattainable standards risks frustration and disengagement. Instead, set *realistic goals* and support students through explanation, practice, and the understanding that mistakes are part of the learning process.[5] Thus, actively teach and practice appropriate behaviours, in a similar way as you would teach arithmetic or other academic subjects.

Pitfalls for Material Reward Systems

Material reward systems can motivate students and reinforce desired behaviours when used thoughtfully, but they come with potential challenges that can negatively affect interpersonal dynamics.

- *Withdrawing privileges*: Material reward systems, such as stickers or points, can be counterproductive if mismanaged by withdrawing privileges for undesirable behaviour, rather than rewarding positive actions. This approach shifts attention away from reinforcing good behaviour and can create a punitive classroom atmosphere. If everybody but a few students can easily earn rewards, to these few students, this may feel like withdrawing a privilege.
- *Pressure to conform*: Students may begin to feel compelled to conform in order to earn rewards, rather than acting out of intrinsic motivation. This can undermine their sense of autonomy and self-worth, potentially straining the interaction between teacher and student.
- *Unhealthy competition and classroom tensions*: Encouragement and rewards from teachers call on certain students (or groups) to outperform others in order to gain rewards. Thus, reward systems invite competition. Without competitiveness in rewards, their meaning and purpose can become skewed. This competition must be guided carefully to avoid that the reward systems foster too much rivalry and disputes, especially when certain students consistently outperform others. Publicly displayed scores or group rewards tied to individual performance can create resentment when students who struggle to meet expectations may feel singled out or excluded. If one student's behaviour prevents the group from earning a reward, it may harm collaboration and lead to public shaming or social isolation for that student, damaging the classroom atmosphere. Thus, overemphasis on competition can undermine teamwork and mutual respect.
- *Manipulation and trust issues*: Some students might exploit loopholes or manipulate the system to earn rewards. This can erode trust, teachers may view students as insincere, and students may lose faith in the fairness of the system. It undermines the purpose, the focus shifts from positive behaviours to gaming the system.
- *Negative impact on teachers*: Managing a material reward system can be time-consuming. The administrative burden, tracking behaviours and managing rewards can overwhelm

Maintaining, Directing, and Redirecting Student Behaviour

teachers. Disputes over perceived fairness can lead to tension between teachers and students. If a teacher inconsistently applies rules or overlooks behaviours, students may question the system's legitimacy, potentially causing frustration or disengagement spilling over into interactions with students, negatively impacting the classroom climate. It is no coincidence that school-wide systems based on the popular Positive Behavioural Support[6] are only effective when accompanied by proper training and a consistent approach by all involved teachers, ensuring a focus on fostering a positive and supportive learning environment for all students.

Strategies to Avoid Negative Interpersonal Effects of Material Reward Systems

To minimise the pitfalls of material reward systems, you can adopt the following approaches:

Focus on Positive Behaviours
- Emphasise rewarding desired actions rather than punishing undesirable ones.
- Highlight specific achievements to encourage continued improvement.

Set Achievable Goals
- Ensure that expectations are realistic and attainable for all students.
- Adjust goals to reflect individual capabilities and progress.

Practice and Explain
- Actively teach the behaviours you want to see, providing clear instructions and opportunities for practice.
- Explain why these behaviours are important to foster understanding and motivation.

Track Positive Behaviours Collectively
- Award points to the class as a group to encourage teamwork and reduce unhealthy competition.
- Avoid publicly displaying individual scores or rankings.
- List behaviours and award points instead of student names.

Collaborate Privately
- Work with individual students on specific goals privately to protect their dignity and ensure tailored support.
- Involve students in creating their behaviour plans to increase their investment and sense of Agency.

Reward Effort, Not Just Outcomes
- Recognise the effort students put into improving, even if the desired behaviour isn't fully achieved.
- Encourage perseverance and growth by valuing progress over perfection.

> **To Keep in Mind**
>
> When using material reward systems, you can create a supportive environment that nurtures trust, autonomy, and meaningful relationships by focusing on positive behaviours, fostering collaboration, and balancing rewards with intrinsic motivators. Actively teach and practice the behaviours you want to increase.

When giving a lesson to colleagues or a group of students in **Activity 8.4**, you can apply strategies for maintaining student behaviour.

Directing Student Behaviour

Two Examples of Lack of Agency

> Frustrated by a lack of order and learning in their chemistry class, the tenth-grade student representatives approached the assistant principal with their concerns. They describe a chaotic environment where the new teacher struggles to maintain control. Students talk amongst themselves, distractions abound, and lessons lack focus. This is especially troubling for students planning to take chemistry as a core subject. They worry that the disorderly classroom dynamics hinder their foundational understanding and leave them unprepared for next year's challenges.

This new teacher was soft-spoken had a hunched posture and focused more on the smartboard than on the students. He rarely scanned the room or addressed disruptions. This low-Agency behaviour led to students talking amongst themselves, shouting, joking, playing on their smartphones and asking non-serious questions to distract the teacher. After a while, the students realised they still needed the teacher's knowledge, but as a group, they could not establish order in the classroom. So, they sought help from the assistant principal.

> Parents of the fifth-grade students voiced their worries to the school principal, describing a classroom that seemed out of control. The teacher's inability to enforce structure made it difficult for children to concentrate and complete their work. Parents feared that this lack of focus and organisation would lead their children to fall behind academically, putting their progress at risk.

This teacher stayed seated at her desk, assisting students individually, and relied on an ineffective system for managing the rest of the class: Students needing assistance were supposed to write their names on the board and return to their desks, but lined up at her desk to receive the teacher's help. When students ignored the procedures—shouting, chatting, and moving around—the teacher failed to intervene. This low-Agency approach left the classroom chaotic and unproductive, prompting concerns from parents.

In both cases, the teachers' lack of Agency created complementary high-Agency responses from students. These behaviours ranged from disruptive to disengaged, further deteriorating classroom dynamics. Both teachers struggled to assert Agency in their classrooms, failing to intervene effectively despite their friendly demeanour. As a result, their classrooms devolved into disarray, resembling the challenges faced by Teacher Tonia, discussed in Chapter 1 (see the profile in Figure 5.4).

Combing High Agency with High Communion

If these teachers were to react to the chaos with frustration and resort to confrontational behaviour—characterised by low Agency and especially low Communion—they might find themselves in a situation like Teacher Dion's lessons, as described in Chapter 1 (see profile in Figure 5.6). This approach would likely lead to heightened conflict and strained relationships, further deteriorating the classroom climate.

Instead, as we explored in the section "Moving Up Counterclockwise" in Chapter 5, the more effective strategy is to regain control by increasing Agency through high-Communion behaviours. This approach, moving upwards and counterclockwise in the Interpersonal Circle (from the lower right quadrant to the upper-right quadrant), emphasises connection and collaboration while establishing authority. In our experience, it is unrealistic to expect a teacher to "jump" from a low-Agency position in the Interpersonal Circle (uncertain or compliant behaviour) to a position with a lot of Agency (directing or imposing behaviour). Moving upwards via the high-Communion side is therefore advisable.

Changing the situation of the two teachers in these examples is very difficult; it is much more productive to prevent chaotic situations to arise. Effective teachers can create an environment where students naturally want to follow their lead by displaying behaviours that project high Agency, such as speaking with clarity and purpose, highlighting key points, actively scanning the classroom, and using persuasive gestures (see Chapter 7 on non-verbal behaviours communicating high Agency). This type of confident and structured behaviour sends a clear message: "I'm in charge, and I'm here to help you succeed." Students are likely to respond complementary, cooperate and align with the teacher's plan.

However, it is important to combine high Agency with high Communion. When teachers emphasise rules and enforce norms with low Communion—focusing solely on authority, setting and enforcing rules without relational warmth —it can create a more guarded or even resistant response from students. Instead of cooperation, the classroom dynamic might lean towards withdrawal or suspicion.

We will now delve into the role of rules in productively directing students that could have helped the teachers above in preventing chaos.

To Keep in Mind

Directing requires Agency and Communion:

- Exhibit confident, clear behaviours that signal leadership.
- Blend structure with warmth to foster trust and cooperation.
- Avoid extremes—neither passively allowing chaos nor harshly enforcing rules.

Directing Students by Setting Classroom Rules

Establishing clear rules is a proactive way for teachers to create an environment that minimises disruptions and keeps lessons running smoothly. By setting expectations upfront, students know what behaviour is expected, which helps maintain order and encourages productive learning.

Every school has overarching guidelines for punctuality, attendance, and other procedural matters. However, teachers often have the autonomy to implement specific rules that suit their teaching style and classroom dynamics. Examples might include informing the teacher in advance if homework is not completed or raising a hand to speak instead of calling out.

In classrooms with a positive atmosphere, many rules are implicit, but teachers often make key rules explicit when meeting a new class to set the tone early. Considerations for rule-setting are:

Deciding on Rules
– Determine which behaviours are most important for classroom harmony. A few well-chosen rules work better than a long list. Students are more likely to follow rules they can easily recall and understand.
– Focus on practical and relevant rules that address common issues, rather than overloading students with unnecessary directives.
– Align rules with existing school norms to make them feel natural and intuitive for students.
– Positively worded rules are more motivating and easier for students to remember. For instance, "Raise your hand to ask a question" is more effective than "Don't talk without permission."

Communicating Rules
– Consider the timing: Will you introduce all rules on day one, or address them as needed? For example, if tardiness is not an issue, there is no need to highlight a rule about arriving on time in the beginning.
– Writing every minor rule on paper or the board can make ordinary expectations feel rigid or excessive. Reserve written documentation for unique or especially important rules.
– Younger students often need more explicit instruction on what is expected. In contrast, older students with more classroom experience may intuitively understand appropriate behaviour.

Motivating Compliance
– Focus on rules that the entire class can realistically follow.
– You could consider offering incentives when the class collectively adheres to the rules. You should certainly remember to praise the class if they (try to) adhere to the rules.
– Avoid punishing the entire class if a few students struggle to comply. Instead, offer additional support to those individuals.

Responding to Violations
– Plan how you will address rule-breaking consistently and fairly to reinforce their importance.

While rules help establish order, they should feel natural rather than overly restrictive. For example, spending an entire lesson discussing basic rules might feel unnecessary to students, especially in secondary school. Instead, integrate rule-setting seamlessly into classroom routines to make expectations clear without overemphasising them. This is also referred to as "pre-teaching"; for example, first recall together what rules apply to doing group work before students start the activity.

> **To Keep in Mind**
>
> Establish a limited number of rules and avoid rules about behaviour that is already widely accepted.

> **Background Information[7]**
>
> *Rules, Norms, and Values*
>
> While *rules* make specific expectations explicit, *norms* and *values* reflect the deeper principles that guide behaviour in the classroom and school community. Schools typically share core values that guide decision-making and interactions, such as:
>
> - Respect for others,
> - Promoting health and well-being,
> - Democratic participation,
> - Holistic development (cognitive, emotional, social, and physical),
>
> These values shape the atmosphere of the school, fostering a space where students and staff feel safe, valued, and motivated. Norms emerge from shared values and define what is considered acceptable or unacceptable. For example:
>
> - A friendly, disturbance-free learning environment is the norm for a respectful school culture.
> - Bullying and racist behaviour are universally unacceptable.
> - A healthy cafeteria aligns with a commitment to student well-being.
> - Lessons that consider emotional expression demonstrate value for students' holistic development.
>
> Rules translate norms into clear, actionable statements, often communicated orally or written down. They clarify expectations for students and reduce ambiguity. For instance:
>
> - *Value*: Respect for others.
> - *Norm*: Everyone should feel safe and supported in class.
> - *Rule*: No interrupting when others are speaking.

> By linking rules to values, students can see the "why" behind expectations, making them more likely to internalise these principles. For instance, explaining that raising hands to speak ensures fairness and respect for others' contributions connects a rule to the broader value of respect.
>
> As a teacher, you embody the school's values and norms in your interactions. Students look to you for consistency and clarity in upholding these principles. When students encounter a new teacher, they often test limits to understand that teacher's norms. This behaviour is a natural way for students to gauge how values are applied in practice. For instance, they may observe whether the teacher enforces rules about raising hands to speak or addresses inappropriate comments.
>
> Rules, norms, and values work together to shape a classroom culture that supports learning and growth. When teachers clearly articulate these elements, students gain a better understanding of what is expected, fostering an environment that aligns with shared principles and promotes positive interactions. By consistently applying rules rooted in meaningful values, teachers not only maintain order but also contribute to the moral and social development of their students.

Involving Students in Rulemaking

Teachers often refer to classroom rules as *agreements* when reminding students of expected behaviour, saying things like, "Didn't we agree that…?" However, this can feel unjust to students, as they may have had little say in setting those rules. By actively involving students in creating classroom expectations, you can foster a sense of ownership, responsibility, and collaboration.

When students contribute to creating rules, they see them as shared agreements rather than imposed restrictions. It also encourages them to take responsibility for adhering to these rules they have helped establish. Collaborative rule-setting demonstrates that their opinions are valued, strengthening the teacher-student relationship. Discuss why you or students think a rule is important.

To facilitate the conversation[8], you could start with identifying the goal by asking, "What makes a lesson enjoyable and productive for everyone?" Then, you can link to their behaviour and discuss which behaviours align and do not align with their vision of an ideal classroom. Try and turn their input into clear, positive, collaborative, and shared rules. Also discuss what actions should be taken in case of violations or what rewards are appropriate in case of success. Using group activities or voting to prioritise key rules, makes the process engaging and democratic. The approach to involving students will vary depending on their developmental level, but even with students as young as 4 or 5 years old, some participation in rule making is possible. For these students, you need to keep it simpler and more guided than for older students who can handle a more open approach.

If your first attempt at collaborative rule-setting—a challenging task—does not go as planned, you need to reflect on what did not work. You can try again later in the school year or future classes after adjusting your strategy. Ask colleagues for advice who are known for being good at this.

> **To Keep in Mind**
>
> By involving students in rulemaking, rules shift to shared agreement. These agreements feel fairer, and students are more likely to embrace them.

Redirecting Undesirable Student Behaviour

Teachers have various tools to guide students back on track, from light-hearted interventions to more direct corrections. These strategies align with different areas of the Interpersonal Circle and have to be tailored to the situation, balancing Communion and Agency to achieve the best outcomes.

When a student's behaviour starts to diverge from expectations, redirecting with kindness and a sense of understanding can be highly effective, a *high-Communion strategy*. For example, if a child begins walking around during a lesson, the teacher might gently say, "Take a seat, buddy," accompanied by a friendly smile or gesture. This approach combines warmth (high Communion) with clear expectations (high Agency), helping students recognise and adjust their behaviour without feeling reprimanded. Using humour, pointing out alternatives, or offering choices also fall into this category, making the interaction feel supportive and non-confrontational.

In some cases, subtle redirection is not enough, and explicit correction is required. If a student continues to disrupt the class despite gentle prompts, the teacher might say firmly, "Please stop interrupting and focus on the task." This intervention falls on the lower-Communion side of the circle, as it involves low-intensity confronting behaviour. Whether redirecting either high or low on Communion, the aim remains ultimately the same, reinforce participation in the lesson and help students master the content by fostering focus and collaboration. In this section, we will delve into more explicit forms of correction.

Correcting student behaviour directly is an inevitable aspect of teaching, though it carries the risk of escalating into a conflict if not handled carefully. When teachers correct behaviour explicitly or address errors, they exhibit moderately low Communion and moderate Agency. In many cultures, this can lead to a complementary low-Communion response from students, potentially spiralling into a negative interaction. While avoiding correction altogether is unrealistic, the goal is to address unwanted behaviour without triggering unnecessary conflict.

> **To Keep in Mind**
>
> Whenever possible, it is preferable to redirect student behaviour using actions on the right, high Communion, side of the Interpersonal Circle.

Background Information

The Illusion of Alternatives

When students are presented with a choice between two options, they often focus solely on those options, particularly when they are younger, and may overlook other possibilities entirely. For example, in Table 6.1, Julia is given two choices: either remain quiet and pay attention to the teacher or risk the rest of the class becoming upset with her if her actions interrupt the lesson. In that moment, Julia might not consider alternative scenarios—perhaps the class will not get angry at all because she says something genuinely funny, or the teacher might find another way to engage her without interrupting the lesson.

This phenomenon, referred to as the *illusion of alternatives* by Watzlawick and colleagues[9], illustrates how framing options can significantly influence decision-making. By offering students two carefully chosen alternatives, teachers can guide their behaviour. For instance, asking, "Would you like to focus on the task, or would you prefer to complete extra work?" subtly encourages students to select the desired behaviour while feeling they have autonomy in their decision.

The Key: Prompt and Subtle Interventions

How do you stop unwanted student behaviour? Ignoring disruptive behaviour for too long usually is not effective, as it can lead to greater unrest in the classroom. Instead, teachers can stop unwanted behaviour by *promptly* and *subtly* signalling their disapproval, allowing students the opportunity to self-regulate.

For instance, if a student begins talking out of turn, a teacher might first move closer to them or look towards the student, signalling that the teacher sees what is happening. This way, the lesson does not need to be interrupted by an explicit verbal warning. If the behaviour persists, non-verbal signals can intensify, such as putting a hand on the student's desk or pausing mid-sentence and looking empathically and firmly at the student. If no effect is sorted, a verbal response may be necessary. By maintaining a calm and empathic tone, the teacher can address the behaviour without escalating tension. For example, a simple statement like "Let's get back on track" can redirect focus without creating confrontation. This gradual move towards low Communion minimises classroom disruption while communicating expectations.

In classrooms with a positive and productive atmosphere, it may appear as though teachers are not correcting student behaviour at all. However, a closer look reveals that these teachers anticipate student behaviours and respond to nearly every instance of behaviour that diverges from the lesson's flow—just in ways that are almost imperceptible.

For instance, a teacher might briefly glance at a student who is becoming distracted or slightly adjust their position to signal awareness. Such subtle interventions are seamless, do not interrupt the lesson, and communicate that the teacher is both observant and in control—a skill often referred to as having "eyes in the back of their head." Kounin, a pioneer in classroom discipline research, described these techniques as *overlapping* and *withitness*. These terms refer to a teacher's ability to manage multiple tasks simultaneously and maintain a comprehensive awareness of the classroom's dynamics.

Prompt and subtle responses are:

Early intervening: Addressing undesirable behaviour as soon as it starts and preventing it from escalating.

Minimally intrusive: These responses are non-disruptive, often go unnoticed by other students, keeping their focus on the lesson and allowing teaching to continue uninterrupted. They avoid drawing unnecessary attention to the misbehaving student, which could reinforce the behaviour through peer reactions. This approach prevents the undesirable behaviour from becoming the focal point, maintaining students' engagement with the lesson.

Promptness and subtlety work hand in hand. Acting quickly allows the correction to be minimal, while subtlety ensures that the response does not overshadow the lesson or create unnecessary tension.

Mastering these techniques requires practice and attentiveness, but they are critical for fostering a classroom environment that encourages learning while maintaining order with minimal teacher interventions.

> **To Keep in Mind**
>
> Prompt and subtle teacher responses to an incipient disruption ensure that this reaction has minimal or no negative impact on the classroom atmosphere.

To become aware of the ways you redirect students, you can ask a colleague to observe this in a lesson (**Activity 8.5**).

A Hierarchy of Interventions

Managing student behaviour effectively requires teachers to have access to a sequence of interventions with increasing intensity, a structured approach we call "climbing the intervention ladder." This progression begins with a subtle signal and, if necessary, advances to more explicit actions. Each step must be designed to minimise disruption and resolve unwanted behaviour without unnecessary escalation. Do what is needed, but not more than is necessary.

Start small with subtle interventions: The first steps on the ladder involve minimal signals and indirect responses to unwanted behaviour as discussed earlier. For example, non-verbal cues like a pointed glance or slight pause in teaching, proximity adjustments, such as moving closer to the student or light verbal prompts, like gently mentioning the student's name.

Intensify when necessary: If the behaviour persists despite subtle cues, the next steps involve more distinct actions such as:
- Addressing the student directly, such as naming the wanted behaviour: "I need you to focus right now."
- Pausing the lesson momentarily to redirect the class's attention back to the task.
- Making expectations clear and issuing clear directives about the required behaviour.
- If directives are not followed, warning of consequences.
- Enforcing consequences, such as relocating the student within the classroom. Make sure that students understand how your sanctions enable learning, such as less distraction for a student and the class.

Last resort: sanctions or removal: When all other options fail, the final steps might involve applying school-wide disciplinary actions, such as removing the student from the classroom, detention, or suspension. These measures are reserved for severe or repeated disruptions and are far removed from day-to-day classroom interactions. In the best case such actions signal to the involved student the seriousness of the problem, but this may not be self-evident.

The principle guiding this ladder is straightforward: *the smaller, the better*. By keeping corrections as low on the ladder as possible, teachers preserve the classroom's focus on learning and minimise the energy expended on discipline. The more intense an intervention is, the more likely it is that the class's attention will be diverted from the lesson. Having a clear understanding of each step- a mental picture- ensures that teachers can act quickly and appropriately when stronger interventions are needed. In the section in Chapter 9 on student disruptive behaviour, we will give examples of interventions with increasing intensity and will delve into enforcing rules and punishment.

In terms of the Interpersonal Circle, moving up the ladder shifts behaviour outwards from its origin, gradually reducing Communion towards the periphery of the circle. Skilled teachers use numerous measures of increasing intensity before resorting to removal or punishment.

To Keep in Mind

- To be able to respond quickly when needed, you need to have your personal intervention ladder in place.
- The lower you stay on the ladder, the easier it is to sustain a supportive atmosphere and lesson focus.

Activity 8.6 lets you think about the intensity of redirections of undesirable student behaviour, which ones you would want to use and creating a hierarchy of interventions.

If you conduct a simulated lesson with a group of students or colleagues, you can in **Activity 8.7** try out redirecting.

Background Information

The Impact of Public Correction on Student Social Standing

Correcting students in front of the class can have consequences for their social relationships with classmates. When a teacher frequently calls out a student's behaviour in public, it can damage the student's social position among their peers. This is especially harmful for vulnerable students who may already struggle with forming friendships.

Positive relationships with classmates are essential for both social-emotional and cognitive student development.[10] Friendships provide a support network that helps students navigate the challenges of school life, enhancing their overall well-being and academic engagement.

Interestingly, disruptive behaviour alone does not significantly affect how students are perceived by their peers. The critical factor is how the teacher handles that behaviour. When a teacher frequently corrects a student in front of the class, the teacher's actions serve as a cue for classmates—a phenomenon known as *social referencing*. In this process, students look to the teacher's responses to form opinions about their peers. Thus, public corrections can inadvertently stigmatise a student, shaping how classmates view and interact with them. Over time, this can isolate the student socially, compounding the challenges they face.

To avoid harming a student's social standing, it is crucial to minimise public corrections. *Choose discreet interventions* whenever possible, such as subtle non-verbal cues or quiet, one-on-one discussions. *Use the intervention ladder*, intensifying interventions only when necessary and in a way that minimises public attention.

Content, Phrasing and Non-verbal Cues of Corrections

Corrections (and compliments) in the classroom do more than conveying instructions or praise—they send interpersonal messages that influence teacher-student interactions. The content and phrasing of what is said, and the accompanying non-verbal cues affect how students perceive the teacher's message.

Messages with an explicit relational content are, for example: "I appreciate that from you," and "I'm in charge here," or less explicitly, "Well done," "Listen up, everyone," and "I need to consult a book for that."

Compliments tied to academic content—"Well done on solving that problem!" —often come across as high in Communion (Cooperative), strengthening positive interactions between teacher and students. Corrections, on the other hand—"Sit down properly"—can feel low in Communion (Confrontational), especially if non-verbal behaviours signal low Communion as well.

Expressions like—"I need to consult a book for that"—might come across as low in Agency (Passive) when spoken hesitantly but can still serve well an interpersonal purpose. The teacher demonstrates taking the question (and thus the student) seriously, which can have positive implications for the interaction.

How teachers phrase corrections plays a vital role in shaping their interpersonal impact. The use of the imperative form is the most evident in this regard. Sentences like "Grab your book" and "Pay attention" are clear and assertive with high Agency, and the latter may also include a correction, making it low on Communion.

The content and phrasing of corrections is only part of the equation. Non-verbal cues—tone of voice, facial expression, body language as discussed in Chapter 7—can strengthen but also undermine their effect.

Teachers can say the sentences in Table 8.2 when they want a student who is sitting backwards on his chair to sit "properly" again. They all address the same issue, yet you can expect these remarks to have different effects on the student (and on the rest of the class, as they also hear these remarks). The effect will also be quite different in the context of a positive versus a more strained teacher-student relationship.

> *Questions*: Some of the statements take the form of *questions*, which can shift the tone of teacher-student interactions. Questions like "What's so interesting behind you?," or "Jerry, why are you sitting turned around?" may engage the student in explaining. Asking, "What did I say about sitting backward?" may prompt students to recall and reflect on the rules. You make the student think about the norm you have set, and by doing so, you might encourage the student to feel more responsible for resolving the situation. While these approaches can land the interaction on the high-Communion side of the Interpersonal Circle by showing interest or curiosity, they might not be the fastest way to achieve immediate behavioural change, because you will also have to do something with the answer.
>
> *Phrasings in strained relationships*: In dealing with students, some phrasings are often more effective than others. Especially in a teacher-student system where the working atmosphere is strained, the teacher's phrasings are of great importance. Open-ended questions or ambiguous corrections can backfire. A question like "What's so interesting behind you?" might provoke a humorous or sarcastic response, such as "The wall, obviously!" A casually phrased request like, "Sit up straight for a moment" might invite a literal, humorous response: "Okay, I did for a moment." Intended humour such as "I'd rather see your face than your back," could provoke playful pushback: "Well, ma'am, everyone has different tastes!"

Table 8.2 Teacher sentences towards a student sitting backwards on his chair

– Could you please look this way for a moment?	– What did I say about sitting backwards?
– Can you look this way for a moment?	– Could you turn around, please?
– Look this way, please.	– Can you turn around?
– Look this way now, please.	– Can you turn around now?
– Could you finally look this way?	– Could you finally turn around?
– Look this way now!	– Turn around for a moment.
– Look this way!	– Turn around now!
– I want you to look this way now!	– Finally, turn around now!
– Look this way or you're out!	– I want you to turn around!
– I'd rather see your face than your back.	– Turn around!
– Why don't you take a picture of the person behind you, so you can look at it all weekend instead?	– Turn around or you're out.
	– Stop looking behind you all the time.
	– Stop sitting backwards.
– What's so interesting behind you?	– Sit up straight for a moment.
– I'm here, you know!	– I'd like to see your face, not the back of your head.
– Do you have eyes on the back of your head or something?	
	– Could you please turn around?
– Am I on screen?	– I find it rude when you constantly have your back to me.
– Hey... I'm right here!	
– Look ahead.	– Don't be so impolite, sit up straight.
– Look straight ahead!	– Jerry I'd like to see your face.
– Jerry, why are you sitting turned around?	– Jerry, I want to see your face.
– Jerry, don't look behind you.	– Jerry, for the thousandth time ....
– Jerry, if you're sitting backwards, I don't know what you're up to.	– Jerry, how many times do I have to warn you?

Phrasing in a positive classroom atmosphere: In a system with a pleasant working atmosphere, students are forgiving of occasional awkward phrasing and will not pay much attention.

Alignment of verbal and non-verbal message: Even when the content and phrasing of a statement are appropriate, non-verbal cues can significantly influence the student response. When verbal and non-verbal messages align, students are more likely to understand and accept the correction. Students pick up on mismatches between verbal and non-verbal cues flawlessly. For example, if a teacher says, "Sit properly" with a nervous smile, the uncertainty will undermine the verbal message. Conversely, when saying "You did that well," with a stern or angry expression, the non-verbal cue (anger) will dominate, outshining the praise.

Background Information

The I-Message: A Constructive Way to Address Behaviour

The I-message, pioneered by Thomas Gordon,[11] is a communication technique designed to express dissatisfaction with a student's behaviour in a way that fosters understanding, avoids defensiveness, and maintains respect. This approach shifts the focus away from mere confrontation towards constructive dialogue, making it an effective tool for teachers to manage classroom behaviour.

Key components of the I-message
Non-judgemental Description of the Student's Behaviour:

– Clearly and objectively describe the specific behaviour that is problematic.
– Avoid labels or accusations.
– Example: "When you sit turned around..."

Expressing Your Feelings:

- Share how the behaviour affects you personally, framing it in a non-accusatory way.
- This helps students understand the emotional impact of their actions.
- Example: "...I feel disrespected..."

Explaining the Consequences:
Highlight the tangible impact of the behaviour, both on you and the broader classroom environment.

- This encourages the student to see the larger context of their actions.
- Example: "[A]nd that distracts me, making it harder for me to teach effectively, which also makes it difficult for the class to understand."

The I-message promotes understanding by focusing on specific actions rather than the student as a person and helps avoid unnecessary defensiveness. It fosters students not to feel attacked and inclined to listen. The concrete consequences make the impact of their behaviour more relatable and encourages self-reflection.

In **Activity 8.8**, you can experiment with different phrasings of corrections and analyse the interpersonal effects.

Addressing Redirection

When redirecting student behaviour, it is crucial that the students understand you are speaking directly to them. Without clear *addressing*, even the best intentions get lost, making redirection less effective. To make sure your message lands, you can use:

Non-verbal signals: A glance, raised eyebrow, or slight pause in your speech can be enough to draw attention. This approach is often least disruptive and works well for subtle interventions.

Verbal cues: Use the student's name to establish direct communication. For example: "Sam, I need your attention right now."

A combination of verbal and non-verbal cues: For added emphasis, you can pair a verbal cue with a non-verbal message, such as saying a name while raising your eyebrows. Start with the smallest, least emphatic intervention. If subtle cues do not work, intensify gradually—mention the student's name or address them more directly.

If multiple students need redirection, ensure you are clear about who you are speaking to. Generalised corrections can confuse students or make them feel unfairly singled out. Instead, look at each student individually and use names if necessary to avoid ambiguity.

Balancing Correction with Respect for the Student

When redirecting students' behaviour, it is important to make a clear distinction between rejecting the *behaviour* and rejecting the *person*. This distinction emphasises respect and acceptance for the individual while guiding them towards desired actions. Students can interpret corrections as personal criticism, especially if the feedback is not carefully phrased or if the relationship is already strained. While the adage *"Don't take it personally"* is common, it rarely communicates this distinction effectively. Instead, the teacher's words and tone must clarify that it is the action being addressed, not the student's worth or character. So, you do not say "I don't like you," but "I don't like this behaviour" or even better, say what you *do* like "I'd like you to listen when someone else is talking."

To Keep in Mind

By framing corrections as alternative actions, you ensure that the student feels respected, even during moments of redirection. This fosters the student to remain open to feedback and motivated to improve.

In Sum

Redirecting and maintaining, primarily react to student behaviour. Directing, aims to support desirable behaviour and at the same time prevent undesirable student behaviour– for example, by setting a rule.

For maintaining desirable student behaviour, you need a broad repertoire in expressing appreciation and giving rewards. Create your own hierarchy of rewards.

To direct desirable student behaviour, you need a few understandable rules aligned with the school rules. Discuss these rules with your students and model desirable behaviour.

Whenever possible, redirect student behaviour using actions high on Communion. When necessary, use prompt and subtle teacher responses to an incipient disruption, ensure that this reaction has minimal or no negative impact on the classroom atmosphere. Always have your intervention ladder available.

Notes

1. Lane et al. (2024).
2. https://www.fastcompany.com/3041739/the-one-word-thats-undermining-everything-else-you-say
3. Ryan and Deci (2000).
4. Deci et al. (2001).
5. Scott et al. (2012).
6. Crone et al. (2015), Scott et al. (2012).
7. See also Bennett (2020).
8. See, e.g., https://www.teachstarter.com/gb/blog/making-classroom-rules/
9. Watzlawick et al. (1974).
10. Endedijk et al. (2022).
11. Gordon and Burch (1974).

9 Responding to Challenging Student Behaviours*

In the earlier chapters, we explored the foundational aspects of teacher-student interactions: How to maintain, direct, and redirect student behaviour effectively. Now, we turn to specific situations that often test teachers' patience and skills. These include disruptive behaviour, (annoying) comments, disappointing performance, and emotional expressions from students during class.

The final section of this chapter focuses on students with significant behavioural challenges. These are students who require more than the usual classroom management techniques and who often do not respond—or only minimally—to traditional interventions.

But before delving deeper into strategies to deal with such behaviours, it is important to reflect on the emotional impact these student behaviours can have on teachers. Negative emotions stemming from challenging classroom situations can influence how you perceive and respond to students and ultimately the enjoyment of teaching. Reframing negative emotions is a critical first step in effectively addressing complex classroom dynamics.

Reappraising Negative Emotions

> Yuval, a student in the fourth year of his teacher education programme, was eager to teach his Grade 5 class about respiration and blood circulation. He had meticulously prepared for the lesson and anticipated engaging the students. However, as he introduced the topic, his student Nikki expressed her disinterest, bluntly stating that she wasn't in the mood. Disappointed, Yuval responded, "Then you'll have to find some motivation, Nikki." Offended, Nikki refused to engage, sitting with a sulking expression. Tensions escalated when Yuval's frustration grew, prompting Nikki to snap back, "I don't have to like this topic, do I?"

This interaction illustrates how challenging student behaviours can provoke strong emotional reactions in teachers. Negative emotions—such as frustration, anger, or helplessness—often affect the classroom atmosphere. When teachers react emotionally, this often shows in their interpersonal behaviour and can spiral into negative complementary interactions on the left

---

* This chapter presents potential teacher responses based on interviews with teachers and observations of their lessons in Dutch multicultural classrooms. The categorization of the types of situations is based on the work of Admiraal et al. (1996).

DOI: 10.4324/9781003563464-9

side of the Interpersonal Circle, feeding into conflict and power struggles. In this case, both Yuval and Nikki became increasingly angry, derailing the lesson and souring the classroom environment.

Transforming Negative Emotions: A Key Professional Skill

When unchecked, emotional responses can perpetuate a cycle of opposition and resistance. Recognising and reframing these feelings is essential for breaking the cycle and steering interactions back to a productive and supportive space. The ability to manage one's emotional response is not just about self-control but also about fostering an atmosphere where conflicts are minimised, and learning can thrive.

It is key to regulate your negative emotions, ensuring that irritation, anger, or frustration do not overly influence your behaviour. When faced with negative emotions, the first step is recognising them. From here, you can actively work to change your emotional response, turning frustration into understanding or disappointment into curiosity. When you know that certain student behaviours affect you negatively, you can try to control that negative emotion or even try to turn it into a more positive one. The latter is known as *reappraising or reinterpreting emotions*.[1] Reappraising emotions allows you to choose *non-complementary responses*—actions that break the cycle of negativity on the left side of the Interpersonal Circle. To do this, you can ask yourself if you can think of a positive outcome from this event.

For instance, in the earlier example in which Yuval and Nikki ended up in a negative interaction, by reflecting on the potential benefits of the situation (e.g., strengthening the teacher-student relationship), Yuval could find an opportunity for growth even in the moment of conflict. Yuval's disappointment likely stemmed from his high expectations for the lesson and the effort he put into preparing it. Meanwhile, Nikki's lack of enthusiasm stemmed from her own perspective, one that Yuval might not have initially considered. For example, Nikki may have had negative experiences with biology lessons in the past and thus anticipate this lesson to be similarly challenging for her. If Yuval could reframe his feelings of frustration into concern for Nikki's disengagement, he might respond more constructively. Instead of reacting defensively, he might try to find ways to convey his own enthusiasm about the topic to students like Nikki, or he could ask her why she is not in the mood, showing empathy and opening a dialogue.

Reflection and Proactive Emotion Management

Reappraising emotions requires practice and may only happen after the emotional moment has passed. Regular reflection on challenging interactions can help you gradually develop the ability and habit to process and reframe negative emotions in real time during lessons. This mindfulness of the moment strengthens your capacity to steer classroom dynamics in a positive direction.

While reappraisal is vital, it is even better of course, to prevent negative emotions from arising in the first place. Awareness of your emotional triggers and the interpersonal messages you convey with your non-verbal cues, particularly *facial expressions* (see Chapter 7), can help you maintain control. When your facial expressions align with your words, students receive clear and consistent signals.

However, there are times when expressing dissatisfaction–communicating behaviour on the oppositional side of the Interpersonal Circle–is necessary. When students' actions cross boundaries, strict or even low intensity confrontational responses are sometimes required to establish limits. The remainder of this chapter explores how to do this effectively while preserving or creating a positive classroom atmosphere.

> **To Keep in Mind**
>
> You need to recognise your own negative emotions, regulate them if necessary, and be able to reinterpret them by looking for alternative explanations for unwanted student behaviour. This will allow you to respond in more responsive ways.

Student Disruptive Behaviour

Redirecting student behaviour is an essential part of teaching. While disruptions are often brief, they can interrupt the learning process and significantly impact the learning environment, and the teacher's relationship with the class. Key to managing these moments lies in preventing escalation and addressing issues early and subtly (also see the section in Chapter 8 on redirecting student behaviour).

Building a good relationship with your students is the foundation for a well-managed classroom and helps preventing unwanted interactions. The alternative approaches to classroom management mentioned in Chapter 2 highlight additional strategies for prevention:

- Creating a motivating curriculum that engages students with meaningful, relevant content.
- Using interactive methods to keep students' attention focussed.
- Creating flow through effective classroom organisation that facilitates a structured, efficient environment minimising opportunities for disengagement and disruption.

Understanding Disruptions

Disruptions can vary widely in scope, severity and impact. *Scope* varies from involving only one or a few students without affecting the entire class to almost everyone in class being off-task or disengaged. *Severity* ranges from low–when students are off-task and daydreaming or doodle–to high, like talking, shouting, or other behaviours that interrupt the lesson. Disruptions thus also differ in their *impact*: Minor distractions that can be ignored without significant disruption to the lesson flow or major ones that require immediate attention to re-establish order.

Intervening

In cases of *off-task behaviour by one or a few students*, the goal is to address the issue with low intensity interventions without disrupting the lesson for other students. Sometimes, this behaviour can be ignored as correcting it might distract more from the lesson than the actual student behaviour. Here are examples of interventions with increasing intensity that teachers can use in this situation:

- Look at the student while continuing the lesson.
- Stand near the student.
- Place a hand on the student's desk.
- Non-verbally correct (raise eyebrows, point, make a stop gesture, make a silence gesture, direct eyes to the book).
- Look at the student.
- Briefly pause your instruction.
- Make a friendly joke.
- Remind the student of the task ("in the book in front of you...").
- Give the student a turn.
- Say the student's name.
- Give compliments to others showing the desired behaviour.
- State the desired behaviour.
- Say the student's name and the desired behaviour.
- Shift attention back to the lesson with an encouraging comment, like: "Let's dive back into this; I know we can finish strong!".

Through these approaches you can ensure that students realise that you notice classroom disruptions (this is related to teacher Agency) and that disruptions are managed in a way that minimises interruptions to the learning process. This maintains a positive classroom atmosphere.

Managing *disruptions that halt the flow of a lesson*—whether caused by one, a few students, or many students—requires a more intensive approach. The teacher's threefold objectives are *ending* the off-task behaviour effectively, *resume* the lesson and *ensuring* interactions do not harm the teacher's relationship with the students, that is, the overall classroom atmosphere.

In addition to subtle interventions discussed earlier, the following methods can help teachers restore lesson focussed student behaviours (i.e., order) and get the lesson back on track:

- Stop speaking, wait, and use a deliberate pause to draw attention to the disruption.
- Ask what is going on.
- Tell the class what behaviour you want to see. ("Take out your notebook and work silently.")
- State the desired behaviour. ("I want you to be quiet and listen when I'm talking.")
- Clearly articulate the observed behaviour. ("You are talking while I am speaking.")
- Positively phrase correction. ("What you're saying is interesting, but it doesn't relate to the topic we're discussing.")
- A quick activity or question to refocus attention. For example: "Everyone, let's take ten seconds to write down your next step in the task."
- State the effect of student behaviour on the class and possibly the teacher. ("You're interrupting me. You are distracting others. I have to start over again, which will make it take much longer.")

- State your own behaviour and the consequences of the class's behaviour. ("I'm waiting too long. I'll warn one more time; if it's not quiet, we'll make up the time during recess.")
- Remind students of the rules, expectations or agreements. ("Remember, we all agreed to listen while others are speaking." "You can sit there, but you need to pay attention.")
- Address the entire class with a reprimand.
- Have the student state the rule. ("What is the rule?")
- Give a paradoxical command. ("Stand up and act silly for a moment. Does anyone else want to act silly?") This should not be used as punishment or humiliation.
- Wait and listen to whether the reprimand has an effect.
- If the behaviour persists, announce a consequence.
- Implement the consequence.

Keep in mind that there is a delicate balance between the flow of the lesson and redirecting students' behaviour. With an unclear flow combined with many reprimands, chances increase that your redirections and reprimands become the new action programme instead of students' engaging in schoolwork. This is one reason why rather "small" redirections with low intensity are advisable.

To Keep in Mind

- Address disruptive behaviour by combining calm, clear interventions with a focus on maintaining relationships.
- Intervene early and subtly.
- Avoid public reprimands that could lead to embarrassment or defensiveness.

It is important, when redirecting student behaviour, to make a clear distinction between imposing and confrontational behaviour. **Activity 9.1** addresses this.

Follow-Through: Ensuring Effectiveness and Restoring Relationships

When implementing interventions, follow-up is crucial. A common mistake after addressing disruptions is to immediately resume teaching or walk away without verifying if your intervention has had its desired effect. Skipping this can diminish the impact of the corrective action, leaving the issue unresolved or inviting further disruptions. Students may learn that what you say as a teacher is not what you will do. Ensure the student understands the intervention's purpose and its expected outcomes, and actually does show the desired behaviour, before moving forward with the lesson.

As said before, effective classroom management is not just about stopping disruptive behaviour—it is also about maintaining a positive relationship with students. After more intensive disciplinary actions, teacher behaviour characterised by high levels of *Communion* can be necessary for rebuilding trust. Without this balance, the teacher-student relationship can suffer, potentially leading to further conflicts or disengagement.

Conversations intended to restore relationships after disciplinary actions, are often more productive outside the immediate classroom environment. This setting removes the public pressure of peers and allows for a more personal and meaningful dialogue. In such a restorative conversation, it is important to show genuine interest in the student's perspective and explore potential reasons behind their behaviour in a calm and non-judgemental manner; "Can you share what was going on earlier?" Together you can work towards a solution: "How can we make sure this doesn't happen again?" Or, "How can I help you deal with this next time?"

Enforcing Rules

Preventing and redirecting undesirable student behaviours involves the effective enforcement of rules. You can assist students by pointing out potential issues before they escalate and before it is late: Be alert and address violation of rules promptly and subtly. If a student still struggles to adhere to a rule, it is crucial to respond with as little confrontation as possible, delivering the reaction swiftly after the violation. Quick responses to (incipient) problematic behaviour usually require a lower intensity of redirection preferably starting with non-verbal cues. The lower the intensity, the more likely the student will find it natural to comply with the rule. When the rule is "listen during instruction," you can assist students with the interventions in the first block of the previous section, starting with looking at the student while continuing the lesson and if necessary, going up to say that it should be quiet during instruction or compliment students who are quiet. Keeping the hierarchy of interventions—discussed in Chapter 8—in mind and knowing how to use it is helpful in this regard.

A challenging aspect for (especially novice) teachers in rule enforcement is the desire for consistency. Both students and colleagues often emphasise the importance of *"being consistent,"* but consistency has multiple interpretations, each with its own challenges:

- *Always do what you say*. Effectiveness of following through what you said depends on what you have said and what happens in the classroom. If you threaten that "The next one talking will be sent to the principal," following through may not always be fair or effective. When a student then asks, "What did he say?," it might not be desirable to send that student out. So, avoid making threats you cannot, do not want or should not enforce; *Be careful what you say*.
- *Treat every student the same*. Equal treatment does not always mean fair treatment. You need to consider individual student needs, behaviour history, and context. For example, a well-behaved student who talks out of turn at one point can possibly be ignored while a clear reminder of what behaviour you expect may be a better response for a chronically disruptive student. So, *take history into account*.
- *Act the same in every situation*. Context matters: Using the same approach in all circumstances is undesirable. For example, your behaviour and focus on silence in class during a test might differ from a Friday afternoon lesson. So, *take the situation into account*.

All of this means that there are exceptions when it comes to enforcing rules. Rule enforcement may need to be adapted to situational and individual factors, for example:

History and future
— Events in the previous lesson.
— Whether a warning has been issued.
— Previous behaviour of the student in different situations.
— Frequency of the behaviour in the past.
— Upcoming break.
— The subsequent lesson or activity.

Student characteristics
— Difficulty of the topic for the student.
— Students' interest in the topic.
— Students' opinion of the teacher.
— Students' home situation, dyslexia, ADHD, etc.
— Whether the student is hungry.
— Student's standing in the class.
— Social media influences on students.

Specific circumstances
— Timing of the lesson on the day, in the week.
— Weather conditions: Storm, hot, cold.
— Completion of homework or not.
— Difficulty of homework.
— Relationship with the class.

It is important that students clearly understand when there is an exceptional situation and why the rule is not being enforced. Lastly, it is essential to adhere yourself to certain rules you have set. If students are not allowed to eat in class, sticking to this rule is easier for students if you refrain from eating as well.

> **To Keep in Mind**
>
> Effective rule enforcement requires:
>
> — Addressing issues promptly and subtly.
> — Considering context and individual needs.
> — Maintaining the core values of fairness and respect.

Activity 9.2 will help you evaluate the rules you have.

Punishment: A Tool to Use Sparingly if at All

Punishment is one of the most intense ways to react to student behaviour in the classroom. It ranks high on the hierarchy of intensity of interventions and should be approached with caution. While it may occasionally seem like the only option for novice teachers striving to restore order, its potential drawbacks—including strained relationships with students and limited effectiveness in changing behaviour—cannot be ignored. It is well-established that rewarding positive behaviour is a far more effective strategy.

Punishments can have counterproductive effects if not handled thoughtfully. They can prompt resentment and resistance; students may rebel or develop negative feelings towards the teacher or the topic, thus disrupting classroom relationships and creating a tense or hostile classroom environment. They also can encourage negative attention; for some students, even negative attention can reinforce (mis)behaviour.

Punishments generally fall into two categories:

Adding an unpleasant task. Examples include writing an essay, completing extra homework, cleaning the classroom or tidying school grounds, retention after school.
Removing a privilege. Examples include losing recess time, denying access to a computer or other enjoyable activities.

Making Punishments Productive

For punishment to work, it should help students learn and encourage better behaviour. Punishments should teach a lesson, make students reflect, or help students to meet classroom expectations. For example:

- Moving a student to a different seat can minimise distractions and help them focus.
- Writing an essay might help a student catch up on missed material or help them reflect on the origin or consequences of their behaviour.

Students need to understand why they are being punished and see a clear connection between their actions and the consequences. For example: "You will stay in during recess to complete the work you missed because you were talking during class time." Therefore, address misbehaviour as soon as possible, but avoid reacting in anger or out of frustration.

While the primary goal of punishment should be to redirect (future) behaviour, it can also serve a secondary purpose: Preserving or restoring a productive learning environment for other students. For example, removing a disruptive student from the classroom can protect the learning environment, but it does not teach the disciplined student how to behave appropriately or help them catch up on missed material.

When deciding on a punishment, key questions are:

Was the student set up for success? For example:
- Did you provide the student with the opportunity to exhibit the expected behaviour?
- Were timely guidance and reminders given before the situation escalated?

Is the punishment fair and age-appropriate? For example:
- Is the severity of the punishment commensurate with the nature of the misconduct?
- Is the punishment developmentally suitable for the student?

Does the punishment have clear boundaries?
- Ensure the punishment has a clear start and end so the student knows when it is resolved.

Is the reason for punishment understood?
- Clearly communicate to the student why they are being disciplined to avoid confusion or resentment.

Making these decisions on the spot during a tense classroom moment is tough and can easily go wrong. An alternative is to administer punishment after class during a calm conversation. You then can use time to reflect on the situation and discuss with the student how they can improve. Such a conversation allows you to engage in proactive discussions about what support students with ongoing behavioural challenges might need and to explain how future issues will be handled. You could involve the student in these decisions.

What to Avoid When Using Punishment

To ensure punishments are fair, constructive, and do not backfire, avoid the following:

Acting out of revenge or frustration: Punishments perceived as retaliation almost always lead to resistance or defiance.

Humiliation: Public punishments can harm a student's dignity and exacerbate behaviour problems. "Losing face" in front of peers can be really frustrating for students. Always apply consequences discreetly to maintain respect. Also, defying the teacher can even boost a student's popularity in class and act as a reinforcer of negative student behaviours.

Punishing with grades: Grades should reflect academic performance and progress, not (mis)behaviour. Using grades as punishment undermines their purpose.

Punishing the whole class: Holding the entire class accountable for one person's actions is unfair and creates unnecessary tension and resentment.

Assigning difficult tasks as retribution: For example, using an unexpectedly hard test to punish disruptive behaviour harms trust and morale.

Repeatedly withholding fun activities in challenging classes: Especially difficult classes need positive, relationship-building activities, not punishment that alienates students even further.

> **To Keep in Mind**
>
> Punishment should never be your go-to solution, so:
>
> - Use it sparingly if at all.
> - Focus on fairness, clarity, and the opportunity for learning.
> - Maintain a calm, measured approach.
> - Protect the learning process for others and help the disciplined student to grow and succeed.
> - Ensure students know what went wrong, how they can do better next time, and how you will support them.

Table 9.1 Overview of Punishments

Social Punishments	Activity-Related Punishments
– Move the student to a different seat – Let the student sit at the teacher's desk / stand in the corner or in the hallway – Give a (stern) reprimand – Remove the student from the lesson/class – Suspend the student – Denying the opportunity to retake an assessment – Informing parents or guardians – Rewarding desired behaviour in another student	– Writing a reflective essay or a letter about what they did or what is needed for a positive class environment – Engage the student in a service project within or outside the school, like organising the library – Doing something for a fellow student, e.g., explain difficult topics – Doing something for a (different) teacher – Implement a restorative justice approach where the student must make amends with those affected by their actions – Let the student create a presentation or poster that teaches peers about the misbehaviour they made and how to avoid it in the future – Cleaning the board – Classroom duties – Sweeping – Extra homework – Repairing material damage – Telling a joke
Material Punishments	
– Confiscation of the phone – A fine – Revoking privileges – Requiring compensation for damages – Donating to a good cause	
Exchange Punishments	
– Point-based punishment system for an individual student (e.g., three points equals one hour of detention) – Point-based punishment system for the class	
Time-Related Punishments	**Physical Punishments**
– Detention – Reporting at eight o'clock the next morning – Returning at a specially designated time	– Doing push-ups – Running a lap around the school

Table 9.1 presents an overview of possible punishments to be evaluated in Activity 9.3.

Activity 9.3 allows you to evaluate the significance of punishments and which ones you want to use

Student Remarks

Content-Related Remarks

> While the teacher is talking about the causes of the Second World War (1939-1945), Steven raises his hand. The teacher gives him the floor, and Steven asks, "Who won that war, sir?" The teacher is caught off guard and says, "That's not what we're discussing right now."

Student remarks in class are an interaction where the student, not the teacher, leads the exchange. Unlike disruptions, these remarks are task-oriented and may reflect curiosity and engagement, or an attempt to connect with the lesson. A student might also offer an unexpected response, ask an unanticipated question, or even make a light-hearted joke related to the topic.

In such moments, the teacher's goal is typically to acknowledge the remark briefly and then guide the class back to the activity. Instead of simply dismissing a question as irrelevant, there are several effective ways to handle these interactions:

Listen first and redirect. Show the student that their comment has been heard by acknowledging it and explaining when the topic can be discussed. For example, "Good question, Steven! We'll get to that shortly. First, we'll focus on the causes." This approach validates the student's curiosity while maintaining lesson flow.

Incorporate the remark. If relevant and time permits, include the comment in the lesson. "The U.S. won, Steven. Now let's explore how the war began and why that outcome happened." This approach keeps the student engaged and connects the remark to the topic. The teacher could also involve the classroom: "Excellent question. Does anybody know how it all ended?"

These strategies maintain the flow of the class while showing students their input is valued. They combine reasonable high Agency and Communion.

A third approach demonstrates a more cooperative action with lower Agency:

Probe. Explore what the student's remark means. "What do you mean exactly, Steven? Why do you want to know that now?" While this might slow the lesson's pace, it provides the student with an opportunity to clarify their thoughts and feel heard. Such interactions can lead to valuable discussions, resolving misunderstandings or delving into related topics.

In case Steven would have tried to make a funny remark by asking, "Can we drink German beer because of that war?" a smile or a quick reply like, "Only if you're over eighteen!" can maintain a positive atmosphere and bring attention back to the subject.

However, not all remarks are benign or constructive. Comments that are discriminatory or offensive, such as "Germans are just less intelligent, that's why they lost!" require immediate and decisive action. For example, "That's not appropriate, Steven. I don't accept remarks like that in this class." In such cases, you must pause the lesson and address the issue thoroughly, making it clear that such remarks are unacceptable and explaining why. This approach reinforces the classroom's commitment to mutual respect and inclusivity while educating students about the impact of their words.

Personal or Challenging Remarks

Student remarks perceived as personally challenging or affecting a teacher can be among the most difficult to handle, as they may touch on sensitive things such as appearance, habits, or (a lack of) authority. These comments frequently arise from a student wanting to maintain a high status in class by defying the teacher or from an ongoing negative dynamic with the student, which can escalate if not carefully managed.

For instance, consider this interaction:

- Teacher: "Shani, Kelly, sit up straight."
- Kelly: "You're not sitting straight either."

- Teacher: "That's not the point right now."
- Kelly: "Yes, it is."
- Teacher: "I'm warning you: sit up straight!"
- Kelly: "No."
- Teacher: "Leave my classroom then."
- Kelly: "You're always unfair, and you look weird."

While such remarks, like Kelly's final jab, can feel deeply personal and provoke anger, staying calm and professional is key. Reacting emotionally could exacerbate the conflict, fuelling the negative dynamic. Instead, try to interpret the comment in the broader context of the ongoing interaction, on the left side of the Interpersonal Circle, view it as a reflection of frustration or resistance rather than a genuine personal attack. This reframing can help you maintain your composure.

To manage such remarks, you can:

Defuse in the moment. A calm response, such as, "Kelly, leave the classroom for now," avoids escalating the interaction. It communicates authority without further engaging in the conflict.

Address the underlying issue later: After the lesson, have a private, calm conversation with the student. Seek to understand the student's perspective, discuss the behaviour, and explain your expectations. This creates space for rebuilding trust and clarifying boundaries.

Prevent escalations. Reflect on what may have led to the situation. Could the original request, like asking Kelly to sit up straight, have been communicated differently? For example, saying in a non-confrontational tone, "Kelly, I notice you're slouching. Sitting up straight helps with focus—can you try that for me?" might yield better results, or an enthusiastic, "Okay everybody, let's sit up straight and tackle these assignments!"

Reinforce positive behaviours. If a student follows instructions or improves behaviour, acknowledge it. For example, compliment Kelly when she sits up straight in the future. This shifts the focus towards constructive interactions.

To Keep in Mind

Students' comments are rarely intended to personally hurt you, but result from an ongoing escalation in an interaction, on the left side of the Interpersonal Circle.

Disappointing Student Performance

A teacher discusses previously covered grammar with the class: "Who can tell me again what an adverbial phrase is?" Various students raise their hands, and the teacher gives Sophia a turn: "That's a part of a sentence that says something about a noun, right?" The teacher responds, "Thank you, almost Sophia. What do you think, Mila?" Mila then provides the correct answer.

Disappointing student performance, such as giving incorrect answers or struggling with material, is a natural part of the learning process. How teachers respond to such performance can significantly impact the student's motivation, confidence, and willingness to participate in the future, as well as the relationship with the teacher.

In the previous example, the teacher acknowledges Sophia's participation and redirects the question to Mila for the correct answer. This approach is moderately high on Communion starts quite high on Agency (thanking and giving a turn) and moves to moderately low Agency (listening to Sophia's and later Mila's answer). It likely keeps Sophia engaged but does not directly address her error. Also, for others it might now be unclear what the correct answer is.

The teacher could have chosen a very different response to express dissatisfaction with Sophia's performance; low on Communion and high on Agency: "Sophia that's wrong, we already covered this, everybody should know by now." With this, the teacher would provide feedback on Sophia's performance but is rather likely to alienate Sophia as well. Or the teacher could correct Sophia's response as well as encourage her and ask, "And what is an adjective phrase? How would you define that?" This allows Sophia to reflect on her mistake, stay involved, and learn from the exchange without feeling dismissed. It also offers a small repetition of the subject matter for other students.

Common scenarios for disappointing student performance include responses low on Agency and high on Communion (understanding behaviour). These responses allow your students to explain their behaviour, what they find difficult or do not understand so that you can then provide better support. Some examples:

> *Lack of task orientation*. If a student is not trying, ask what might be causing their disengagement and offer support. Example: "It seems like you're distracted today. Is there something on your mind; can I help clarify anything about this topic?"
> *Non-responsiveness*: Encourage participation without putting the student on the spot. Example: "It's okay if you're unsure. Let's revisit this idea after we discuss it as a class." However, starting with high Agency and varying amounts of Communion can be useful too.
> *Incorrect answers and low grades*: Provide constructive feedback without discouragement: Example: "That's not quite right, but it's a good start. Let's break it down together."

In classrooms with positive teacher-student relationships, students feel respected and safe and thus are willing to ask for help and engage in feedback. This helps teachers to turn underperformance into valuable learning opportunities.

> **To Keep in Mind**
>
> Responses low on Agency and high on Communion help students to explain their behaviour so that you can then provide better support.

Student Emotional Expressions

Students can sometimes react unexpectedly and emotionally to actions taken by a teacher or a peer. These reactions, particularly when directed at the teacher, risk damaging the teacher-student relationship and disrupting the learning environment. Whether the teacher's action involved addressing disruptive behaviour, providing feedback on performance, or delivering content, the response on emotional actions must be handled with care to accommodate a students' feelings, help them to calm down, and to avoid further escalation and the interruption of the task-oriented behaviour of other students.

> In the history lessons, most content has been for months on European and North American topics. A student from an Asian background rather suddenly shouts in class in anger, "Why do we never hear about Asia or Africa"? The teacher says, "Well, we can talk about that at another moment" and puts a hand on the student's shoulder.

Emotional reactions may stem from underlying frustrations or feelings of exclusion, as illustrated in this example. While the teacher's response attempts to acknowledge the student's frustration, it risks dismissing a valid concern and may inadvertently escalate the situation. A more intensive acknowledgement of the emotion and concern could be: "I think I understand why you feel that way. You raise an important topic, and we should certainly include perspectives from Asia and Africa." You could turn a situation like this into a learning opportunity by inviting the student to share specific topics or histories they think should be included.

> Teacher Renz has ordered Jim in front of class to do a mathematical assignment. Jim makes a mistake, and the teacher tells him, "Again you cannot do it, too bad." Jim starts crying.

Here the teacher's action has likely escalated an already strained relationship. The teacher's response reflects low Communion and possibly frustration, worsening the relationship and further discouraging the student. The situation demands restorative actions to rebuild trust through acknowledging the inappropriate comment and reassure the student of their worth.

In **Activity 9.4**, you try to find out what causes students to react emotionally.

Responding to Emotional Student Remarks

In moments when a student reacts emotionally, teachers face the challenge of managing the immediate situation, calm the student or the class and restore the relationship with them. In terms of the Interpersonal Circle, maintaining high Communion while adjusting Agency to the situation is essential.

When a student expresses frustration or anger, as in the first example, you can calm the situation by acknowledging the student's feelings. A simple acknowledgement like, "I see this is important to you," can diffuse tension. Offering to address the student's concern in more detail later ensures the issue is not dismissed while keeping the lesson on track.

Escalation often occurs when the teacher responds defensively or dismissively, which may invalidate the student's feelings and provoke further reaction. To prevent this, you can keep a calm and neutral tone, and set boundaries respectfully: "This is important, let's discuss this directly after this lesson."

The teacher in the example puts a hand on the shoulder to convey support and help to quiet. While this might work well for some students, it could feel intrusive or unwelcome to others. You must consider individual and cultural preferences and customs before using touch.

In the example of teacher Renz, high Communion and low Agency is essential for calming down the student and restoring a positive relationship. This involves active listening that would allow Jim to express his feelings and concerns, acknowledging one's own behaviours, and patience and encouragement to build the student's confidence step by step. A private follow-up after class will be necessary.

> **To Keep in Mind**
>
> After an emotional incident:
>
> – Meet with the student privately to revisit their concern.
> – Offer an opportunity to share their perspective while explaining the teacher's viewpoint or constraints.
> – Use the discussion to rebuild trust and clarify expectations for future interactions.
> – If possible and warranted, use the student's feedback.

Managing Physical Altercations

Classrooms are lively spaces, and occasionally, emotions can boil over—sometimes to the point of physical confrontations between students or even towards a teacher. Fortunately, these moments are rare at most schools. However, they are intense, and they raise an important question: When, if ever, should you physically intervene?

Even with a robust school safety policy in place, situations may arise where the safety of a student, teacher, or the entire classroom is immediately at risk. While fostering a positive classroom environment and using effective teaching strategies can prevent many issues, it can be important to be prepared for those rare, critical moments that require action. Make sure that you know the school's regulations and procedures regarding physical altercations.

Physical intervention by the teacher should always be a last resort and only used to prevent immediate harm. For example, if a student's behaviour poses a clear and imminent danger to themselves or others, stepping in may be the only way to ensure safety. However, such decisions must be made with caution and understanding that they will always be subject to later scrutiny.[2]

Students with Special Needs[3]

Generally, most students adapt well to the rules, engage with lessons, and find joy in learning. They respond positively to a teacher's strategies, including constructive feedback, clear lesson plans, and effective classroom management. When minor distractions or occasional misbehaviour occur, most students can typically be redirected without much difficulty.

Responding to Challenging Student Behaviours 137

However, some students present unique challenges—students with special needs. These individuals may in some ways require special education and display a range of disruptive or withdrawn behaviours that demand attention and strategies on top of the usual classroom management. In this section, we briefly discuss dealing with these behaviours, but we want to emphasise that addressing these challenges often requires specific, professional knowledge and skills, and this book does not cover that.

Behaviour of Students with Special Needs

While some students may easily be triggered and frequently exhibit frustration, anger, or other emotional responses, others might seem quiet, detached or withdrawn. It is essential to recognise that these students often struggle internally with their behaviour and its impact, just as much as the teacher and classroom environment are affected. Behavioural challenges can manifest in various ways, including:

- *Defiant, disruptive or oppositional behaviour*: Arguing, refusing to comply, actions that disturb others or challenging authority.
- *Aggressive behaviour*: Physical or verbal aggression towards peers or teachers.
- *Extreme withdrawal*: Marked by intense shyness or reluctance to engage socially or academically.

Behavioural issues often manifest as more *extreme positions* on the dimensions of the Interpersonal Circle, Agency and Communion. For example:

- Expressions of anger may be louder, more abrupt, or prolonged.
- Displays of shyness or withdrawal might be deeply entrenched and harder to alleviate.

Such behaviours may appear maladaptive and unusual, ranging from overly affectionate or excessively friendly to defiant or oppositional. Figure 9.1 illustrates how these behaviours can be viewed as positioned further from the centre of the Interpersonal Circle (grey ring), indicating the greater intensity compared to typical students' behaviour.

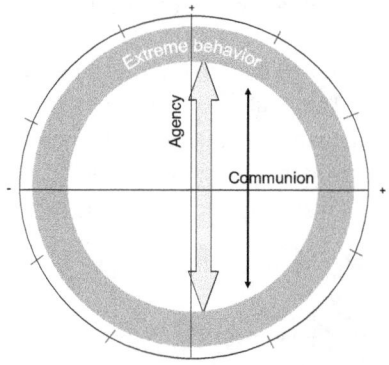

Figure 9.1 More intense student behaviour of students with special needs and complementarity displayed in the Interpersonal Circle student

Moreover, these students often do not respond predictably—for example in line with the complementarity principles—to teacher actions. While other students may adapt quickly to *authoritative behaviour* (thick arrow in Figure 9.1), a student with behavioural challenges may show only little or no complementarity after a prolonged authoritative guidance (thin arrow).

Establishing Positive Relationships with Students with Behavioural Challenges

Building and maintaining a good relationship with students with behavioural challenges can be particularly demanding. Difficult interactions often strain the teacher-student relationship, leading to a cycle where strained relationships perpetuate challenging behaviour. However, focusing on cultivating a positive, friendly relationship can serve as a powerful tool to improve classroom dynamics and reduce future conflicts.

A positive relationship acts as a stabilising foundation for interactions. When students feel valued and respected, they are more likely to respond positively to guidance, feedback, and classroom norms. Establishing a good relationship increases the likelihood of productive interactions, even in challenging situations. If negative interactions occur, they are more easily restored if the general relationship is characterised by trust and understanding.

Strategies for building connections with these students include:

Spontaneous positive interactions. Brief, informal moments during the school day can strengthen relationships. For example:
— Smile and greet the student warmly in the hallway.
— Share a light-hearted joke during class downtime.
— Compliment the student when they demonstrate positive behaviour, however small.

Intentional positive interactions. Purposefully engage with the student in ways that are separate from academic expectations. These moments help establish trust and show that you value them beyond their behaviour or classroom performance. For example:
— Discuss a shared interest, like sports or music.
— Ask about their weekend or hobbies.
— Share a brief story about yourself to build rapport.

The *Banking Time strategy*, developed by Bob Pianta,[4] suggests scheduling regular informal conversations with the student. The goal is to foster trust and rapport without the pressure of academic tasks or behaviour management. You set aside time weekly or bi-weekly for a short, relaxed chat, where the student steers the conversation, focusing on their interests and avoid school-related topics unless the student brings them up.

> **To Keep in Mind**
>
> While establishing a good relationship with students with behavioural challenges takes time and effort, it is one of the most effective ways to improve classroom interactions and foster long-term success.

Supporting Students with Behavioural Challenges

Ultimately, the goal is to help students with behavioural challenges to access the lesson, learn effectively, and experience success. How can you, from an interpersonal perspective, support these students? The foundations of effective relationships remain consistent with all students, but standard strategies—such as positive reinforcement, redirecting, enforcing rules—often prove less effective for students with behavioural issues. While these methods work well for most students, those with behavioural challenges require more specialised and targeted support. Even something as straightforward as rewarding good behaviour might not yield the same results as easily. These students face additional barriers that make accessing the productive and enjoyable aspects of the lesson more difficult for them.

Managing their behaviour often requires teachers focussed assistance by:

Persisting longer with their strategies: For example, maintaining a calm yet authoritative tone even when patience wears thin.

Avoiding falling into complementary escalation: A defiant student may tempt you into escalating the interaction by becoming overly strict or punitive. This reactive escalation can strain the teacher-student relationship and derail classroom dynamics. You must consciously guard yourself, especially against the temptation to mirror extreme low Communion student behaviour.

For some students, interventions may include individualised treatment plans or specialised lesson adjustments designed to meet their unique needs. In some cases, a student's requirements might surpass what can be managed by the teacher within the general classroom setting and you need to seek expert assistance from behavioural experts such as a psychologist or special education teacher.

Figure 9.2 provides a schematic representation of the varying levels of support required by students across different classrooms.[5] Not all classes will encounter the full spectrum of

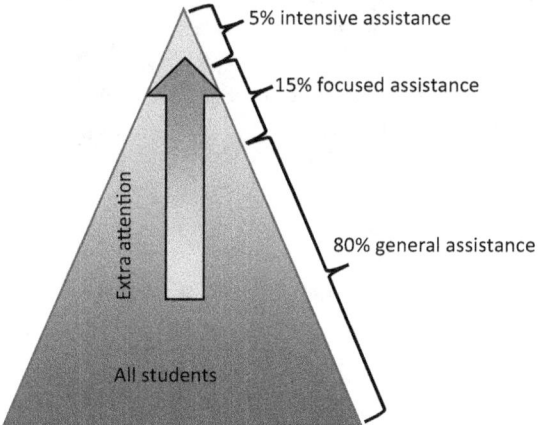

Figure 9.2 Distribution of students according to their need for support

Adapted from Fox et al. (2010)

behavioural challenges, but understanding these distinctions helps in tailoring effective responses.

Dealing with students with special needs requires patience, empathy, and specialised skills. Effective interventions often begin before any challenge arises. Use calm moments to anticipate potential behaviours and organise lessons or tasks that minimise triggers. You might assign specific roles or tasks that engage the student and provide structure. Consider in advance how to respond constructively if certain behaviours occur repeatedly. For example, if a student is prone to outbursts, you might plan to redirect their energy by assigning a hands-on task rather than engaging in confrontation.

> **To Keep in Mind**
>
> Students with special needs often ask for a different kind of support to unlock their potential and participate fully in the learning process. While this chapter introduces the topic, seek expert advice when necessary.

> **In Sum**
>
> In response to student behaviours that you perceive as challenging:
>
> – Re-evaluate your own negative emotions by looking for alternative explanations for the student behaviour. Stay calm.
> – Address issues promptly and subtly.
> – Combine calm, clear interventions with a focus on maintaining relationships.
> – Consider context and individual needs.
> – Maintain the core values of fairness and respect.
> – Help students to explain their behaviour with interventions low on Agency and high on Communion so that you can then provide better support.
> – Use punishment sparingly if at all.
>
> Students with special needs may respond little or not at all to teachers' interventions and may require different strategies.

Notes

1 Chang and Taxer (2021).
2 https://www.justice.gov/crs/highlight/preventing-bias-hate-in-school
3 See, for more information, Green (2008).
4 Pianta and Hamre (2001).
5 Scott et al. (2012).

10 Dealing with Situations That Are Important for the Classroom Atmosphere

A teacher moves around the classroom, offering help as students quietly work on their assignments. Those not receiving assistance remain focused, working independently. After making her rounds, the teacher claps her hands and announces, "Attention, please...Helen, Michael...I'm going to go over a few things I noticed."

This teacher is described by her students as both *strongly leading, friendly*, and *understanding*. While students often take the initiative—asking plenty of questions and driving their learning—the teacher when moving around the class, combines her understanding with an active role in keeping everyone engaged. She does not hesitate to step in when participation falters.

Teaching Moments That Are Important for the Classroom Atmosphere

Why is she seen as strongly leading? The key lies in *whole-class teaching moments*. These moments—when the teacher takes centre stage, addressing the entire class—have a profound impact on how students perceive the teacher's Agency (leadership and authority). Even though the teacher may display a more collaborative and supportive style during group or one-on-one interactions, her behaviour during whole-class moments strongly defines her overall level of Agency in students' eyes. When she speaks to the whole class, her role becomes more directive: managing student behaviour, leading discussions, and guiding the flow of the lesson. Whole-class teaching moments hold much weight in shaping students' perception of a teacher as a leader.[1]

While Agency is more strongly established via whole-class moments, Communion (warmth and friendliness) *shines much more through in informal interactions*. Think about moments such as chatting with students as they walk into the classroom, sharing a laugh in the hallway or building rapport during a school trip. These casual interactions build trust and connection.

To Keep in Mind

Whole-class teaching moments are where a teacher's leadership truly shines. These moments define students' perception of Agency. Therefore, when in front of class, exhibit behaviour in the upper-right quadrant of the Interpersonal Circle, such as:

- Moving and speaking calmly, yet consciously and decisively.
- Positioning yourself upright in front of the class.
- Providing structure in the lesson content.
- Making notes on the smartboard without looking at it for too long.
- Directing your face towards the class, looking toward students, and scanning the classroom to maintain an overview.

Furthermore, it is important to avoid getting too much into the lower half of the circle by:

- Being easily distracted.
- Not having materials ready.
- Looking around tensely.
- Leafing through your book or rummaging in your bag.
- Looking down or constantly at the board.
- Mumbling.
- Appearing restless (for example, looking at the clock, speaking loudly, walking quickly, and with small steps, fidgeting).

As discussed in Chapter 7, non-verbal cues play a crucial role in how students perceive Agency during whole-class teaching. For example, looking at students during whole-class discussions (or eye contact in Western classrooms) communicates authority and attentiveness more effectively than during one-on-one interactions. Teacher talking during whole-class moments signals a high level of Agency. However, during decentralised learning (e.g., group work), extended teacher talk can come across as overbearing, reducing the perception of Agency.[2]

We identify six critical categories of classroom scenarios that determine the classroom atmosphere, each with its unique dynamics and potential challenges: Starting the lesson, whole-class instruction, managing individual or group work, instructional conversation, transitions between lesson parts, and ending the lesson. The situations have common characteristics that we will discuss first. For each of these categories, practical strategies are presented to help teachers navigate challenges effectively and maintain a productive, respectful learning environment.

Managing Whole-Class Teaching Moments

When a teacher steps to the front of the classroom and begins to speak, the unspoken rule in most schools is that students should fall silent. Yet, this does not always happen effortlessly, particularly for novice teachers. Whole-class teaching moments—while central to instruction—can often feel like the most nerve-wracking parts of a lesson. These moments require juggling multiple demands: Delivering content effectively, employing sound pedagogy, and maintaining control over student behaviour. For teachers still building their routines, this balancing act can feel overwhelming.

Whole-class teaching moments often *run too long* in lessons led by novice teachers. Consider the example of discussing homework collectively. For students who have already completed their homework correctly, this segment may feel redundant. Bored and disengaged, they might start chatting, prompting the teacher to redirect them, which further extends the discussion. A more effective approach might involve working directly with students who struggled with the homework, while allowing others to move on to independent tasks.

Similarly, open-ended learning conversations can sometimes become unruly. While these discussions are valuable, they can lead to a flood of off-topic or unserious comments if not carefully managed. Redirecting the class back to the main topic takes extra time, and novice teachers may find it challenging to regain control.

The Power of Strong Relationships and Preparation

Occasional missteps—such as an explanation that runs too long or a lesson moment that loses focus—are not catastrophic if the overall classroom atmosphere is positive. A teacher who fosters a good relationship with students can recover from these moments without harming the class dynamic. The strength of the teacher-student relationship often shapes how students interpret and respond to your behaviour. When trust and rapport are strong, students are more forgiving, and minor lapses have little lasting impact.

Preparation is key to navigating these moments successfully. For beginners, investing time in thoroughly planning both the content and the pedagogical approach can provide a solid foundation. A well-structured and interesting lesson does not just make it easier to maintain control; it also gives students a clear reason to stay engaged. When lessons feel meaningful and valuable, students are naturally more inclined to listen. For example, to prevent distractions before they even arise, consider starting with a quick, engaging activity that captures students' attention and sets the tone for the lesson. By using effective teaching strategies, you can minimise potential disruptions and create a positive flow that reduces the need for constant behavioural interventions.

> **To Keep in Mind**
>
> In whole-class teaching moments, there should be something for students to gain. To achieve this, you can, for example:
>
> – Choose motivating content.
> – Structure the material effectively.
> – Emphasise the relevance of the material for an upcoming test.

Redirecting

Even in the best-prepared lessons, there will be times when students require redirection. When this happens, the challenge is not just about addressing the behaviour; it is also about keeping the class focused on the lesson. The consequences of disruptions can ripple through the classroom. Correcting one student often shifts the class's attention away from the lesson to the correction itself. Even those not involved may lose focus, requiring additional effort from the teacher to re-engage them. This can set off a cycle of interruptions that frustrates both students and teacher.

Corrections, however, are an unavoidable part of teaching. Experienced teachers manage them seamlessly by addressing issues promptly and subtly, as explained in Chapter 8. A quick glance, a name casually mentioned, or a strategic pause in talking can often redirect students without derailing the lesson. These subtle strategies are less likely to disrupt the flow of the class or draw attention away from the content.

Capturing Attention and Keeping Students Focused

In any whole-class teaching moment, one of the teacher's essential tasks is *capturing the attention of the students* and *keeping them engaged* with the lesson. From an interpersonal perspective, this involves combining high Agency with, as much as possible, high Communion to create a productive and positive classroom environment. It is not just about commanding attention but doing so in a way that fosters respect and cooperation—even with students who are less inclined to participate. However occasionally, it may also be necessary to redirect students with less cooperative behaviour, as discussed in Chapters 8 and 9.

Strategies for gaining attention. When starting a whole-class activity, students are often restless. Effective ways to grab their attention include:

- *Stand prominently*: Position yourself visibly at the front of the class and stand still, keep silent, glancing around at the students, particularly those who are restless.
- *Gesture*: Use gestures like clapping or a clear "stop" motion to signal the start of the activity.
- *Adjust your voice*: Start speaking loudly, then lower your voice so students notice when others are still talking.
- *Pause strategically*: Slow down or stop mid-sentence if students are not participating. Silence can be a powerful tool.
- *Clearly state expectations*: Let students know exactly what behaviour you expect—such as sitting down quietly or facing forwards.
- *Lighten the mood*: A well-placed joke can quickly direct attention and set a positive tone.
- *Show enthusiasm*: Let students experience your enthusiasm for starting the activity, its content, and for communicating with your students.

It is often necessary to wait for silence before proceeding, but do not wait too long. Once the majority of students are paying attention, begin the lesson to engage the rest. Avoid overreacting to minor noises or disruptions; this can escalate issues unnecessarily. Address lingering distractions only when most of the class is focused.

Strategies for keeping students focused. Maintaining focus and motivation throughout the lesson requires clarity and predictability. As explored in Chapter 8, strategies for maintaining, directing, and redirecting students' behaviour are essential. Interactions should help establish a calm atmosphere while keeping students engaged with the task at hand.

Tailoring Response to Your Strengths

It is important to recognise that no single strategy works universally. The effectiveness of any intervention depends on the context, your relationship with the class, and your behavioural strengths. Teachers are most successful when they lean into behaviours within their areas of

Table 10.1 Eight ways for a teacher to respond when a class enters noisily

Sector	Response to a noisy entrance of class. The teacher:
Directing	Informs that she has noticed something has happened and clearly indicates that the lesson is about to begin: "Okay, something has happened, but now, everyone, quickly take your seats so we can start. We have a full lesson today, bags off the tables, we'll begin with some independent reading."
Helping	Talks to the students about the situation and offers to mediate between the quarrelling students: "I'm curious about what happened ... Michelle, Hava, Karen, and Cynthia, if you all come see me later, we can try to work things out together."
Understanding	Listens with interest to what the students have experienced without giving advice or expressing an opinion: "What happened?"
Compliant	Walks calmly through the class and gives students the opportunity to vent.
Uncertain	Hesitantly rummages in her bag without asking students why they are so excited.
Dissatisfied	Stands in the centre of the class, silent with a frown, and stern, scanning the class until it becomes quiet.
Confrontational	Actively corrects the noisy behaviour of students and prohibits further discussion of the incident: "Everyone, be quiet now ... Silence ... Michelle and Hava, listen to me instead of continuing to quarrel..."
Imposing	Indicates without addressing what concerns the students that she wants to start now: "We are here for the lesson now, and we're starting."

confidence and expertise in the Interpersonal Circle. When teachers use behaviour from a part of the circle where they have an extensive repertoire, without allowing behaviour from the left side of the Interpersonal Circle to dominate, the chance of successful intervention is greater.

In this context, it is crucial to understand that behaviour in nearly any sector of the Interpersonal Circle can be effective if used wisely. Table 10.1 provides an example of eight ways a teacher can respond when a class enters very noisily after an argument on the schoolyard during recess. In most cases, as in this example, responses rooted in insecurity are less likely to succeed.

Starting the Lesson: Setting the Tone for Success

The start of a lesson is a crucial moment where teachers establish connection with the class and focus students on the learning ahead. This process typically unfolds in three phases.

Establishing Contact with Students

As students enter the classroom and take their seats, this initial phase is an opportunity to connect with them on a personal level. These informal interactions help foster a strong teacher-student relationship characterised by a high degree of Communion (see Figure 10.1). Even small signals at this stage can have a significant impact on classroom dynamics. For example:

- *Welcome at the door*: Stand by the door, greet students with a "Good morning" or "Hello," or even offer a handshake.
- *Positive body language*: Make eye contact, smile, and maintain an open posture that conveys approachability.

- *Informal conversations*: Engage in light, informal chats to learn about your students' interests or mood that day.
- *Time to unwind*: Allow students to chat briefly, settle in, and prepare their materials. This helps them transition into the learning environment.

These moments, though brief, are powerful for creating a welcoming atmosphere that encourages students to feel valued and respected. However, it is crucial to approach this phase with cultural sensitivity. Not all classroom traditions or gestures are universally appropriate. For instance, while eye contact or shaking hands might be seen as signs of respect in some cultures, they could be uncomfortable or even inappropriate in others.

Different cultural contexts often have their own unique ways of beginning lessons. For example, in many Chinese primary and middle school classrooms, the start of the lesson reflects a deep-rooted emphasis on *respecting teachers*. The process is formal and coordinated:

- After the teacher enters the room, students are required to stand up, standing firmly in place as a sign of discipline and respect.
- The class monitor—usually one of the top-performing students—leads by calling out, "Stand up!" This prompts all students to rise together and greet the teacher loudly with, "Hello, teacher!"
- The teacher responds with, "Hello everyone!" to acknowledge the students' greeting.
- Finally, the class monitor announces, "Sit down," signalling that the students can take their seats and the formal instruction can begin.[3]

This structured routine not only reinforces respect but also establishes a clear and unified transition into the learning phase. Teachers need to understand different cultural practices when considering how to start a lesson effectively.

Gaining the Class's Attention

Once students are settled, the focus shifts to transitioning from informal interactions to the structured part of the lesson. The teacher needs to signal that the lesson is about to begin

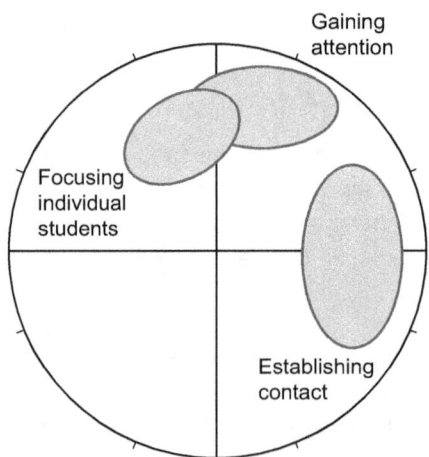

Figure 10.1 Teacher behaviour in the Interpersonal Circle at the start of the lesson

and guide students to shift their focus. At this stage, the goal is to transition smoothly into the lesson while maintaining a positive atmosphere through a combination of high Communion with high Agency (see Figure 10.1).

The previous section provided some interventions for directing attention. For the start of the lesson, here are some specific interventions:

- *Attendance check*: Take a quick roll call or visually scan the classroom to ensure everyone is present.
- *Clear signals*: Use verbal or non-verbal cues to mark the end of the welcoming phase. Examples include closing the door, clapping hands, making a gesture, or saying something like, "Alright, let's get started!"
- *Lesson plan cues*: Point to the lesson agenda displayed on the screen or hand out materials such as worksheets or tasks.
- *Address latecomers*: Politely but firmly acknowledge students who arrive late, ensuring they integrate smoothly into the class, and understand that late coming is not appropriate.

Focusing Individual Students

After most of the class is paying attention, there may still be a few students who remain disengaged. This phase requires the teacher to shift to behaviours, which may involve a reduction in Communion (see Figure 10.1) to assert classroom norms. For example:

- Show with a wink or smile or verbally that you trust the student to go and pay attention.
- Use subtle, non-verbal cues like a direct glance, standing near the student, or pausing your speech.
- Call out the student's name briefly but without making it the centre of attention.
- Politely but firmly ask the student to refocus or put away distractors.

These interventions should help avoid unnecessary escalation while signalling that the learning environment requires focus.

Transitions Between Phases of the Lesson Start

Moving through these phases can happen naturally, with subtle cues like the ringing of a bell, handing out worksheets, or closing the classroom door. However, transitions can also require a more abrupt approach if students struggle to shift their attention. In such cases, repeating the second and third phases may be necessary to ensure the entire class is ready to learn.

> **To Keep in Mind**
> - By thoughtfully managing the phases of the start of the lesson, you can set a positive and productive tone for the lesson, laying the groundwork for both engagement and effective learning.
> - Starting the lesson combines initial high Communion with gradually increasing Agency and if necessary lowering Communion.

Whole-Class Instruction

Whole-class instruction is in many classrooms a cornerstone of teaching, where teachers take centre stage to introduce new topics or content. These moments might be brief and occur once during a lesson, or they could span a significant portion, reappearing at various points. Regardless of their duration, the effectiveness of whole-class instruction depends on keeping students engaged and focused. By combining interpersonal skills with clear instructional strategies, teachers can make whole-class instruction moments more effective, ensuring that students stay on track both behaviourally and academically. When instruction is unclear or drags on, students may grow restless, leading to disruptions that can derail their attention and the flow of the lesson. To avoid this, whole-class instruction must balance two key goals.

Directing Students' Learning Process

The first goal is to guide the students' learning journey effectively. Achieving this requires teacher behaviour that exudes high Agency—clear, confident, and directive actions that establish authority and structure. A positive degree of Communion is also essential, as it fosters a sense of comfort and motivation among students. By combining such levels of Agency and Communion (see Figure 10.2), teachers can create an environment where students feel both guided and supported.

To direct learning effectively during instruction, consider employing the following techniques:

- Emphasise key words to draw attention to important points.
- Vary your tone and volume to maintain interest and signal significance.
- Use structuring phrases like "firstly," "next," and "finally" to organise information clearly.
- Pause strategically to give students time to process, take notes, or ask questions.
- Display trust in the students' ability to master the content.
- Show enthusiasm to engage students with the material.

These strategies not only clarify content but also maintain the rhythm of the lesson, reducing the chances of disengagement.

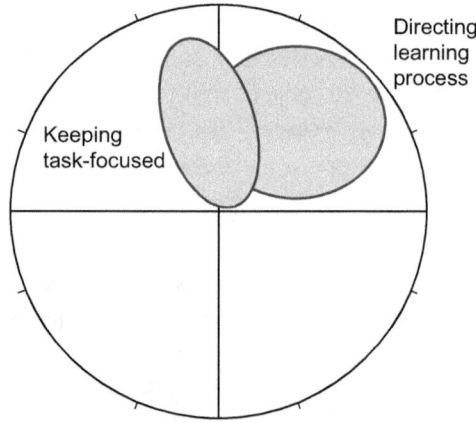

Figure 10.2 Teacher behaviour in the Interpersonal Circle during whole-class instruction

Keeping Students Task-Focused

The second goal is to ensure students stay focused and actively engaged with the material. The section on managing whole-class teaching moments highlighted how to maintain attention involving high Agency and occasionally a bit lower Communion (see Figure 10.2). During instruction, you can take additional steps to foster active participation and reduce passivity. For instance:

- *Encourage active engagement* by having students read aloud, explain concepts to their peers, or lead parts of the discussion.
- *Maintain a brisk pace* to avoid lulls that can lead to distraction.
- *Involve all students*, not just those who raise their hands. Techniques such as:
  - Using mini whiteboards for all students to write their answers.
  - Leveraging digital tools that allow students to respond quickly and anonymously.
  - Pairing students for brief discussions after a thought-provoking question.
  - Having students move to different areas of the classroom to indicate their chosen answer to a multiple-choice question.

These activities are not only engaging but also serve a dual purpose: they help you gauge the students' understanding and encourage them to think critically about the material.

> **To Keep in Mind**
> - Whole-class instruction requires high Agency; the level of Communion may vary.
> - You need to keep students task-focused and direct their learning process.
> - Integrating interactive elements helps in sustaining focus and meeting pedagogical goals.

Managing Individual or Group Work

Managing independent or group work is a delicate balance of guidance and oversight, where the teacher transitions from leading whole-class instruction to supporting students as they work independently. This process involves three key aspects: *initiating independent work*, *maintaining task-focused behaviour*, and *redirecting off-task behaviour*. Each aspect requires a blend of interpersonal strategies to ensure students remain engaged and productive.

Initiating Independent Work

The shift from whole-class instruction to independent work is crucial for setting the tone and focus of the student activities. At this stage, teachers aim to ensure that students understand the task and begin working with purpose. To initiate independent work effectively after the whole-class instruction, consider these interventions that combine high Agency with high Communion (see Figure 10.3):

- *Move around the classroom*: Circulate to give brief, procedural instructions through both verbal and non-verbal cues (e.g., pointing or gesturing, asking questions in a non-demanding way).

150 An Interpersonal Perspective on Classroom Management

- *Systematically scan the room*: Alternate between observing individual students or groups and maintaining a whole-class perspective. This creates a sense of presence and accountability. Keep scanning the classroom even if you help an inidividual student.
- *Engage closely*: Stand near students, leaning in or moving within touching distance, if culturally appropriate, to provide a calm but focused start to their work.
- *Encourage involvement*: When moving around compliment students with their engagement.

Maintaining Task-Focused Behaviour

Once students are working, it is the teacher's role to sustain their focus and momentum. This requires a balance of interpersonal strategies, leaning more towards high Communion to encourage and support, with occasional moments of high Agency and somewhat lower Communion when stronger intervention is needed (see Figure 10.3). Key strategies include:

- *Make classroom rounds*: Teachers typically conduct systematic passes through the classroom. Pause to observe, provide encouragement, or address individual needs.
- *Adjust your approach based on context*: Adopt a more approachable and calmer demeanour (high on Communion) to inspire confidence or a more controlled, directive style (high on Agency) when necessary. Pay attention to student signals—such as raised hands, (sloughed) posture, or verbal cues—to determine how to approach them.
- *Address common issues collectively*: If multiple students have the same question or struggle with the instructions, take a moment to clarify for the entire class. This prevents repeated explanations and minimises confusion.
- *Anchor yourself strategically*: Occasionally sit in a central location in the classroom, which makes you accessible to students while also maintaining a view of the overall activity.

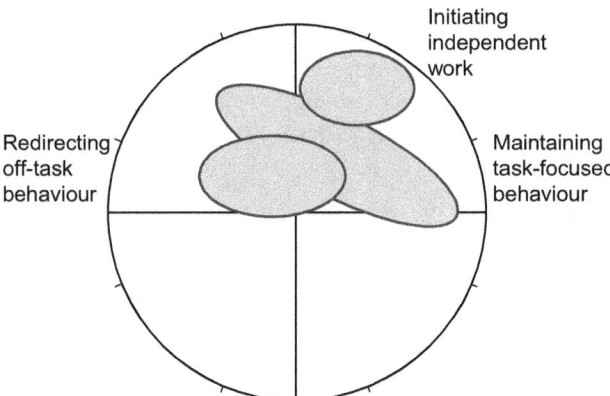

Figure 10.3 Teacher behaviour in the Interpersonal Circle when managing individual or group work

Redirecting Off-Task Behaviour

During independent or group work, there can be moments when students lose focus. Whether they are chatting, waiting for clarification, or moving around the room, you must intervene to refocus their attention.

Strategies for addressing non-task-focused behaviour include interventions discussed in the section on redirecting in Chapter 8 and the section on managing whole-class teaching moments in this chapter. Remember, that gentle, non-confrontational cues like a subtle glance, a soft verbal reminder, or standing near off-task students can be enough to redirect them without disrupting others. However, occasionally, you might need to intervene with lower Communion actions (see Figure 10.3).

Finally, be sure to have additional challenges or alternative activities prepared for students who finish early. This keeps them engaged and prevents disruptions.

> **To Keep in Mind**
>
> To manage individual or group work you need to give clear instructions at the start and circle class deliberately.

Whole-Class Instructional Conversation

Instructional conversations—where teachers guide discourse by asking for and responding to students' input—are a valuable yet challenging teaching method. These interactions can enhance conceptual understanding and linguistic skills by engaging all students in meaningful dialogue. However, without careful classroom management, they may devolve into side conversations, fail to capture the attention of the whole class, or lead to unproductive or unserious answers. To maximise their pedagogical value, instructional conversations must involve the entire class and maintain focus on the learning objectives.

Engaging Students

To prevent an instructional conversation from turning into a one-on-one dialogue or losing the attention of other students, you need to *engage the entire class*. Consider these strategies:

- *Change your physical position*: Step away from the responding student to encourage others to stay engaged and avoid turning the exchange into a private conversation.
- *Vary speaking turns unpredictably*: Randomly call on students to answer questions to maintain focus and accountability.
- *Pose questions to the entire class*: Instead of addressing a specific student, direct questions to everyone. Follow up by calling on a student after giving them time to think.
- *Include quieter students*: Encourage participation by specifically calling on students who might not typically volunteer.
- *Foster a supportive atmosphere*: Show warmth and openness to reduce any anxiety students may feel about participating, thereby encouraging active involvement. Model making mistakes and *thinking* out loud.

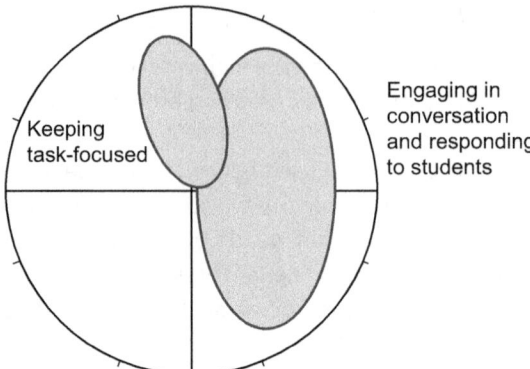

Figure 10.4 Teacher behaviour in the Interpersonal Circle during instructional conversation

By structuring the conversation this way, teachers through their high Communion and varying Agency behaviour (see Figure 10.4) ensure that all students are engaged and benefit from the discussion.

Responding to Student Input

Student responses in an instructional conversation can vary widely—from insightful contributions to unexpected or incorrect answers. Regardless of the quality of input, the teacher must guide the learning process while maintaining focus and motivation. For instructional conversations to succeed, teachers must use a combination of high Communion—to foster a supportive, open environment—and appropriate Agency—to maintain structure and focus (see Figure 10.4). For example, you can:

- *Provide positive reinforcement*: Frequent affirmations to keep students motivated. Use verbal and non-verbal encouragement, such as nodding, saying "yes," or giving a thumbs up, if culturally appropriate, to acknowledge students' contributions.
- *Deepen the discussion*: Gentle guidance to encourage deeper thinking.
- *Refocus where necessary*: If a student's response veers off-topic or is incomplete, use a stopping gesture or brief intervention to refocus their answer.
- *Correct and build*: When a response is incorrect or incomplete after multiple students' attempts., provide the correct answer yourself. Avoid repeating the incorrect phrasing, as this risks reinforcing the mistake; instead, reframe it in your desired terms and expand on it to build understanding. Do not repeatedly call on the smartest students to set things right.

Keeping Students Task-Focused

In case of a student inattentiveness or disruption, somewhat lower Communion (see Figure 10.4) might be needed.

To Keep in Mind

Be sure to engage all student during whole-class instructional conversations.

Transitions Between Lesson Parts

Transitions between different parts of a lesson—such as moving from one activity to another or switching work formats—are moments that can easily disrupt classroom order. These transitions usually involve some movement and noise as students shift focus and adjust to the new activity. To ensure smooth and effective transitions, minimise downtime to avoid gaps between activities that might lead to unnecessary distractions. It is helpful to divide the process into three phases.

Initiating the Transition

This phase signals the end of the current activity and introduces the next one. Clear communication and assertive behaviour help to manage this phase effectively. You should employ behaviour characterised by high Agency and some Communion (see Figure 10.5) to guide students through the shift. Strategies include:

- *Standing prominently*: Position yourself at the front of the classroom and request the students' attention to emphasise the transition.
- *Using clear signals*: For example, ringing a bell, clapping hands, turning off a smartboard, wiping the board clean, or setting up materials for the next activity. With younger children, a "transition song" that is always sung while cleaning up, may also be effective.
- *Referring to prior instructions*: Remind students about a pre-scheduled activity shift or timeline discussed earlier in the lesson.
- *Walking around*: If transitioning from individual or group work, walking through the classroom can help gather attention and prepare students for the change.

Directing the Class

Once the transition has been initiated, the teacher might be a bit lower on Agency (see Figure 10.5) and focuses on directing the entire class toward the new activity. This phase involves clarifying what students need to do and ensuring they are attentive. Techniques such as standing prominently, verbal cues, non-verbal gestures, adjusting your voice, structured instruction and clearly stated expectations are especially relevant here.

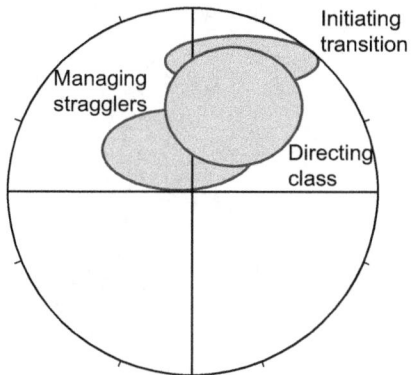

Figure 10.5 Teacher behaviour in the Interpersonal Circle during transitions between lesson parts

Managing Stragglers

Even with a well-executed transition, some students may take longer to refocus. The final phase involves addressing these stragglers, usually lowering Communion (see Figure 10.5) to ensure everyone is fully engaged in the new activity. Again, strategies from the section on managing whole-class teaching moments apply, for example:

- *Providing individualised assistance*: Help students find the correct page in their book or clarify the next steps.
- *Repeating instructions*: Briefly restate the organisational or task-related directions for students who missed them.
- *Adjust your position*: Standing near off-task students can encourage them to re-engage without requiring verbal correction.

Ending of the Lesson

The ending of a lesson serves as a critical moment to wrap up learning activities, provide closure, and set the tone for subsequent lessons or the end of the school day. Effective lesson conclusions combine high Agency to maintain structure and discipline with high Communion to reinforce positive teacher-student relationships.

Bringing the Task to an End

Before concluding the lesson, teachers often need to refocus students' attention to ensure tasks are properly completed. This requires behaviour characterised by high Agency and may sometimes involve slightly confrontational actions (see Figure 10.6) to regain attention. For example:

- *Clearly state expectations*: Emphasise how students should behave during the final moments. Inform students that it is time to finish their work or prepare for the next steps.
- *Calling out specific students*: Mentioning names if individuals are not paying attention.

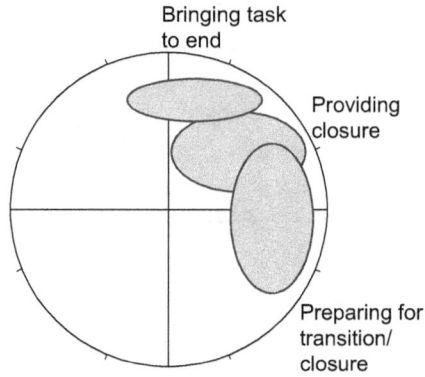

Figure 10.6 Teacher behaviour in the Interpersonal Circle at lesson conclusion

Providing Closure

To effectively conclude the lesson, teachers typically summarise the key points covered or provide a brief preview of what comes next. This is an opportunity to transition from neutral or low Communion to a higher level of Communion (see Figure 10.6). Common practices include:

- *Summarising the lesson*: Highlight the major topics or learning outcomes to reinforce understanding. You can include students by posing reflective questions about the lesson, such as:
  o "What was the most important thing we learned today?"
  o "What will you practice for next time?"
- *Previewing future lessons*: Give students an idea of what to expect in upcoming sessions, creating continuity in learning.
- *Assigning homework*: Clearly communicate homework expectations by:
  o Verbally stating the assignment if necessary multiple times.
  o Writing the homework on the board for visual reinforcement.

Preparing the Classroom for Transition or Closure

In secondary education, the teacher often transitions the classroom to prepare for the next class or the end of the day. To manage this effectively:

- *Model expected behaviour*: Push in chairs, straighten tables, or tidy up personal areas.
- *Praise positive actions*: Compliment students for adhering to classroom norms, such as leaving their workspaces tidy.

In primary education, lesson conclusions typically also involve more relational and routine elements. Teachers may:

- *Involve students in cleanup*: Encourage collaborative tidying of the classroom, reinforcing a sense of responsibility and teamwork.
- *Affirm the relationship*: Make personal connections by saying goodbye to each student or acknowledging their contributions during the day.

Like the start of the lesson, different cultural contexts may have their own unique ways of closing a lesson, for example, in a formal and coordinated process involving students stand up and thanking and greeting the teacher.

> ### In Sum
> Student perceptions of teacher Agency are mostly based on whole-class teaching moments whereas student perceptions of teacher Communion are based on more informal interactions.

> Whole-class moments require balancing delivering content clearly, employing sound pedagogical strategies, and maintaining control over student behaviour. You need to keep students task-focused and direct their learning process.
>
> When in front of the class, exhibit behaviour in the upper-right quadrant of the Interpersonal Circle, such as:
>
> - Moving and speaking calmly, yet consciously and decisively.
> - Positioning yourself upright.
> - Providing structure in the lesson content.
> - Making notes on the smartboard without looking at it for too long.
> - Directing your face towards the class, looking toward students, and scanning the classroom to maintain an overview.

Notes

1 van Tartwijk et al. (1998).
2 van Tartwijk et al. (2010).
3 Liu personal communication.

11 Answers to Frequently Asked Questions about Teacher-Student Interactions and Relationships

Classrooms are complex ecosystems where the dynamics of teacher-student interactions and relationship plays a central role in shaping the learning environment. Over the years, extensive research has been conducted to better understand these dynamics, focusing on both teacher and student perceptions of their interactions and relationships. While much of this research originates in the Netherlands (home of the authors of this book), it spans across diverse countries including Canada, China, Indonesia, Iran, Italy, Pakistan, Spain, the Nordic countries, the United Kingdom, the United States, and Turkey. The findings, revealing insights into how relationships influence classroom climates worldwide, generally focus more on classes in secondary education than in primary education.

Results in Earlier Chapters

In Chapter 2, we discussed how positive teacher-student relationships benefit both students and teachers, fostering better learning outcomes for students and greater satisfaction for teachers. Other chapters explored key findings, including:

- *Students' shared perspectives*: Students tend to agree with one another in how they perceive the relationship with their teacher (Chapter 4).
- *Differing views*: Teachers and students often see the relationship differently, with two-thirds of teachers rating themselves closer to their ideal than students do (Chapter 4).
- *Mutual interaction changes*: Both teachers and students contribute equally to shifts in the relationship over time (Chapter 6).
- *Impact of extreme behaviours*: Repeated marked behaviours, especially those at the left side of the Interpersonal Circle diminish long-term Agency and Communion, profoundly harming relationships (Chapter 5).
- *First impressions matter*: Students' initial impressions of a teacher are strongly related to their perceptions later in the year (Chapter 5).
- *The importance of starting high on Communion*: Teachers who begin the school year with a high level of Communion are more likely to see their relationships improve, while those starting with low Communion face greater risk of deterioration (Chapter 5).

DOI: 10.4324/9781003563464-11

- *Experience levels and consistency*: Veteran teachers generally maintain consistent relationships across classes, whereas novice teachers often experience significant variability (Chapter 5).
- *Career-long trends*: As teachers progress in their careers, Agency tends to increase quickly in the early years, while Communion remains relatively stable. Later in their careers, Communion may slightly decline (Chapter 5).

Overview of the Current Chapter

We frequently have to answer the same questions on what is known from research on teacher-student interactions and relationships. Now we dive deeper into these frequently asked questions, providing answers rooted in research. Key topics include: The link between relationships and outcomes: How do teacher-student dynamics impact student motivation, academic performance, and teacher job satisfaction? Cultural differences: How do interpersonal behaviours and classroom climates vary across cultures, and what do student perceptions look like in multicultural classrooms? Related factors: How are characteristics such as student age, class composition, and teacher experience related to these perceptions? Developing interpersonal behaviour: Can specific interpersonal behaviours be developed or improved to enhance classroom relationships?

Most of the research we will discuss used the *Questionnaire on Teacher Interaction (QTI)*, a tool used to visualise the dynamics in teacher-students communication processes with a focus on the relationship aspect of these dynamics. Underlying the presentation of these relationships, are the two dimensions of the Interpersonal Circle: Agency (how assertive a teacher is) and Communion (how warm or supportive they are). While individual QTI-questions like "Is this teacher patient?" or sectors like "Uncertain" can offer valuable insights as feedback for teachers, focusing on the overarching dimensions provides a more reliable and comprehensive view of how teacher-student relationships connect to other factors, such as student motivation or teacher gender.

What is in the Teacher-Student Relationship for Students and Teachers?[1]

How Are Student Outcomes and Relationships Connected?

A great deal of research has been conducted on the connections between teacher-student relationships and student learning outcomes. Students who perceive their teacher as both high on Agency and Communion tend to thrive.

In most studies, the Agency dimension tends to be associated with students' performance on academic tasks and tests. When teachers are clear about expectations and provide structured guidance, students are more task-oriented and perform better. The Communion dimension is more strongly related to students' motivation and interest. By connecting with students on a personal level and addressing their needs, teachers create a positive classroom atmosphere that enables students to focus on their work. The teacher behaviours on the two dimensions complement each other. Agency relates to structure and focus, while Communion relates to a supportive environment where students feel valued and understood. Together, dynamics in the communication positively related to these dimensions contribute to a positive social climate, where students feel empowered to engage with academic tasks.

When teacher-student relationships are characterised by both high levels of Agency and Communion, students not only are more engaged in their learning, but students also behave more socially in class. There is, for instance, less bullying among them.[2]

Interestingly, the impact of Agency and Communion on student outcomes may vary slightly across cultural groups. Research suggests that minority students often benefit more from teachers who score highly in both dimensions.[3] For instance, studies in Dutch multicultural classrooms found that the positive effects of high Agency and Communion were stronger for students whose parents were born in Morocco than for students whose families have been in the Netherlands longer. This highlights the importance of culturally responsive teaching, where both structure and connection are tailored to meet diverse student needs.

Motivation: How Does It Bridge Between Relationships and Performance?

The connection between teacher-student relationships and academic outcomes can be understood through the lens of motivation. Motivation may act as the link between interpersonal relationships and students' academic performance. Clarity about what is expected of students and the targeted guidance of student behaviour (Agency) ensure that students work in a task-oriented manner. Connecting with students' world and personal needs (Community) fosters a positive experience in the classroom and creates mental space to engage with academic tasks.

Teachers who take both high Agency and high Communion positions in the relationship with their students, tend to use a wider variety of teaching strategies, switching between whole-class instruction, group work, and independent activities.[4] This flexibility may help strengthen student motivation. It allows them to adapt to diverse learning needs and keep students engaged. Positioned in the upper-right quadrant of the Interpersonal Circle, these teachers create dynamic and effective learning environments that benefit all students.

This process is illustrated in Figure 11.1, which highlights the connections between teacher behaviour, teacher-student relationships, student behaviour, and academic outcomes. As indicated in Chapter 3, the student's personal perception of what is happening in the classroom plays a central role, as does the teacher's interpersonal behaviour.

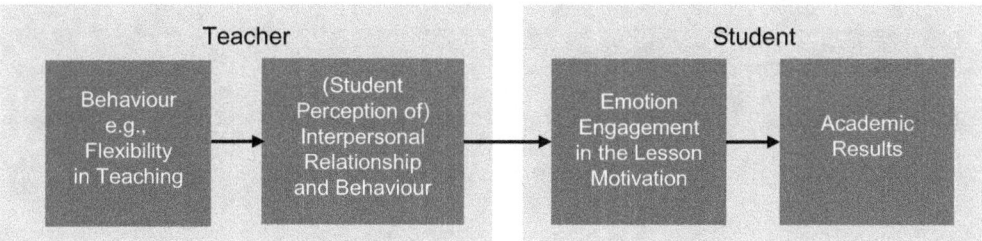

Figure 11.1 Connections between teacher behaviour, the teacher-student relationship and behaviour and outcomes for students

Four Relationship Types: What Do They Mean for Students?

Different combinations of teacher Agency and Communion in the relationship with their students produce distinct classroom dynamics, as seen in the examples from Chapter 1:

- *High Agency and high Communion* (Teacher August): Students learn effectively and enjoy the process. This is the ideal combination, fostering both strong academic performance and motivation.
- *Low Agency and low Communion* (Teacher Dion): Students are neither motivated nor achieving, leading to poor outcomes.
- *Low Agency and high Communion* (Teacher Tonia): While students feel comfortable and enjoy the classroom environment, they lack the drive to engage deeply with academic tasks.
- *High Agency and low Communion* (Teacher Renz): Students may perform well due to external pressures, such as fear or obligation, but their intrinsic motivation and enjoyment of learning suffer.

> **To Keep in Mind**
>
> Students gain the most—academically, socially, and emotionally—from teachers they consider to be high on both Agency and Communion.

What Is in the Teacher-Student Relationship for the Teacher?

The teacher-student relationship does not only benefit students, but it also plays a critical role in teachers' well-being, satisfaction, and overall experience in the classroom.[5] When teachers experience high levels of Agency (leading with confidence) and Communion (connection and trust) in their interactions with students, they tend to:

- Enjoy their lessons more and feel fulfilled by their profession.
- Report higher motivation and a stronger sense of purpose.
- Experience relatively less stress and greater self-efficacy—the belief in their ability to influence student learning positively.
- Stay open to trying new teaching strategies and approaches, as their confidence allows for more experimentation.

> **To Keep in Mind**
>
> A strong teacher-student relationship is not just good for students; it directly enhances teachers' job satisfaction, confidence, and emotional well-being.

A Peek Inside the Classroom: What Do Teacher Heart Rates Tell?

To explore how teacher-student interactions affect teachers' emotions and stress, researchers measured teachers' heart rates during some of their lessons.[6] Heart rate changes can signal moments of psychological significance, where teachers are actively processing or responding to what is happening in the classroom. Findings revealed:

- *Agency and positive emotions*: Teachers whose heart rates increased when they exerted more Agency reported feeling more satisfied and positive about their lesson. This suggests that, while taking charge can feel exciting or even a little stressful, it is also rewarding. These teachers view their leadership and structure-setting as successful and fulfilling moments.
- *Communion and emotional labour*: Teachers whose heart rates increased when displaying more Communion tended to feel negative about the lesson afterward. They were relieved the lesson was over and described feeling emotionally drained. This may indicate they experienced too much emotional labour. Teachers displayed positive behaviours—like patience or kindness—even when they were not naturally feeling them. For example, smiling at a student while internally feeling frustrated about time constraints.

The findings highlight an important insight for teachers. Being high on Agency can feel energising and empowering when you view it as a tool for success. Being high on Communion, while essential, can sometimes require emotional effort, especially when you feel pressured to maintain positivity or connection while balancing other demands (e.g., time management or lesson progression). When you experience this emotional labour, you may benefit from strategies that help you align your outward behaviour with your internal state, ensuring that the warmth and connection you show feels authentic and less draining. The beginning of Chapter 9 elaborated this reappraising of emotions.

Do Behaviours and Relationships Differ Between Countries and Cultures?

Comparisons Between Countries and Cultures: Are These Valid?

When comparing teacher-student interactions across different countries and cultures, it is important to interpret the findings carefully, as several issues may threaten the validity of such comparisons.

- *Relative comparisons*: When students answer questions about the interpersonal behaviour of teachers or their relationship with those teachers, their answers are shaped by comparisons to other teachers within their context. This affects comparisons of teachers across different countries. For example, Chinese students will compare the leadership of their teacher to that of other Chinese teachers, while British students will do the same in relation to their other British teachers. As a result, a Chinese teacher viewed as 'not very authoritative' in China may, upon observation, show more authority than a British teacher seen at a similar level of being 'authoritative' in Britain.
- *Cultural norms and expectations*: Perceptions of teacher behaviour are influenced by cultural norms and expectations. For example, a Dutch teacher perceived as strict by Dutch students appeared lenient to an Indian colleague, illustrating that the standard for strictness varies between cultures. Each culture has implicit standards for appropriate teacher

behaviour. These cultural norms influence what is perceived as "ideal" or "acceptable" in teacher-student relationships, affecting how students respond to surveys or assessments. Statements like "Dutch teachers are stricter than Indian teachers" cannot be validly made based on QTI data alone. Such statements would ignore the relativistic nature of student perceptions and cultural expectations for teacher behaviour.

Representativeness of study samples: To compare countries meaningfully, studies must use representative samples–groups of teachers that accurately reflect the population of teachers in each country. Unfortunately, many studies lack this level of representation. Without a representative sample, we cannot reliably claim that the findings reflect the broader patterns in that country's classrooms. So, when interpreting comparisons between countries, it is crucial to question: Who was included in the study, and how well do they represent teachers in their country?

Equivalence of questionnaires: A last challenge comes from comparing scores on the QTI across languages and cultures. While the QTI consistently identifies the two key dimensions Agency and Communion, there is often no proof of scalar equivalence. Scalar equivalence means that the same score ensures the same thing across different versions of the QTI. For example, a score of '4' on a specific behaviour in Britain might not carry the same meaning as a score of '4' in Indonesia. Without this proof, two identical scores on the QTI might not reflect the same perception or behaviour in different cultural contexts.

These relativisations do not mean that comparisons between countries are impossible. Despite cultural differences, the Interpersonal Circle remains a universal model for describing relationships,[7] and this framework allows for comparisons of teacher behaviours across cultures at a structural level.

With these considerations in mind, we will now proceed to share some results of studies on similarities and differences in QTI profiles in different countries and with students from different countries.

To Keep in Mind

While interpretations of differences between cultures and countries must account for cultural relativity and contextual nuances, the structural framework provided by the Interpersonal Circle allows meaningful cross-cultural comparisons of teacher-student relationships.

Are There Also Similarities Between Countries and Cultures?

While much discussion focuses on cultural differences in teacher-student interactions and relationships, it is equally important to recognise similarities across countries and cultures. These are:

- The two dimensions of Agency and Communion in the Interpersonal Circle provide a universal way to describe interpersonal communication in classrooms worldwide. This universality provides a common ground for examining teacher-student interactions and relationships in different cultural contexts.

- Teachers in all cultures tend to score in the upper-right quadrant of the Interpersonal Circle (positive Agency and Communion) on average, and this combination of directing and connection is widely considered desirable.
- The association between teacher behaviour (Agency and Communion) and student outcomes—such as motivation, engagement, and academic performance—holds true across cultures.

This high degree of similarity highlights that, despite cultural differences, the fundamental dynamics of positive teacher-student relationships are shared globally.

Do Ideals of Teacher-Student Relationships Differ Between Countries or Cultures?[8]

While universal similarities exist, cultural norms can shape specific elements of what constitutes appropriate teacher behaviour. Regarding students' ideals of the interpersonal relationship with their teachers, studies in international schools showed some ethnicity related differences. Whereas students from Nordic countries preferred more Agency from their teachers than students from other countries, South Africans preferred less Communion. Teachers in the Netherlands and the United States did not differ much in their ideals of their relationship with their students, although teachers in the United States ideally wanted to be somewhat stricter than their Dutch colleagues, who, in turn, wanted to be slightly more compliant.

These cultural nuances suggest that while the dimensions of Agency and Communion are universal, the ideal combination of them can vary based on students' and teachers' cultural backgrounds.

Do Perceptions of Actual Relationships Differ Between Countries or Cultures?

The QTI has been used in many different countries for single-nation research, and a few studies directly compared levels of teacher's Agency and Communion in different countries.[9] Figure 11.2 shows the scores in different countries for the data from 12 samples in 11 countries; we included two Chinese studies with different QTI versions. We marked the countries where the same 48 questions version of the QTI was used.[10]

Students everywhere tend to rate their teachers in the upper-right quadrant of the Interpersonal Circle, indicating generally high Agency and Communion.

Some country-level variations can be noted:

- Teachers in *Brunei*, *Singapore*, *China*, and *Estonia* generally score higher on both Agency and Communion, indicating that they are perceived as both effective leaders and highly supportive in their interactions with students.
- *Italian* teachers are noted for lower scores on Communion, meaning they may connect less with students on an interpersonal level. However, their Agency scores remain like those of other countries, suggesting consistent leadership and control in the classroom.
- Teachers in *Turkey* exhibit mid-range scores on Communion but are rated lower on Agency, suggesting a moderate level of interpersonal connection but relatively less assertiveness or control compared to other countries.

- *Dutch* teachers tend to score somewhat lower on both Agency and Communion than teachers in most other countries. This may result from differences in sample composition. In many studies, teachers volunteer to participate, and volunteers tend to be perceived more favourably on both dimensions. The Dutch sample was randomly selected, which might explain the relatively lower scores.
- The two studies conducted in *China* produced different outcomes. This may be due to variations in teacher-student relationships within the country, and to variations in the QTI versions used. This highlights the need for caution when interpreting cross-country findings, as methodology, sampling differences and within country variations can significantly affect results.
- Interestingly, while *Chinese* teachers displayed more stable Agency in their classrooms, *Dutch* teachers were observed to vary their Agency more and often giving students additional responsibility. These differences reflect implicit cultural expectations about effective teacher behaviour.[11]

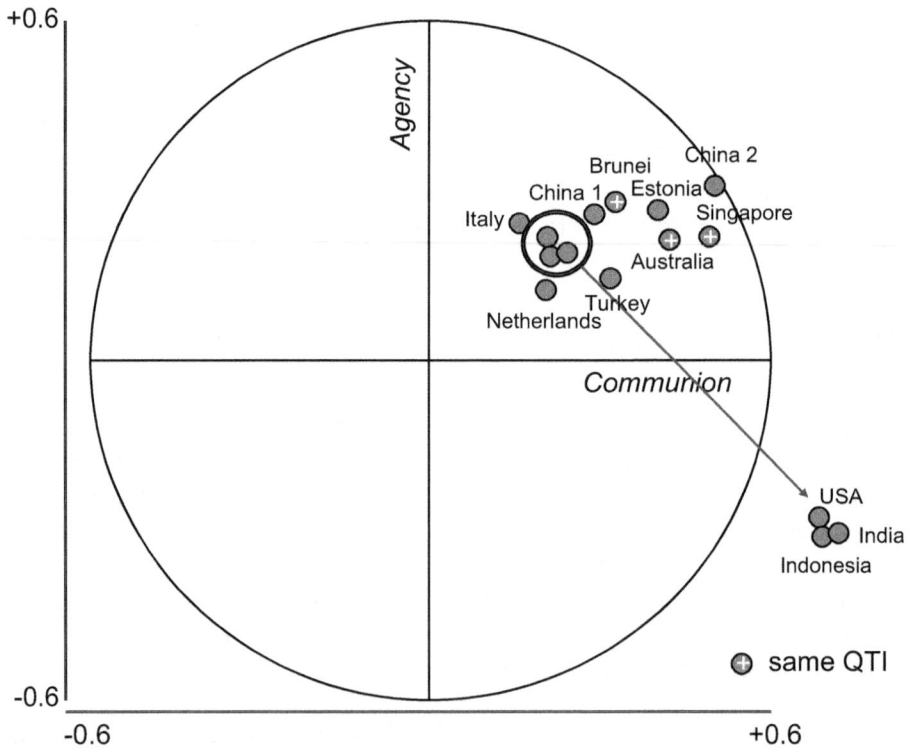

Figure 11.2 Student QTI scores in different countries. Dimension scores can run from -1.0 to +1.0

Adapted from den Brok and van Tartwijk (2015) and based on Maulana et al. (2012), Den Brok and van Tartwijk (2015), Sun et al. (2018), Wei et al. (2009), Passini et al. (2015), Palk et al. (2024)

We note *that the variation in Agency and Communion scores within a single country is often much larger than the average difference between countries.*[12] Variability within a single country may outweigh the average differences between countries. In other words: If teachers in Country A score, on average, higher on Agency than teachers in Country B, this does not mean that every teacher in Country A is higher than those in Country B. Individual differences between teachers can easily be reversed from these averages. For example, one teacher in Country B might score much higher on Agency than many teachers in Country A. This means that country-level averages tell us little about the actual behaviour of a specific teacher in that country.

How Do Students from Various Ethnic Backgrounds Perceive Teacher-Student Relationships?

Research, often in multicultural classrooms, is available focusing on connections of students' and teachers' cultural backgrounds and teacher-student relationships. Various measures are used for cultural backgrounds, such as the language spoken at home, the country of birth, or how teachers and students identify themselves—for example, as British, non-British, or British with a migration background. Which criterion for cultural background is used makes little difference. We summarise the findings from these studies:[13]

- *Higher ratings in multicultural classrooms*: Students in diverse, multicultural urban classrooms tend to score teachers higher on both Agency and Communion. This may result from teachers adapting their strategies to individual student needs and their awareness of their interactions.[14] Greater cultural diversity in a classroom appears linked to more cooperative teacher behaviours.[15]
- *Ethnicity-specific differences*: Western students often perceive lower Agency from teachers compared to students from other countries. Findings for Communion are mixed. Some studies show Western students perceive higher Communion., but others report no differences or the opposite trend. In Dutch multicultural schools, Moroccan and Turkish students rated teachers higher on Agency than their Dutch and Surinamese peers. Students with a Moroccan background perceived their teacher lower on Communion than their Dutch classmates.[16]
- *Gender and ethnicity interactions*: In the Netherlands, Moroccan boys rated teachers higher on Agency than Moroccan girls, whose scores aligned more closely with Dutch students. Teachers, in turn, reported that they had to reprimand boys more often, which could explain the higher scores given by the boys.

Do Teachers Treat Students Differently Based on Ethnicity?[17]

Evidence from observational studies reveals that teachers' treatment of students can influence their perceptions of teacher relationships. In the USA, primary school teachers tend to be more critical of African American males and praise black female students less frequently than their white peers. Also, they often exhibit biases, giving black students more negative feedback and less praise.

166 An Interpersonal Perspective on Classroom Management

In the Netherlands, teachers were reported to correct Moroccan students' behaviour more often than that of students from other countries. These teachers explained this by citing the need for greater structure and discipline in multicultural classrooms. They also emphasised that collectivistic cultural factors, such as preserving face and re-establishing rapport after redirecting students, were more important in the teaching of students in multicultural classrooms.

Does Teacher Ethnicity Influence Student Perceptions?

Research also indicates that students' perceptions of teachers can vary based on the teacher's ethnicity:

- In the USA, *Asian* teachers were perceived as having lower Agency compared to teachers from other ethnic groups.[18]
- *Euro-American* teachers were seen as higher on Communion compared to African American teachers,[19] though another study reported that Western teachers were viewed as less immediate and emotionally close than teachers from other countries.[20]
- In the *Netherlands*, students rated Dutch-background teachers higher on both Agency and Communion compared to non-Dutch teachers. Students also reported difficulties in interpreting the emotions of teachers from different cultural backgrounds. Some described perceiving less emotion or warmth from non-Dutch teachers, suggesting that cultural differences in communication styles may influence these perceptions.

Are Teacher-Student Relationships Associated with Class, Teacher, or Student Characteristics?[21]

Studies using the QTI have examined various characteristics of classes, students, and teachers that may be related to perceptions of Agency and Communion. However, it is crucial to note that the differences in perceptions of various categories are generally small and represent subtle nuances rather than drastic variations. The differences between individual teachers tend to be far more significant than those associated with general characteristics such as subject taught, gender, or school type. For example, when teachers of one subject are perceived by students to show slightly more Agency on average than teachers of another subject, it does not mean that every teacher teaching that subject scores higher on Agency than those of the other subject: the variation within the group of teachers teaching a subject is so large that, between two individual teachers of these subjects, the difference could easily be reversed. This underscores the importance of focusing on personalised teacher assessments rather than generalised group characteristics.

- *Class size*: Students in larger classes tend to rate their teachers higher on Agency and lower on Communion, probably due to a greater emphasis on maintaining order and less opportunity for individual connections. The relationship between class size and the interpersonal climate is most significant in classes with fewer than 20 or more than 30 students. In mid-range class sizes, the differences are negligible.

- *Student age*: Students in the lower years of secondary education and in primary education rate teachers slightly higher on Agency and Communion than older students in the upper years of secondary education.
- *Student gender*: Boys perceive slightly less Agency and Communion in teachers compared to girls. So, girls tend to view teachers more positively on both dimensions. Consequently, classrooms with more boys generally result in lower overall ratings of teachers on Agency and Communion. Gender differences may also interact with cultural backgrounds, affecting perceptions, as discussed in the previous section.
- *Teacher gender*: Female teachers are generally perceived as slightly higher on Agency and Communion than male teachers.
- *Teacher subject*: In secondary education, the subject taught by the teacher has a small impact. Mathematics and science teachers scored lower on both Agency and Communion than other teachers.
- *Teacher personality*: Research is inconclusive on the role of teacher personality traits. Some studies found no connection between personality and teacher-student relationships, while others suggested that traits like *neuroticism* and *conscientiousness* may lead to higher ratings on Agency and Communion.
- *Schools*: The way teachers and students perceive the teacher-student relationship is similar across different types of schools (such as vocational, general, or academic tracks).[22] Progressive or alternative schools (e.g., Montessori, Steiner-Waldorf) show no distinct trends in the interpersonal climate other than in traditional schools. This probably even applies to very alternative schools, such as Summerhill. So, specific educational or pedagogical philosophies are not significantly linked to student perceived teacher-student relationships. Across all types of schools, diverse teacher-student relationship styles exist, including stricter and more lenient approaches, even in Montessori or other progressive schools.

However, when examining differences or similarities in teacher-student relationships between schools, it is important to consider the relativity in perceptions. Students' responses on the QTI are not absolute but relative to their experiences with other teachers at the same school. For example, a teacher demonstrating a particular level of strictness might be perceived differently depending on the school context. At a stricter school, the teacher may be seen as one of the least strict compared to their colleagues, whereas at a less strict school, the same teacher could be perceived as very strict. While it is possible to assess relative differences within a school, making absolute comparisons across schools based on perceived Agency and Communion is problematic without accounting for the contextual norms that shape these perceptions.

Can Good Interpersonal Behaviour Be Learned?

Research suggests that good interpersonal behaviour is learnable for teachers, even though individual student teachers vary in their ability to establish positive teacher-student relationships. While some student teachers naturally excel—often due to prior experience with group dynamics, such as coaching a sports team—others encounter challenges but can improve significantly with targeted training and practice.

What Are Effective Approaches for Developing Teacher-Student Relationships During Student Teaching?

Learning interpersonal behaviour requires a combination of practice, theoretical knowledge, reflective observation, and feedback. Key contributors to student teachers' development in the school practicum are school mentors who inspire and encourage experimentation with new approaches and teacher educators who can provide connections between classroom practice and underlying theory, enhancing understanding and skill development.

To accelerate the development of positive relationships with students and improve classroom management, a three-pronged approach is recommended:[23]

- *Student feedback*: Use tools like the QTI to gather feedback from yourself and students about the teacher's interpersonal behaviour at least twice during placement. Discuss results with mentors (Activity 4.3) and, where possible, students (Activity 4.4).
- *Video analysis*: Analyse recordings of your own lessons to evaluate both verbal and non-verbal communication, using the Interpersonal Circle framework (Activities 4.1 and 4.2, as well as various activities in Chapters 8 and 9).
- *Informal conversations*: Engage in regular, spontaneous discussions with mentors, colleagues and students to share insights and strategies for improving teacher-student relationships.

Research in this area suggests that intensive training in observing teaching fragments (such as through virtual environments) can reduce teacher anxiety, boost confidence, and lead to more reflective and well-founded evaluations.[24] For example, when theory is combined with virtual scenarios, it helps student teachers better understand, interpret, and quickly resolve classroom situations.

What Are Learning Approaches Among Student Teachers?

Research identifies four main approaches that student teachers adopt during placements:

- *Knowledge-oriented*: These students primarily seek knowledge and theory, looking to experts for guidance on classroom management and fostering good relationships with students. They are proactive and focused on developing new behaviours.
- *Feedback-oriented*: Like the knowledge-oriented approach, this approach also involves seeking content and theory with an active, developmental mindset. However, in this case, students rely more on their school mentors and teacher educators for feedback and as a sounding board.
- *Inspiration-oriented*: These students actively seek knowledge and theory but view their school mentors more as role models and sources of inspiration. Their approach tends to be more reflective, focusing on reviewing past experiences.
- *Practice-oriented*: In this more passive approach, students primarily seek simple tips and advice. They rely on school mentors as role models and sources of inspiration but are less actively engaged in seeking theory or knowledge.

The first three approaches generally result in faster and more growth compared to the practice-oriented approach.

How Can Experienced Teachers Develop?

Even experienced teachers can benefit from observing their colleagues to identify behaviours and strategies that foster better relationships. Effective observation involves paying attention to *non-verbal communication* (see the overview in Chapter 7), such as:

- Body posture.
- Facial expressions, gestures, eye contact with students.
- Physical proximity to students.
- Utilisation of available space.
- Non-linguistic aspects of speech, such as volume, intonation, pauses, and pitch.

When analysing *verbal communication*, consider:

- Approving or disapproving tone.
- Questioning or directing style.
- Addressing students clearly.
- Using concise or expansive language.

From an interpersonal perspective, it is important to assess where the teacher would be placed on the two dimensions of the *Interpersonal Circle*:

- Agency.
- Communion.

While almost all *classroom situations* can be evaluated in this way, certain situations (as detailed in Chapter 10) are particularly important. These include:

- Starting the lesson.
- Transitions between different lesson elements.
- Providing instructions.
- Managing classroom disruptions or unexpected student behaviour.

To observe, you can use the observation forms 8.1 for rewarding, 8.5 for redirecting, and 11.1 for non-verbal behaviours.

Long-term, intensive interpersonal behaviour training has been shown to significantly improve classroom climates. However, this process requires patience.[25] Though in the first year of training, teachers initially became more uncertain and exhibited less Agency, in the following year, they showed substantial growth in Agency and Communion.

Classroom climates tend to be stable and changes in teacher behaviour (e.g., showing less anger or less insecurity) may not immediately alter student perceptions of their relationship with the teacher. Selective attention plays a role here, as students may seek confirmation of their existing opinions of the teacher. Therefore, when a negative classroom climate is deeply ingrained, a fresh start with a new class, combined with thorough preparation, support, and targeted practice, may be more effective. For example, ingrained patterns—such as repeated escalation during transitions like walking to gym class—may be significantly reduced, in a new classroom setting.

In Sum

The Interpersonal Circle with its dimensions Agency and Communion provides a way to describe interpersonal communication in classrooms worldwide.

Students in all cultures tend to score their teachers in the upper-right quadrant of the Interpersonal Circle, and this position is widely considered the most desirable.

Students who perceive their teacher high on Agency and Communion tend to thrive. Students of teachers who are clear about expectations and provide structured guidance (high on Agency), are more task-oriented and perform better. Students' motivation and interest are higher when teachers show friendly and understanding behaviour.

A strong teacher-student relationship enhances teachers' job satisfaction, confidence, and emotional well-being.

Teacher gender, subject taught, school type, and class size are related to student perceptions of the teacher-student relationships. The differences in perceptions represent subtle nuances rather than drastic variations and tend to be far smaller than differences between individual teachers.

Student gender, age, and ethnic background have a minor association with their perceptions of the teacher-student relationships.

Good interpersonal behaviour is learnable for (student) teachers.

Notes

1. Wubbels et al. (2006, 2023), Roorda et al. (2011, 2017), Spilt et al. (2011), Quin (2017).
2. Hendrickx et al. (2017).
3. Den Brok et al. (2010); Sanders and Wiseman (1990).
4. Den Brok (2001); Van der Lans et al. (2020).
5. Spilt et al. (2011).
6. Donker et al. (2020).
7. Horowitz and Strack (2010).
8. Den Brok and van Tartwijk (2015), Wubbels et al. (2023).
9. Maulana et al. (2012), Den Brok and van Tartwijk (2015), Wubbels et al. (2023).
10. Wubbels (1993).
11. Sun et al. (2019).

12 Maulana et al. (2012).
13 Den Brok and van Tartwijk (2015).
14 den Brok et al. (2010).
15 Den Brok and van Tartwijk (2015).
16 den Brok et al. (2010).
17 Den Brok and van Tartwijk (2015).
18 Levy et al. (1996).
19 Levy et al. (1996, 2003).
20 McCroskey et al. (1996), Neuliep (1995).
21 Wubbels et al. (2023).
22 Créton and Wubbels (1984).
23 Adams (2023).
24 Theelen (2021).
25 Van Amelsfoort (1999).

Appendix 4.1
The QTI for Secondary Education

Below are 24 statements about your teacher. For each statement, please select the option that best reflects your opinion by marking the corresponding circle.

		Completely disagree				Completely agree
1.	This teacher is a good leader	O	O	O	O	O
2.	This teacher is someone you can depend on	O	O	O	O	O
3.	This teacher is patient	O	O	O	O	O
4.	This teacher lets students get away with a lot	O	O	O	O	O
5.	This teacher's discipline is weak	O	O	O	O	O
6.	This teacher is dissatisfied	O	O	O	O	O
7.	This teacher gets angry quickly	O	O	O	O	O
8.	This teacher controls when students can speak	O	O	O	O	O
9.	This teacher is respected	O	O	O	O	O
10.	This teacher has a sense of humour	O	O	O	O	O
11.	This teacher is understanding	O	O	O	O	O
12.	This teacher can be influenced by us	O	O	O	O	O
13.	This teacher is uncertain	O	O	O	O	O
14.	This teacher is grumpy	O	O	O	O	O
15.	This teacher threatens to punish students	O	O	O	O	O
16.	This teacher imposes silence in class	O	O	O	O	O
17.	This teacher acts confidently	O	O	O	O	O
18.	This teacher's class is pleasant	O	O	O	O	O

(continued)

Below are 24 statements about your teacher. For each statement, please select the option that best reflects your opinion by marking the corresponding circle.

		Completely disagree				Completely agree
19.	This teacher is easy-going	O	O	O	O	O
20.	This teacher tolerates a lot of student behaviour	O	O	O	O	O
21.	This teacher is hesitant	O	O	O	O	O
22.	This teacher is unhappy	O	O	O	O	O
23.	This teacher gets angry unexpectedly	O	O	O	O	O
24.	This teacher is strict	O	O	O	O	O

Displaying the Scores in the Interpersonal Circle for the Teacher

After completing the questionnaire, assign numerical values to the selected responses according to the following key:

Completely disagree				Completely agree
O	O	O	O	O
0	1	2	3	4

Next, add up the numerical values assigned to the responses for the following questions, then divide the total by 3:

Question 1, 9 and 17 = ...Directing
Question 2, 10 and 18 = ...Helping
Question 3, 11 and 19 = ...Understanding
Question 4, 12 and 20 = ...Compliant
Question 5, 13 and 21 = ...Uncertain
Question 6, 14 and 22 = ...Dissatisfied
Question 7, 15 and 23 = ...Confrontational
Question 8, 16 and 24 = ...Imposing

The eight scores can then be plotted on the Interpersonal Circle for the Teacher below. For example: if the score for Directing is 2, draw a straight line (or even better, a curved line) from the second mark on the Agency axis to the second mark between Directing and Helping. Similarly, if the score for Helping is 3, start at the third mark on the Communion axis and connect it to the third mark on the line between Helping and Directing. Repeat this process for each total score, placing them in the corresponding sectors.

174 Appendix 4.1

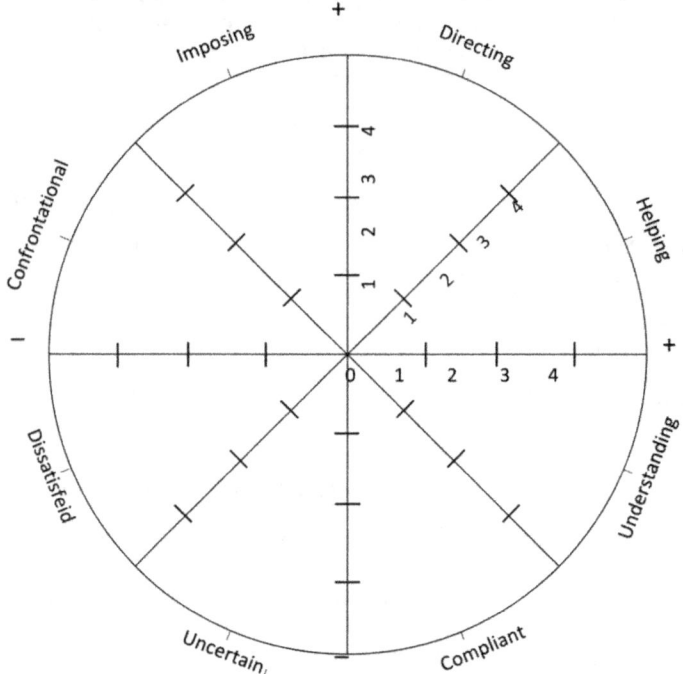

Disclaimer

This questionnaire is intended for personal reflection. The 24 statements and their results are not meant for formal evaluation or judgment.

Appendix 4.2
The QTI for Primary Education

Below are 16 statements about your teacher. For each statement, please select the option that best reflects your opinion by marking the corresponding circle.

		Completely disagree				*Completely agree*
1.	This teacher is a good leader	O	O	O	O	O
2.	This teacher's class is pleasant	O	O	O	O	O
3.	This teacher is patient	O	O	O	O	O
4.	This teacher lets students get away with a lot	O	O	O	O	O
5.	This teacher's discipline is weak	O	O	O	O	O
6.	This teacher is unhappy	O	O	O	O	O
7.	This teacher gets angry quickly	O	O	O	O	O
8.	This teacher controls when students can speak	O	O	O	O	O
9.	This teacher is respected	O	O	O	O	O
10.	This teacher has a sense of humour	O	O	O	O	O
11.	This teacher is understanding	O	O	O	O	O
12.	This teacher tolerates a lot of student behaviour	O	O	O	O	O
13.	This teacher is hesitant	O	O	O	O	O
14.	This teacher is grumpy	O	O	O	O	O
15.	This teacher threatens to punish students	O	O	O	O	O
16.	This teacher is strict	O	O	O	O	O

Displaying the Scores in the Interpersonal Circle for the Teacher

After completing the questionnaire, assign numerical values to the selected responses according to the following key:

Completely disagree				Completely agree
○	○	○	○	○
0	1	2	3	4

Next, add up the numerical values assigned to the responses for the following questions, then divide the total by 2:

Question 1 and 9 = ...Directing
Question 2 and 10 = ...Helping
Question 3 and 11 = ...Understanding
Question 4 and 12 = ...Compliant
Question 5 and 13 = ...Uncertain
Question 6 and 14 = ...Dissatisfied
Question 7 and 15 = ...Confrontational
Question 8 and 16 = ...Imposing

The eight scores can then be plotted on the Interpersonal Circle for the Teacher below. For example: if the score for Directing is 2, draw a straight line (or even better, a curved line) from the second mark on the Agency axis to the second mark between Directing and Helping. Similarly, if the score for Helping is 3, start at the third mark on the Communion axis and connect it to the third mark on the line between Helping and Directing. Repeat this process for each total score, placing them in the corresponding sectors.

Appendix 4.2

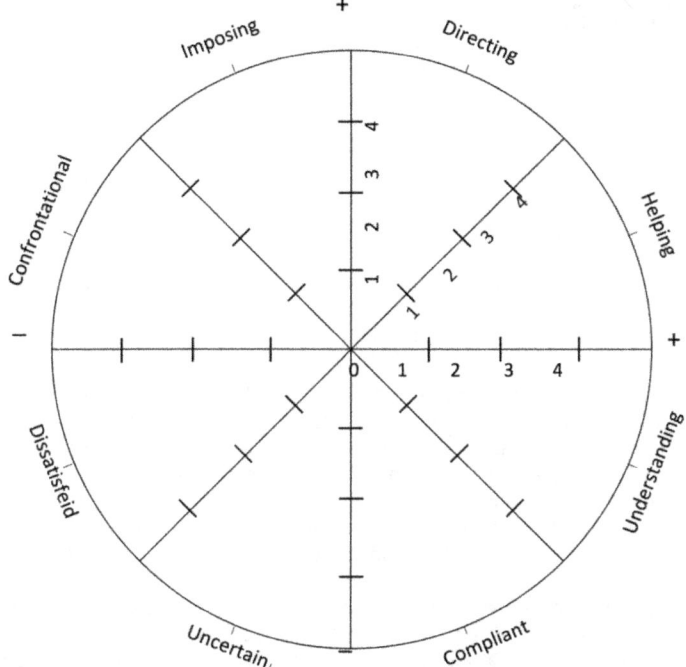

Disclaimer

This questionnaire is intended for personal reflection. The 16 statements and their results are not meant for formal evaluation or judgment.

References

Adams, T. (2023). *Learning to navigate classroom dynamics: studying student teachers' classroom management learning during their teacher education internship* [Doctoral dissertation, Wageningen University and Research]. Education and Learning Sciences (ELS). http://edepot.wur.nl/591327

Admiraal, W.F. (1994). *Reacties van docenten op aandachteisende situaties in de klas* [Teacher responses to attention demanding situations in class, doctoral dissertation, Universiteit Utrecht]. W.C.C.

Admiraal, W.F., Wubbels, T., & Korthagen, F.A.J. (1996). Student teacher behaviour in response to daily hassles in the classroom. *Social Psychology of Education*, 1(1), 25-46. https://doi.org/10.1007/bf02333404

Andersen, J.F. (1979). The relation between teacher immediacy and teacher effectiveness. In D. Nimmo (Ed.), *Communication yearbook 3* (pp. 543-559). Transaction Books.

Andersen, P., & Andersen, J.F. (1982). Nonverbal immediacy in instruction. In L.L. Barker (Ed.), *Communication in the classroom* (pp. 98-120). Prentice-Hall.

Bateson, G. (1958). *Naven; A survey of the problems suggested by a composite picture of the culture of a New Guinea tribe drawn from three points of view*. Stanford University Press.

Bennett, T. (2020). *Running the room: the teacher's guide to behaviour*. John Catt Educational Ltd.

Blatt, S.J., & Luyten, P. (2010). Relatedness and self-definition in normal and disrupted personality development. In L.M. Horowitz & S. Strack (Eds.), *Handbook of interpersonal psychology: Theory, research, assessment, and therapeutic interventions* (pp. 37-56). John Wiley & Sons. https://doi.org/10.1002/9781118001868.ch3

Bondy, E., & Ross, D.D. (2008). The teacher as warm demander. *Educational Leadership*, 66, 54-58. https://doi.org/10.1037/e517642009-020

Brekelmans, M. (1989). *Interpersoonlijk gedrag van docenten in de klas* [Teacher interpersonal behaviour in class, doctoral dissertation, Universiteit Utrecht]. W.C.C.

Brekelmans, M. (2010). *Klimaatverandering in de klas* [Climate change in class]. Universiteit Utrecht. https://dspace.library.uu.nl/handle/1874/44903

Brekelmans, M., Wubbels, T., & van Tartwijk, J. (2005). Teacher-student relationships across the teaching career. *International Journal of Educational Research*, 43(1-2), 55-71. https://doi.org/10.1016/j.ijer.2006.03.006

Burgoon, J.K., Manusov, V., & Guerrero, L.K. (2022). *Nonverbal communication* (2nd ed.). Routledge. https://doi.org/10.4324/9781003095552

Chang, M.L., & Taxer, J. (2021). Teacher emotion regulation strategies in response to classroom misbehavior. *Teachers and Teaching*, 27(5), 353-369. https://doi.org/10.1080/13540602.2020.1740198

Chen, G.M., & Starosta, W.J. (2003). Asian approaches to human communication: A dialogue. *Intercultural Communication Studies*, 12(4), 1-15.

Chuang, Y.C. (2005). Effects of interaction pattern on family harmony and well-being: Test of interpersonal theory, relational-models theory, and Confucian ethics. *Asian Journal of Social Psychology*, 8(3), 272-291. https://doi.org/10.1111/j.1467-839x.2005.00174.x

Claessens, L. (2016). *Be on my side, I'll be on your side: Teachers' perceptions of teacher-student relationships* [Doctoral dissertation, Universiteit Utrecht]. Utrecht University Repository.

Créton, H.A., & Wubbels, T. (1984). *Ordeproblemen bij beginnende leraren* [Discipline problems of beginning teachers, doctoral dissertation, Universiteit Utrecht]. W.C.C

Crone, D.A., Hawken, L.S., & Horner, R.H. (2015). *Building positive behavior support systems in schools*. Guilford Press.

De Jong, R. (2013). *Student teachers' practical knowledge, discipline strategies, and the teacher-class relationship* [Doctoral dissertation, Universiteit Leiden]. ICLON. https://hdl.handle.net/1887/20734

Deci, E.L., Koestner, R., & Ryan, R.M. (2001). Extrinsic rewards and intrinsic motivation in education: Reconsidered once again. *Review of Educational Research*, 71(1), 1-27. https://doi.org/10.3102/00346543071001001

Den Brok, P. (2001). *Teaching and student outcomes: A study on teachers' thoughts and actions from an interpersonal and a learning activities perspective* [Doctoral dissertation Universiteit Utrecht]. W.C.C. https://Alexandria.tue.nl/openaccess/metis211815.pdf

Den Brok, P., & van Tartwijk, J. (2015). Teacher-student interpersonal communication in international education. In M. Hayden, J. Levy, & J.J. Thompson (Eds.), *The SAGE handbook of research in international education* (pp. 309-324). Sage.

Den Brok, P., van Tartwijk, J., Wubbels, T., & Veldman, I. (2010). The differential effect of the teacher-student interpersonal relationship on student outcomes for students with different ethnic backgrounds. *British Journal of Educational Psychology*, 80(2), 199-221. https://doi.org/10.1348/000709909x465632

Donker, M.H. (2020). *In DEPTh: Dynamics of emotional processes in teachers–An exploration of teachers' interpersonal behavior and physiological responses* [Doctoral dissertation, Universiteit Utrecht]. Utrecht University Repository. https://Dspace.library.uu.nl/handle/1874/400084

Donker, M.H., van Gog, T., Goetz, T., Roos, A.L., & Mainhard, T. (2020). Associations between teachers' interpersonal behavior, physiological arousal, and lesson-focused emotions. *Contemporary Educational Psychology*, 63, 101906. https://doi.org/10.1016/j.cedpsych.2020.101906

Doyle, W. (1986). Classroom organization and management. In M.C. Wittrock (Ed.), *Handbook of research on teaching* (3rd ed., pp. 392-431). McMillan.

Doyle, W. (2006). Ecological approaches to classroom management. In C.M. Evertson & C.S. Weinstein (Eds.), *Handbook of classroom management: Research, practice, and contemporary issues* (pp. 97-126). Lawrence Erlbaum Associates.

Ekman, P., & Friesen, W.V. (2003). *Unmasking the face: A guide to recognizing emotions from facial clues*. Malor Books.

Elias, M., & Schwab, Y. (2006). From compliance to responsibility: Social and emotional learning and classroom management. In C.M. Evertson & C.S. Weinstein (Eds.), *Handbook of classroom management: Research, practice, and contemporary issues* (pp. 309-342). Lawrence Erlbaum Associates.

Endedijk, H.M., Breeman, L.D., van Lissa, C.J., Hendrickx, M.M.H.G., den Boer, L., & Mainhard, T. (2022). The teacher's invisible hand: A meta-analysis of the relevance of teacher–student relationship quality for peer relationships and the contribution of student behavior. *Review of Educational Research*, 92(3), 370-412. https://doi.org/10.3102/00346543211051428

Evertson, C.M., & Weinstein, C.S. (2006). Classroom management as a field of inquiry. In C.M. Evertson & C.S. Weinstein (Eds.), *Handbook of classroom management: Research, practice, and contemporary issues* (pp. 3-16). Lawrence Erlbaum Associates.

Fox, L., Carta, J., Strain, P.S., Dunlap, G., & Hemmeter, M.L. (2010). Response to intervention and the pyramid model. *Infants & Young Children*, 23(1), 3-13. https://doi.org/10.1097/iyc.0b013e3181c816e2

Gifford, R. (2010). The role of nonverbal communication in interpersonal relations. In L.M. Horowitz, & S. Strack (Eds.), *Handbook of interpersonal psychology: Theory, research, assessment, and therapeutic interventions* (pp. 171-190). John Wiley & Sons.

Gordon, T., & Burch, N. (1974). *TET teacher effectiveness training*. David McKay Company.

Green, R.W. (2008). *Lost at school: Why our kids with behavioral challenges are falling through the cracks and how we can help them*. Scribner.

Hendrickx, M.M.H.G. (2017). *The role of the teacher in classroom peer relations* [Doctoral dissertation, Universiteit Utrecht]. Utrecht University Repository. https://Research.portal.uu.nl/publications/the-role-of-the-teacher-in-classroom-peer-relations

Hendrickx, M.M.H.G., Mainhard, M.T., Boor-Klip, H.J., Cillessen, A.H.N., & Brekelmans, M. (2016). Social dynamics in the classroom: Teacher support and conflict and the peer ecology. *Teaching and Teacher Education*, 53, 30-40. https://doi.org/10.1016/j.tate.2015.10.004

Hendrickx, M.M.H.G., Mainhard, T., Boor-Klip, H.J., & Brekelmans, M. (2017). Teacher liking as an affective filter for the association between student behavior and peer status. *Contemporary Educational Psychology*, 49, 250-262. https://doi.org/10.1016/j.cedpsych.2017.03.004

Hickey, D., & Schafer, N.J. (2006). Design-based, participation-centered approaches to classroom management. In C.M. Evertson & C.S. Weinstein (Eds.), *Handbook of classroom management: Research, practice, and contemporary issues* (pp. 281-308). Lawrence Erlbaum Associates.

Horowitz, L.M., & Strack, S. (2010). Introduction. In L.M. Horowitz & S. Strack (Eds.), *Handbook of interpersonal psychology: Theory, research, assessment, and therapeutic interventions* (pp. 1-14). John Wiley & Sons. https://doi.org/10.1002/9781118001868.ch1

Kiesler, D.J. (1983). The 1982 interpersonal circle: a taxonomy for complementarity in human transactions. *Psychological Review, 90*, 185-214. https://doi.org/10.1037//0033-295x.90.3.185

Landrum, T.M., & Kauffmann, J. (2006). Behavioural approaches to classroom management. In C.M. Evertson & C.S. Weinstein (Eds.), *Handbook of classroom management: Research, practice, and contemporary issues* (pp. 47-72). Lawrence Erlbaum Associates.

Lane, K.L., Baldy, T., Becker, T., Bradshaw, C., Dolan, V., McIntosh, K., Nese, R., Payno-Simmons, R., Sutherland, K., Dymnicki, A., Freeman, B., Lemire, S., Moulton, S., Porowski, A., & Holian, L. (2024). *Teacher-delivered behavioral interventions in grades K-5. A practice guide for educators.* WWC 2025001. What Works Clearinghouse.

Leary, T. (1957). *An interpersonal diagnosis of personality*. Ronald Press Company.

Levy, J., Créton, H., & Wubbels, T. (1993). Perceptions of interpersonal teacher behavior. In T. Wubbels & J. Levy (Eds.), *Do you know what you look like? Interpersonal relationships in education* (pp. 29-45). Falmer Press. https://doi.org/10.4324/9780203975565

Levy, J., Wubbels, T., & Brekelmans, M. (1996) *Cultural factors in students' and teachers' perceptions of the learning environment.* Paper presented at the annual meeting of the American Educational Research Association, San Francisco.

Levy, J., Wubbels, T., den Brok, P., & Brekelmans, M. (2003). Students' perceptions of teacher interpersonal aspects of the learning environment. *Learning Environments Research, 6*(1), 5-36. https://doi.org/10.1023/a:1022967927037

Lewin, K. (1952). *Field theory in social science: Selected theoretical papers*. Tavistock.

Lizdek, I., Sadler, P., Woody, E., Ethier, N., & Malet, G. (2012). Capturing the stream of behavior: A computer-joystick method for coding interpersonal behavior continuously over time. *Social Science Computer Review, 30*(4), 513-521. https://doi.org/10.1177/0894439312436487

Lonner, W.J. (1980). The search for psychological universals. In H.C. Triandis & W.W. Lambert (Eds.), *Handbook of cross cultural psychology* (vol. 1, pp. 143-204). Allyn and Bacon.

Mainhard, M.T. (2009). *Time consistency in teacher-class relationships* [Doctoral dissertation, Universiteit Utrecht]. Utrecht University Repository. https://Research.portal.uu.nl/publications/time-consistency-in-teacher-class-relationships

Mainhard, M.T., Brekelmans, M., den Brok, P., & Wubbels, T. (2011a). The development of the classroom social climate during the first months of the school year. *Contemporary Educational Psychology, 36*(3), 190-200. https://doi.org/10.1016/j.cedpsych.2010.06.002

Mainhard, M.T., Brekelmans, M., & Wubbels, T. (2011b). Coercive and supportive teacher behaviour: Within- and across-lessons associations with the classroom social climate. *Learning and Instruction, 21*(3), 345-354. https://doi.org/10.1016/j.learninstruc.2010.03.003

Maulana, R., Opdenakker, M.C.J.L., den Brok, P., & Bosker, R. J. (2012). Teacher-student interpersonal relationships in Indonesian lower secondary education: Teacher and student perceptions. *Learning Environments Research, 15*, 251-271. https://doi.org/10.1007/s10984-012-9113-7

McCroskey, J.C., Fayer, J.M., Richmond, V.P., Sallinen, A., & Barraclough, R.A. (1996). A multi-cultural examination of the relationship between nonverbal immediacy and affective learning. *Communication Quarterly, 44*(3), 297-307. https://doi.org/10.1080/01463379609370019

Neuliep, J. (1995). *Human communication theory: Applications and case studies*. Pearson College Division.

Palk, K., Leijen, Ä., Baucal, A., & Lepp, L. (2024). Adaptation and evaluation of an Estonian version of the Questionnaire on Teacher Interaction (QTI). *Learning Environments Research, 27*(3), 557-578. https://doi.org/10.1007/s10984-023-09491-9

Passini, S., Molinari, L., & Speltini, G. (2015). A validation of the questionnaire on teacher interaction in Italian secondary school students: The effect of positive relations on motivation and academic achievement. *Social Psychology of Education, 18*(3), 547-559. https://doi.org/10.1007/s11218-015-9300-3

Pennings, H.J.M. (2017). *Interpersonal dynamics in teacher-student interactions and relationships* [Doctoral dissertation Universiteit Utrecht]. Ipskamp. https://Dspace.library.uu.nl/handle/1874/351050

Pennings, H.J.M., Brekelmans, M., Sadler, P., Claessens, L.C.A., van der Want, A.C., & van Tartwijk, J. (2018). Interpersonal adaptation in teacher-student interaction. *Learning and Instruction*, 55, 41-57. https://doi.org/10.1016/j.learninstruc.2017.09.005

Pennings, H.J.M., van Tartwijk, J., Wubbels, T., Claessens, L.C.A., van der Want, A.C., & Brekelmans, M. (2014). Real-time teacher-student interactions: A dynamic systems approach. *Teaching and Teacher Education*, 37, 183-193. https://doi.org/10.1016/j.tate.2013.07.016

Pianta, R.C., & Hamre, B.K. (2001). *Banking time: Pre-K manual*. The Center for Advanced Study of Teaching and Learning at the University of Virginia.

Polderdijk, S., Henrichs, L.F., & van Tartwijk, J. (2025). Warm and demanding teacher practices reviewed from an interpersonal perspective: A qualitative synthesis of urban classroom management. *Teaching and Teacher Education*, 155, 104898. https://doi.org/10.1016/j.tate.2024.104898

Quin, D. (2017). Longitudinal and contextual associations between teacher-student relationships and student engagement. *Review of Educational Research*, 87(2), 345-387. https://doi.org/10.3102/0034654316669434

Roorda, D.L., Jak, S., Zee, M., Oort, F.J., & Koomen, H.M.Y. (2017). Affective teacher-student relationships and students' engagement and achievement: A meta-analytic update and test of the mediating role of engagement. *School Psychology Review*, 46(3), 239-261. https://doi.org/10.17105/spr-2017-0035.v46-3

Roorda, D. L., Koomen, H.M.Y., Spilt, J.L., & Oort, F.J. (2011). The influence of affective teacher-student relationships on students' school engagement and achievement. *Review of Educational Research*, 81(4), 493-529. https://doi.org/10.3102/0034654311421793

Ryan, R.M., & Deci, E.L. (2000). Self-determination theory and the facilitation of intrinsic motivation, social development, and well-being. *American Psychologist*, 55(1), 68-78. https://doi.org/10.1037//0003-066x.55.1.68

Sanders, J.A., & Wiseman, R.L. (1990) The effects of verbal and nonverbal teacher immediacy on perceived cognitive, affective and behavioral learning in the multicultural classroom. *Communication Education*, 39(4), 341-353. https://doi.org/10.1080/03634529009378814

Scott, T.M., Anderson, C.M., & Alter, P. (Eds.). (2012). *Managing classroom behavior using positive behavior supports*. Pearson.

Spilt, J.L., Koomen, H.M.Y., & Thijs, J.T. (2011). Teacher wellbeing: The importance of teacher-student relationships. *Educational Psychology Review*, 23, 457-477. https://doi.org/10.1007/s10648-011-9170-y

Sullivan, H.S. (Ed.). (2013). *The interpersonal theory of psychiatry*. Routledge. https://doi.org/10.4324/9781315014029

Sun, X. (2019). *Teacher-Student Interpersonal Relationships in Chinese Secondary Education Classrooms* [Doctoral dissertation, Universiteit Utrecht]. Utrecht University Repository. https://Research.portal.uu.nl/publications/teacher-student-interpersonal-relationships-in-chinese-seondary

Sun, X., Mainhard, T., & Wubbels, T. (2018). Development and evaluation of a Chinese version of the Questionnaire on Teacher Interaction (QTI). *Learning Environments Research*, 21(1), 1-17. https://doi.org/10.1007/s10984-017-9243-z

Sun, X., Pennings, H.J.M., Mainhard, T., & Wubbels, T. (2019). Teacher interpersonal behavior in the context of positive teacher-student interpersonal relationships in East Asian classrooms: Examining the applicability of western findings. *Teaching and Teacher Education*, 86, 102898. https://doi.org/10.1016/j.tate.2019.102898

Theelen, H. (2021). *Looking around in the classroom: developing preservice teachers' interpersonal competence with classroom simulations*. [Doctoral dissertation, Wageningen University & Research]. Education and Learning Sciences (ELS). https://Edepot.wur.nl/539846

Timmermans, A.C., Rubie-Davies, C.M., & Rjosk, C. (2018). Pygmalion's 50th anniversary: The state of the art in teacher expectation research. *Educational Research and Evaluation*, 24(3-5), 91-98. https://doi.org/10.1080/13803611.2018.1548785

Van Amelsfoort, J. (1999). *Perspectief op instructie, motivatie en zelfregulatie*. [Perspective on instruction, motivation and self-regulation; in Dutch)]. [Doctoral dissertation, Radboud University Nijmegen]. Nijmegen University Press.

Van der Lans, R.M., Cremers, J., Klugkist, I., & Zwart, R. (2020). Teachers' interpersonal relationships and instructional expertise: How are they related? *Studies in Educational Evaluation*, 66, 100902. https://doi.org/10.1016/j.stueduc.2020.100902

Van der Want, A.C. (2015). *Teachers' interpersonal role identity* [Unpublished doctoral dissertation, Universiteit Eindhoven]. ESoE. https://Pure.tue.nl/ws/files/80915502/20171117_want.pdf

Van Tartwijk, J. (1993). *Docentgedrag in beeld: De interpersoonlijke betekenis van nonverbaal gedrag van docenten in de klas* [A View of the teacher: The interpersonal meaning of non-verbal teacher classroom behaviour, doctoral dissertation Universiteit Utrecht]. W.C.C.

Van Tartwijk, J., Brekelmans, M., Wubbels, T., Fisher, D.L., & Fraser, B.J. (1998). Students' perceptions of teacher interpersonal style: The front of the classroom as the teacher's stage. *Teaching and Teacher Education, 14*(6), 607-617. https://doi.org/10.1016/s0742-051x(98)00011-0

Van Tartwijk, J., Wubbels, T., Brekelmans, M., & Mainhard, T. (2010). *Teacher nonverbal behavior and student perceptions of teacher interpersonal styles*. ICLON. Paper presented at the Annual Meeting of the American Educational Research Association, Denver CO.

Van Tartwijk, J., Zwart, R., & Wubbels, T. (2017). Developing teachers' competences with the focus on adaptive expertise in teaching. In J. Husu & J.D. Clandinin (Eds), *The SAGE handbook of research on teacher education* (pp. 820-835). Sage. https://doi.org/10.4135/9781526402042.n47

Veldman, I.M.J. (2017). *Stay or leave?: Veteran teachers' relationships with students and job satisfaction* [Doctoral dissertation, Universiteit Leiden]. ICLON. https://Scholarlypublications.universiteitleiden.nl/handle/1887/57992

Watzlawick, P., Beavin, J.H., & Jackson, D.D. (1967). *The pragmatics of human communication*. Norton.

Watzlawick, P., Weakland, J.H., & Fisch, R. (1974). *Change: Principles of problem formulation and problem resolution*. Norton.

Wei, M., den Brok, P., & Zhou, Y. (2009). Teacher interpersonal behaviour and student outcomes in English as a Foreign Language classrooms in China. *Learning Environments Research, 12*(3), 157-174. https://doi.org/10.1007/s10984-009-9059-6

Woolfolk, A.E., & Brooks, D.M. (1985). The influence of teachers' nonverbal behaviors on students' perceptions and performance. *The Elementary School Journal, 85*(4), 513-528. https://doi.org/10.1086/461418

Wubbels, T. (1993). *Teacher-student relationships in science and mathematics classes*. What Research Says to the Science and Mathematics, number 11. Curtin University of Technology.

Wubbels, T. (2011). An international perspective on classroom management: What should prospective teachers learn? *Teaching Education, 22*(2), 113-131. https://doi.org/10.1080/10476210.2011.567838

Wubbels, T., Brekelmans, M., den Brok, P., Levy, J., Mainhard, T., & van Tartwijk, J. (2012). Let's make things better: Development in research on interpersonal relationships in education. In T. Wubbels, P. den Brok, J. van Tartwijk, & J. Levy (Eds.), *Interpersonal relationships in education: An overview of contemporary research* (pp. 225-250). Sense Publishers.

Wubbels, T., Brekelmans, M., den Brok, P., & van Tartwijk, J. (2006). An interpersonal perspective on classroom management in secondary classrooms in the Netherlands. In C. M. Evertson & C. S. Weinstein (Eds.), *Handbook of classroom management: Research, practice, and contemporary issues* (pp. 1161-1191). Lawrence Erlbaum Associates. https://doi.org/10.4324/9780203874783.ch45

Wubbels, T., Brekelmans, M., den Brok, P., Wijsman, L., Mainhard, T., & van Tartwijk, J. (2014). Teacher-student relationships and classroom management. In E.T. Emmer & E.J. Sabornie (Eds), *Handbook of classroom management* (2nd ed., pp. 363-386). Routledge.

Wubbels, T., Créton, H.A., & Hooymayers, H.P. (1985). *Discipline problems of beginning teachers: interactional teacher behavior mapped out*. Paper presented at the annual meeting of the American Educational Research Association, Chicago.

Wubbels, T., Mainhard, T., den Brok, P., Claessens, L., & van Tartwijk, J. (2023). Classroom management at different time scales: an interpersonal perspective. In E. Sabornie & D. Espelage (Eds.), *Handbook of classroom management: Research, practice, and issues* (3rd ed., pp. 388-414). Routledge. https://doi.org/10.4324/9781003275312-25

Zijlstra, H., Wubbels, T., Brekelmans, M., & Koomen, H.M.Y. (2013). Child perceptions of teacher interpersonal behavior and associations with mathematics achievement in Dutch early grade classrooms. *The Elementary School Journal, 113*(4), 517-540. https://doi.org/10.1086/669618

Index

Pages in *italics* refer to figures and pages followed by n refer to notes.

academic tasks 138, 158-160
Adams, T. 7, 171n23
Admiraal, W.F. 7, 122n*
affection 27
age *see* student: age, teacher: age
agency: change in 65-72; and class characteristics 166; with communion 31-32, 77-81, 109; and complementarity 76; and countries *see* and cultures; and cultures 76-77, 161-165; defined 27; in interpersonal circle 30, *35*, 37; and non-verbal 92-95; observing 38-39; in QTI 45; and student characteristics 167; and student ethnicity 165-166; and student initiative 85; and student outcomes 158-160; and teacher characteristics 167; and teacher satisfaction 160; and teaching methods 33; in whole-class teaching 141-155
Andersen, J.F. 98n1
Andersen, P. 98n1
appreciation 100-103, 121; *see also* rewards
assertive 27, 96; defined *30*
authority 27, 62-64
autonomy 15-16
awareness 23, 26, 29, 92, 97, 114-115, 123, 165

Bateson, G. 87n2
behaviour: content aspect of 25, 29, 35; defined 11; desirable 14, 102, 121; disruptive 11, 99, 114, 116-117, 122, 124, 126-127, 129-130, 135, 137; dysfunctional 32-33; extreme 32, 66, 90, 137, 157; functional 32-33, 83, 90; momentary 12, 34; relationship aspect of 25-26, 29, 158; repertoire 33, 63-64, 100, 103, 121, 145; undesirable 14, 99-100, 105-106, 115

beginning teachers *see* novice teachers
beliefs *see* teacher: thoughts
belongingness *see* relatedness
Bennett, T. 13, 18n3, 121n7
Blatt, S.J. 36n6
Bondy, E. 98n8
Brekelmans, M. 7, 69, *71*, 72n7-72n8
Brooks, D.M. 98n10
bullying 111, 159
Burch, N. 121n11
Burgoon, J.K. 36n8, 98n2

care 14, 27, 56, 67, 80, 96
challenging student behaviour 83-84, 101, 122, 132, 138, 140; disappointing performance and 133-134; disruptive behaviour and 124-130; emotional reactions to 122; personal remarks and 132-133; physical altercation and 136; student emotional expressions and 134-136; student remarks and 131-132
Chang, M.L. 140n1
Chen, G.M. 87n9
Chuang, Y.C. 87n1
Claessens, L. 7, 72n1
classroom atmosphere 4, 10, 12-13, 20, 27, 56, 58, 62, 67-68, 73, 100, 106, 115, 121-122, 125, 141-143; challenging 20; negative 17, 46, 61, 66, 170; positive *see* productive; productive 26, 75, 82-83, 97, 101, 124-125, 158; punitive 106; unfavourable 72
classroom climate *see* classroom atmosphere
classroom management: defined 12-13; approaches to 13-14
class size 166, 170

closeness 27, 32
communion: with agency 31-32, 77-81, 109; change in 65-72; and class characteristics 166; and complementarity 74-75; and countries see and cultures; and cultures 75, 161-165; defined 27; and gaining authority 62-64; in individual student relationships 53-55; in interpersonal circle 30, 35, 37; and non-verbal 88-92; observing 38-39; in QTI 45; and redirecting students 83-84, 86, 100-105, 113-114, 116, 118; and student characteristics 167; and student ethnicity 165-166; and student outcomes 158-160; and teacher characteristics 167; and teacher satisfaction 160; and teaching methods 33; in whole-class teaching 141-155
competence 15-16
competition 80, 106-107
complementarity 73; in agency 76-77; in the combination of agency and communion 77-81, 109; in communion 74-75; cultural nuances in 75-77; and escalation 139; mirroring 74, 77, 139; and negative interactions 113, 122; non-complementarity 123; and professional teacher behaviour 83-85; reciprocity 74-78, 83; and reinforcement 75, 78, 85; and special needs students 137-139
compliments see praise
conflict 54, 59, 78, 81, 109, 113, 123, 127, 133, 138
confrontation 32, 80-82, 84, 89, 96, 114, 119, 127, 136, 140; see also strictness and
consistency 52, 112, 127
content aspect see behaviour: content aspect of
context: cultural 75, 77, 90, 96, 146, 155, 162; (Non-)Western 4, 6, 57, 77, 83, 104; relational 53, 55
cooperative: defined 30
correcting student behaviour see redirecting student behaviour
country see culture
Créton, H.A. 7, 40, 70, 72n6, 171n22
Crone, D.A. 18n7, 121n6
cultural: background 10, 40, 42, 75, 163, 165-167; differences 6, 75, 77, 91, 158, 162-163, 166; diversity 165; norms and expectations 23, 75, 77, 90, 92, 96-97, 161-164; preferences 136
cultural context see context

culture 41, 75-77, 88-92, 96, 98, 102, 113, 146, 158, 161-163, 170; measure for 165

Deci, E.L. 15, 18n11, 121n3-121n4
De Jong, R. 7
Den Brok, P. 7, 36n4, 164, 170n3-170n4, 170n8-170n9, 170n13-170n14, 171n15-171n17
dimensions see interpersonal circle
directing student behaviour 33-34, 78, 99-100, 108-111, 121-122, 144, 148-149, 153, 163, 169
discipline 5, 13, 115-116, 146, 154, 166
disorder 2, 61-64, 68, 82, 86
disruptions 12-13, 15, 26, 52, 56, 59, 73, 83, 99-100, 105, 108, 110, 115, 124-126, 131, 143-144, 148, 151-152, 169; see also student disruptive behaviour; student problematic behaviour
diversity see cultural: diversity
Donker, M.H. 7, 170n6
Doyle, W. 10, 18n1, 18n9

Ekman, P. 98n5
Elias, M. 18n8
emotional labour 17, 161
emotion(s) 16, 21-24, 90-91, 97, 122-124, 135-136, 159-161, 166; transforming negative 123
encouragement 25, 30, 58, 67, 102-103, 106, 136, 150, 152; see also rewards
Endedijk, H.M. 121n10
engagement see student: engagement
engaging: activity 112, 143, 149; students 32, 122, 151
escalation 75, 80, 115, 124, 133-136, 139, 147, 170
ethnicity see student: ethnicity
experienced teacher 42, 62, 67-72, 144, 169
external behavioural control 13-14
Evertson, C.M. 12, 18n2

feedback 7, 40, 43, 55, 60, 63, 73, 100, 102-105, 121, 134-138, 158, 165, 168
first impression 65, 157
flow 19, 26, 78, 103, 110, 114, 124-126, 132, 141-144, 148
fondness 27
Fox, L. 139
Friesen, W.V. 98n5
Fuller F. 5

gender see student: gender, teacher: gender
Gifford, R. 98n4, 98n6

Gordon, T. 119, 121n11
Green., R.W. 140n3
group work 63, 102, 111, 142, 149-153

Hamre, B.K. 140n4
heart rate 22, 160-161
Hendrickx, M.M.H.G. 7, 47n4, 170n2
Hickey, D. 18n10
hierarchy: of interventions 115, 127, 129; of rewards 103
Horowitz, L.M. 36n1, 87n8, 170n7
human needs 15

informal conversations 138, 146, 168; see also informal interactions
instructional conversation 142, 151-152
intentions 21-24, 54, 57-58, 120
interactions: challenging 123; chains in 19-22; changing or improving 24, 34-35, 85-86; complementary 121; constructive, positive or productive 15, 23, 27, 73, 84, 105, 112, 118, 133, 138; defined 11; escalating 73, 75, 85, 133, 139; informal 141, 145-146, 155; location of 53, 55, 150; negative, strained or unwanted 53-54, 100, 124, 138; one-on-one 86, 117, 141-144
interpersonal: behaviour training and learning 167-170; circle 29-35, 39-43, 54-64, 70-74, 80, 83, 137, 141-142, 158-159, 162-163; climate 27, 40, 47, 166-167; meaning 28-29, 41, 75, 88-89, 95; message 11, 25-26, 28-30, 38, 88, 91, 95, 98, 118, 123; perspective 4, 9-12, 15, 17, 139, 144, 169; profile 43-44; style 12, 34, 42, 48-49, 67-72; theory 4, 8, 13, 19, 26, 28-29, 32; theory universal significance 4, 26, 162-163
interventions 84, 113-117, 120, 124-129, 139-140, 143, 147-151

Joystick method 39, 82

Kauffmann, J. 18n6
Kiesler, D.J. 87n3, 87n7
Kounin, J. S. 115

Landrum, T.M. 18n6
Lane, K.L 121n1
learning environment 4, 57-58, 78, 107, 124, 129, 135, 142, 157, 159
Leary, T. 19, 31, 36n2, 36n7

lesson: components 14; first 65-66, 72; starting a 145-147, 169; transitions in 153-154, 169; ending a 154-155, 169
Levy, J. 36n4, 171n18-171n19
Lewin, K. 18n4
Lonner, W.J. 36n7
Luyten, P. 36n6

McCroskey, J.C. 171n20
Mainhard, M.T. 7, 65, 72n5
Maulana, R. 72n2, 87n5, 98n7, 164, 170n9, 170n12
maintaining student behaviour 99-102, 115, 121, 144
misbehaviour see student: misbehaviour
moment-to-moment behaviour 34, 49
motivation see student: motivation
multicultural classrooms 4, 88, 91, 96, 158-159, 165-166

non-verbal behaviour see non-verbal communication
non-verbal cues see non-verbal communication
non-verbal communication: and agency 92-95; alignment verbal and 97-98, 119, 123; and body orientation 88-92; and body posture 25, 28, 57, 60-61, 78, 88-89, 92-96, 102, 108, 145, 150, 169; and calmness 92-94, 102; channels of 25, 88-89; combing verbal and 93, 102, 120, 126; and combination of signals 89, 92, 95; and communion 88-92; and emphasis 92, 94, 120; and eye contact 11, 25-26, 28, 57, 88-91, 96, 98, 102, 142, 145-146, 169; and facial expressions 25, 27-28, 51, 60, 88-92, 97-98, 118, 123, 169; and gestures 11, 25, 59-60, 88, 92-93, 95-98, 100, 109, 144, 146, 153, 169; and leaning 25, 88-89, 150; and non-linguistic aspects of speech 25, 88, 98, 169; and physical distance/proximity 25, 88-92, 96, 98, 169; and touch 89-90, 136, 150; and utilization of space 25, 88, 92-94, 97-98, 169; and voice 27-28, 60-61, 88-92, 98, 118, 144, 153
norms 11, 14, 109-112, 118, 138, 149, 155; see also cultural: norms and expectations
novice teachers 5, 8, 40, 42, 49, 62-64, 66-72, 127, 129, 142-143, 158

observation 7, 11, 43, 168-169
one-on-one relationships *see* relationships: one-on-one
oppositional: defined 30
order 13, 15, 25, 27, 73, 81, 108, 110-112, 115, 124-125, 129, 153, 156, 166
overlapping 115

pace 10, 61, 90-91, 132, 149
Palk, K. 164
Passini, S. 164
patience 53, 85, 122, 136, 139-140, 161, 169
passive: defined 30
pedagogy 5, 9, 15, 17, 33, 142-143, 149, 151, 156, 167
peer relationships *see* relationships
Pennings, H.J.M. 7, 39, 47n1, 82, 87n10
perception: *see* teacher and student 43, 46, 69, 165; determine responses 21, 50; differences in 56, 67-68, 166, 170; gap 69; student 22, 42, 50, 57, 65, 69, 155, 157-158, 162, 166, 170; teacher ideal 43-46, 68-70, 157, 163; teacher self- 22, 42-47, 50, 69
Pianta, R.C. 138, 140n4
Polderdijk, S. 98n8
Positive Behaviour Support 14, 107
power 27
practicing 6-7, 64, 66, 97, 115, 167-170
praise 34, 51, 63, 101-105, 110, 118-119, 155, 165; compliments 52, 125, 127, 133, 138, 150; and grades 102-103; *see also* appreciation; encouragement; rewards
procedures 14, 106, 136
professional teacher behaviour 33, 83, 85, 92, 97, 103, 123, 133
proximity *see* non-verbal communication: physical distance/proximity
punishment 116, 129-131

QTI (Questionnaire on Teacher Interaction): country differences 162-165; development 40-42; different language versions 41-42; excel scoring sheets 42; ideal 42; primary education version 42; in research 43-44, 46-47, 65-68, 70, 158, 162-168; scoring 43; secondary education version 42; self-perception 42; student perception 42
Quin, D. 170n1

reappraisal *see* emotion(s): transforming negative
reciprocity *see* complementarity: reciprocity
redirecting student behaviour 26, 32, 83-84, 88, 99, 105-129, 132, 134, 136, 140, 143-144, 149-151, 169
reinforcement 15, 26, 29-30, 50, 54, 56, 61, 73, 75, 78, 85-88, 91-93, 97, 99-106, 110, 113, 115, 133, 139, 152, 154-155
reinterpreting emotions *see* emotion(s): transforming negative
relatedness 15
relationship: aspect *see* behaviour: relationship aspect of; development 49-51, 64-70, 168; with entire class *see* teacher-class relationship; with individual students 11, 34, 48, 53, 56, 61; negative 17; one-on-one 53; peer 12, 117; quality 23, 73; *see also* classroom atmosphere: productive; positive 12, 15-17, 27, 34, 48, 53-56, 64, 66, 72, 81, 84, 86, 99, 101, 118, 127, 134, 138, 154, 157, 163, 167-168; problematic 53-56, 72; restoring 32, 80, 126, 136; types of 57-61; undesirable 61-62; unfavourable 72
rewards 100-101, 103; hierarchy of 103; pitfalls of 105-107; systems 105-107; types of 104
Roorda, D. L. 170n1
Ross, D.D. 98n8
routines 5, 11, 111, 146, 155
rules 14, 63, 81, 106, 109-113, 121; enforcing 127-128
Ryan, R.M. 15, 18n11, 105, 121n3

Sanders, J.A. 170n3
Schafer, N.J. 18n10
School type 166, 170
Schwab, Y. 18n8
Scott, T.M. 121n5-121n6, 140n5
self-determination theory 15
Skinner B.F. 13
social climate 159; *see also* classroom atmosphere
special needs 136-140
Spilt, J.L. 18n13, 170n5
Starosta, W.J. 87n9
start *see* lesson: starting a
status 27, 93, 132
Strack, S. 36n1, 87n8, 170n7
strictness and confrontation 81-82
student: academic performance 16-17, 60, 130, 158-160, 163; age 97, 101, 106, 129, 158, 167, 170;

challenging behaviour *see* challenging student behaviour; development 5, 117; disruptive behaviour 11, 99, 114, 116-117, 124, 127, 130, 135; engagement 15, 26, 32, 62, 76, 93, 95, 105, 115, 117, 131, 147, 149-150, *159*, 163; gender 97, 165, 167, 170; ethnicity 163, 165-166; internal control 14; misbehaviour 12, 54-55, 83-84, 129, 131, 136; motivation 15-17, 32, 43, 54-56, 102-103, 105-107, 134, 158-160, 163, 170; outcomes 158-159, 163; *see also* student academic performance; student wellbeing; problematic behaviour 12-15, 55, 72, 119, 127; with special needs *see* special needs; well-being 5, 9, 13, 27, 32, 58, 111, 117, 160, 170

student teacher 42, 62, 70, 167-168, 170

Sullivan, H.S. 19, 36n2

Sun, X. 7, 87n6, 164, 170n11

support 27

sympathy 27

Taxer, J. 140n1

teacher: age 69-70; approachable and accommodating 57-58; approachable and authoritative 58-59; authoritarian 60-66; class relationship 11, 34, 48; concerns 5; confidence 49, 70, 92-93, 97, 145, 160, 170; in different cultures 163-165; expectations 16, 27-28, 51, 61, 66, 83, 96, 99, 106-107, 110-116, 123, 126, 129, 133, 136, 138, 144, 153-155, 158; experience 69, 158, 169; gender 90, 97, 158, 166-167, 170; ideal 43-46, 68-70, 157, 163; insecure and oppositional 59-60; interpersonal style *see* interpersonal style; job satisfaction 156, 160, 170; personality 167; self-efficacy 160; self-perception *22*, 42-47, *50*, 69; sense of purpose 160; subject taught 166-167, 170;

student interactions *see* interactions; student perception *22*, 42, *50*, 57, 65, 69, 155, 157-158, 162, 166, 170; student relationship *see* relationship; thoughts 5, 12, 21-23; veteran 70, 158; warm demander 96; well-being 15-16

teaching: culturally responsive 159; effective 100; method 33, 151; perspectives on 9-12; strategies 74, 136, 143, 159-160; student 168; style 7, 57, 61, 110; whole-class 63, 86, 141-144, 148-152, 154-156, 159

Theelen, H. 7, 171n24

time scales 34, 48-49

Timmermans, A.C. 36n9

topic of conversation 53-55

transition *see* lesson: transitions in

values 14, 77, 111-112, 128

Van Amelsfoort, J. 171n25

Van der Lans, R.M. 170n4

Van der Want, A.C. 7

Van Tartwijk, J. 7, 8n1, 156n1, 156n2, 164, 170n8-170n9, 170n13, 171n15, 171n17

Veldman, I.M.J. 7

verbal 25-26, 28-29, 95, 97, 102, 104

Watzlawick, P. 36n3, 36n5, 87n4, 98n9, 114, 121n9

Wei, M. 164

Weinstein, C.S. 12, 18n2

Wijsman L. 7

Wiseman, R.L 170n3

wishful thinking 46

withitness 115

whole-class instruction *see* teaching whole-class

Woolfolk, A.E. 98n10

Wubbels, T. 7, 18n5, 18n12, 40, 47n3, 47n5, 49, 70, 72n3, 72n6, 170n1, 170n8-170n10, 171n21-171n22

For Product Safety Concerns and Information please contact our EU
representative GPSR@taylorandfrancis.com
Taylor & Francis Verlag GmbH, Kaufingerstraße 24, 80331 München, Germany

www.ingramcontent.com/pod-product-compliance
Lightning Source LLC
Chambersburg PA
CBHW082100230426
43670CB00017B/2905